Trump and Us

Why did 62 million Americans vote for Donald Trump? *Trump and Us* offers a fresh perspective on this question, taking seriously the depth and breadth of Trump's support. An expert in political language, Roderick P. Hart turns to Trump's words, voters' remarks, and media commentary for insight. The book offers the first systematic rhetorical analysis of Trump's 2016 campaign and early presidency, using text analysis and archives of earlier presidential campaigns to uncover deep emotional undercurrents in the country and provide historical comparison. *Trump and Us* pays close attention to the emotional dimensions of politics, above and beyond cognition and ideology. Hart argues it was not partisanship, policy, or economic factors that landed Trump in the Oval Office but rather how Trump made people feel.

Roderick P. Hart holds the Shivers Chair in Communication and is Professor of Government at the University of Texas at Austin. Former dean of the Moody College of Communication and founding director of the Annette Strauss Institute for Civic Life, Hart is the author or editor of fifteen books, most recently *Civic Hope: How Ordinary Americans Keep Democracy Alive* (2018). Hart has been named a Fellow of the International Communication Association and a Distinguished Scholar by the National Communication Association. He has received the Edelman Career Award from the American Political Science Association.

Communication, Society and Politics

Editors
W. Lance Bennett, University of Washington
Robert M. Entman, The George Washington University

Politics and relations among individuals in societies across the world are being transformed by new technologies for targeting individuals and sophisticated methods for shaping personalized messages. The new technologies challenge boundaries of many kinds – between news, information, entertainment, and advertising; between media, with the arrival of the World Wide Web; and even between nations. Communication, Society and Politics probes the political and social impacts of these new communication systems in national, comparative, and global perspective.

(*continued after the Index*)

Trump and Us

What He Says and Why People Listen

Roderick P. Hart

University of Texas at Austin

CAMBRIDGE
UNIVERSITY PRESS

CAMBRIDGE
UNIVERSITY PRESS

University Printing House, Cambridge CB2 8BS, United Kingdom

One Liberty Plaza, 20th Floor, New York, NY 10006, USA

477 Williamstown Road, Port Melbourne, VIC 3207, Australia

314–321, 3rd Floor, Plot 3, Splendor Forum, Jasola District Centre,
New Delhi – 110025, India

79 Anson Road, #06–04/06, Singapore 079906

Cambridge University Press is part of the University of Cambridge.

It furthers the University's mission by disseminating knowledge in the pursuit of
education, learning, and research at the highest international levels of excellence.

www.cambridge.org
Information on this title: www.cambridge.org/9781108490818
DOI: 10.1017/9781108854979

First published 2020

Printed in the United States of America by Sheridan Books, Inc.

A catalogue record for this publication is available from the British Library.

Library of Congress Cataloging-in-Publication Data
NAMES: Hart, Roderick P., author.
TITLE: Trump and us : what he says and why people listen / Roderick P. Hart,
    University of Texas, Austin.
OTHER TITLES: What he says and why people listen
DESCRIPTION: Cambridge, United Kingdom ; New York, NY : Cambridge University Press,
    2020. | Includes index.
IDENTIFIERS: LCCN 2019038249 (print) | LCCN 2019038250 (ebook) |
    ISBN 9781108490818 (hardback) | ISBN 9781108796415 (paperback) |
    ISBN 9781108854979 (epub)
SUBJECTS: LCSH: Trump, Donald, 1946–Language. | Trump, Donald, 1946–Influence. | Political
    culture–United States. | Communication in politics–United States–History–
    21st century. | Press and politics–United States.
CLASSIFICATION: LCC E912 .H37 2020 (print) | LCC E912 (ebook) | DDC 973.933092–dc23
LC record available at https://lccn.loc.gov/2019038249
LC ebook record available at https://lccn.loc.gov/2019038250

ISBN 978-1-108-49081-8 Hardback
ISBN 978-1-108-79641-5 Paperback

To the Dealey, Denius, Moody, and Strauss families of Texas

For their wisdom, generosity, and friendship

CONTENTS

Part I   Feeling Conflicted

Part II   Feeling Ignored

Part III   Feeling Trapped

Part IV   Feeling Besieged

Part V   Feeling Tired

Part VI   Feeling Resolute

FIGURES

TABLES

ACKNOWLEDGMENTS

On the morning of November 9, 2016, I found myself in a crowded hotel lobby in Philadelphia as the annual meeting of the National Communication Association (NCA) got underway. The convention attracts some 5,000 attendees each year, most of whom hold faculty appointments at the nation's colleges and universities. On that Wednesday morning, however, it attracted only lacrimation. Sans credentials, I found myself playing the role of grief counselor, as friend after friend complained about the election. Like most academics, NCA attendees largely vote Democratic and, because the field of communication attracts so many women, the outcome of the 2016 campaign hit them particularly hard. Searching for a sliver of optimism, I told the bereaved that the next four years would be a boon to scholarship, helping us unravel mysteries about language, politics, and media in the United States. From what I could tell, my brave pronouncements buoyed up not a single spirit in the City of Brotherly Love on that crisp fall morning.

When pontificating at the time, I had no intention of writing a book about Donald Trump. Inevitably, though, he won me over. What especially perplexed me was how half the nation, every other person I knew, could vote for such a complicated fellow, such an impossible fellow, and stay loyal to him during his first three years in the White House. What did Mr. Trump know that I did not know? Why had so many Americans jumped aboard the Trump Express and how did they make sense of the quirky things he said? Who were these people? Nonvoters suddenly galvanized by Trump? Longstanding Republicans or Hillary haters? Incipient revolutionaries or people just tired of Barack Obama? Above all, I wondered, what did they hear when listening to Trump? Irresistibly, Donald Trump became a question for me.

This book is my answer to Trump-the-question. Because Mr. Trump stirs up so much controversy, I knew that only hard evidence could keep me from being tossed about in his wake. So I have assembled a great quantity of data here, looking exhaustively at Trump's speeches, his press conferences, his debates, and his incessant tweets. But these data mean little by themselves. It is only when one compares them to what the press has written that one begins to get the full measure of the man, a project also advanced by looking at what everyday citizens have said when writing letters to the editors or when responding to nationwide surveys. Donald Trump, I came to believe, can be understood only by triangulation.

To do such work, I depended on many good people. I am especially indebted to the graduate research assistants who helped code some of the messages gathered here, help provided by Kristyn Goldberg (especially) as well as by Ana Aguilar, Sarah Blumberg, Yujin Kim, and Heló Aruth Sturm. I have also been flattered by the interest of faculty colleagues, including Lance Bennett, Matt Grossman, Sharon Jarvis Hardesty, Jay Jennings, Kate Kenski, Susan Nold, Talia Stroud, and Mary Stuckey. I deeply appreciate the help of two university administrators – Jay Bernhardt and Barry Brummett – who lightened my load by supporting a research leave.

I spent that leave at the Shorenstein Center on Media, Politics, and Public Policy at Harvard University. Not only did I get a lot of writing done during that semester (Fall 2018), but I also profited from the wisdom of my longtime friend and colleague, Tom Patterson, the Center's academic visionary. Spending time at Shorenstein gave me a chance to try out my ideas with a delightful medley of colleagues, including Kyla Fullenwider, Nancy Gibbs, James Harkin, Sarah Jackson, Heidi Legg, Gabe London, Nicco Mele, Richard Parker, and George Twumasi. I am also indebted to Tim Bailey, Susan Mahoney, Rebecca Roach, and Setti Warren who made my stay in Cambridge especially pleasant.

When personal friends heard that I was working on a book about Trump they offered me their condolences but also their political opinions. I especially appreciate the thoughts of Vic and Marie Arnold; Carole Buckman; Rick Cherwitz and Katherine Moser; Babs and John

Davis; Kay Hopper; Bob and Carolyn Krasawski; Carol and John Mullaly; Howard and Karen Owen; Linda, Tom, and Ashley Putnam; and, memorably, Daune and Randy Smith.

I hasten to add special thanks to my editor at Cambridge University Press, Sara Doskow, who is as insightful as she is creative and blessedly tolerant of my prose. I profited considerably from the feedback of two anonymous reviewers who were both wise and gracious. Finally, I am indebted to my wife of fifty-three years, Peggy McVey Hart, who said she would divorce me if I said anything kind about Donald Trump in this book. Unwisely, perhaps, I have stuck to the middle of the road here and, hence, may be enrolling in eHarmony. com when the book is published.

Part I
FEELING CONFLICTED

1 TRUMP'S ARRIVAL

Hillary Clinton had a thousand reasons to be upset by the 2016 presidential election. Her book, *What Happened*, lists them all. In Chapter 16 (helpfully entitled *Why*), Clinton lays out her reasons in 120 well-crafted paragraphs. FBI director James Comey is her star performer, far outdistancing Vladimir Putin & Co. Clinton also acknowledges her own shortcomings as a candidate and recounts other popular explanations for the election's outcome – angry blue-collar workers in the Midwest, a disorganized Democratic Party, fear of immigrants swarming the southern border, etc.[1] *What Happened* is a conflicted book, as Clinton tries to explain "how sixty-two million people – many of whom agreed Trump was unfit for the job – could vote for a man so manifestly unqualified to be President."[2]

Feeling conflicted is surely an appropriate emotion when one wins a popularity contest by 2.9 million votes but gets only 43 percent of the Electoral College's delegates. But it is not the former secretary of state and U.S. senator we find seething in *What Happened*; it is the left-brained Wellesley College political science major. How, Mrs. Clinton asks, could she have lost to a man who bragged "about repeated sexual assault," who attacked "immigrants, Muslims, Mexican Americans, prisoners of war, [and] people with disabilities," who was "accused of scamming countless small businesses, contractors, students, and seniors," and who took advantage of the media's silly fascination with her emails?[3] Armed though she is with a raft of statistical, demographic, and socio-logical facts about the election, Clinton concludes her book where she began – mystified by the sheer illogicality of the 2016 campaign.

Hillary Clinton has written an honest, if incomplete, account of one of the most tortured elections in American history. But two things are missing in her story: (1) what Donald Trump said during the campaign and (2) why people listened to him. When quoting Trump (a rare occurrence), Clinton features his misogyny and bombast and, when describing Trump voters, she showcases their irredeemable biases, but she mostly ignores the campaign's rhetorical and emotional dynamics. In doing so, Mrs. Clinton reflects mainstream media coverage as well.

I take a different approach in this book although I share Clinton's question: How could 62 million Americans – half the nation (or at least half of those who voted) – vote for Donald Trump? But rather than focus on what the media calls "Trump's base," I seek a broader, cultural understanding of the American polity and of those who support the Trump presidency.

To do so, I examine a large swath of materials – campaign speeches, press conferences, media interviews, letters to the editor, open-ended polls, political news coverage, person-on-the-street interviews, Trump's tweets, and citizens' reactions to social media. Throughout the book, I will offer alternative explanations for the Trump phenomenon. To do so, I will take political language seriously, placing special faith in *word patterns* that go unnoticed by the casual observer and even by seasoned White House reporters. Crass though he can be, Trump's language shows a surprising cultural awareness. We need to learn what his gut tells him.

What Happened is a homunculus for the Clinton campaign itself. In both cases, voters' feelings, especially their inchoate feelings, are rarely discussed. To be fair, Mrs. Clinton claims throughout her book that she enjoyed chance meetings with her fellow citizens, but the effects of those encounters seem to fade into the mist for her. As a result, *What Happened* is a brittle book, written by a consummately intelligent and well-intentioned person who does not relate easily to ordinary people. In that way and more she provides a sharp contrast to her husband, he of the legendary interpersonal skills. Hillary Clinton is all cognition – briefing papers, polling reports, policy options, and the sociology of the fifth Congressional district.

Although *What Happened* frequently mentions Mr. Trump's bigoted fans, it fails to explain why a retired high school teacher married to a Methodist choir director in Omaha would vote for him.

I shall attempt that feat here. In the chapters to follow, I explore four primary emotions that drove many voters into the Trump camp, emotions that continued to hold sway four years later. For example, Donald Trump knew that many Americans felt *ignored* so he acknowledged them with an accessible, populist style. He knew that some folks felt *trapped* and he uplifted them via emotion-filled storytelling. Others of his constituents felt *besieged* – by elites, especially by the media – so he offered them public therapy by becoming an alternative news source for them. Mr. Trump also sensed that many Americans were *weary* of the political establishment so he used his distinct personality and a barrage of tweets to energize them. The Trump presidency cannot be understood, I shall argue, without understanding this comingling of words and emotions.

Before getting into such details, let us reflect on the questions posed by the 2016 presidential race. Was it the worst political contest in history or did it do what all good campaigns do – activate the citizenry? Was the emergence of Donald Trump a mere fluke or did it provide broad hints about where the nation was heading? What made Trump so different from other politicians and, pivotally, why does he continue to stir up such intense emotions among his fellow citizens? And what about his supporters? Where had such people been hiding in the past and why did they suddenly emerge – full-throated and unrelenting? The 2016 presidential campaign and its aftermath are indeed mysterious.

A Useful Campaign?

"Friends stopped talking to one another. Husbands and wives broke up. Parent groups at schools frayed as people looked anew at neighbors and said 'I thought I knew you.'"[4] According to many, the 2016 presidential campaign was horrific. Columnist Leonard Pitts, Jr., explains why: "Donald Trump is a lying, narcissistic, manifestly incompetent child man who is as dumb as a sack of mackerel."[5] "This is a fundamental rewriting of the map," said CNN's John King on election night,[6] and the pollsters, it seems, were to blame: "It's a debacle on the order of Dewey defeats Truman," opined the University of Virginia's Larry Sabato.[7] "A lot of people feel more emboldened – because someone like Trump is in the White House – to speak their minds on topics that formerly had been taboo," observed secessionist Michael Hill.[8] "People feel it is not their country anymore," noted the University of

Georgia's Cas Mudde and, "to a certain extent, it is not their country anymore."[9] "I don't care what [Trump] says, you're attacking Muslims here," declared Iowan Steventjie Hasna, "and that's not American at all. We stand for American values and that's the exact opposite of what he stands for."[10]

The post-campaign rhetoric ranged from the heartfelt to the histrionic. A sense of urgency filled the air and broad, cultural questions emerged: What did the campaign say about us? Who is an American, really? Will the center hold? The country's very essence, its comprehensiveness, seemed at stake:

- "In my opinion, unless the country gets back together, things just can't work the way they should" (Queen Jones, retired teacher's assistant, Mount Pleasant, North Carolina).[11]
- "The most troubling outcome could be our willingness to retreat deeper into self-interested and self-idolizing divisions that pay little attention to our 'other' neighbors" (Thabiti Anyabwile, church planter, Washington, DC).[12]
- "The results of the 2016 elections bring to mind the words of abolitionist William Lloyd Garrison, who once condemned the slaveholder-dominated American government as 'a covenant with death and an agreement with hell'" (Manisha Sinha, college professor, Storrs, Connecticut).[13]

Eight years earlier, things were different; the country had validated its birthright. One might have expected former secretary of state Colin Powell to be upbeat about that election ("The world wondered, can America really do this? Aren't they too divided? Can they really pull something like this off? And we said to the world, yes, we can, and we did"), but a broader sense of coherence also existed.[14] If the United States was on the brink of collapse in 2016, the nation had found its storied self eight years earlier. Everyone, it seemed, felt the change:

- "[Barack Obama's] campaign of hope and change really stuck with folks, and you see it in the designs that are being fed back. It's as if folks are already nostalgic about this time" (Amy Maniatis, marketing executive, San Francisco, California).[15]
- "The inauguration represents a tangible example of the American spirit, testimony to the indisputable fact that our nation is the greatest on earth" (Patrick Gendron, attorney, Bryan, Texas).[16]

- "I really didn't think the country was ready for an African-American president, but they fooled me, for which I'm glad. We have really come a long way" (Merlin Bragg, administrative assistant, Linden, New Jersey).[17]

Two different elections, two different countries? To be sure, many Americans felt uneasy when Barack Obama became president in 2008 but the 2016 campaign seemed different, as if half the citizenry had suddenly emerged full-form and crazed, demanding that their nation be returned to them. These denizens of the dark – racists, sexists, homophobes, nationalists – seemed constituents of a nation reinvented.

The reality, of course, is that Donald Trump won the presidency in a squeaker. A few more miners in western Pennsylvania, a few more industrial workers in Michigan, and the United States would have had its first female president. That, too, would have been heralded as apocalyptic by some, the full-flowering of the American planting by others. As *Washington Post* columnist Robert Pierre observed, "Whether Donald Trump is impeached or serves out a full term or two, what happens with our nation depends more on how we deal with one another in our divided nation. Barack Obama is who we are. Donald Trump is who we are."[18]

Americans have always cast a furtive eye on one another. Fourth of July celebrations try to paper over that fact but the 9/11 tragedy, and the church bombings, and the Nazis marching remind us it is true. If, as Walt Whitman said, we as individuals contain multitudes, things are far more complicated at the level of the nation-state: Religious freedom as long as it is Christian. Public disclosure accepted, a prying press denounced. Patriotism yes, socialism no, unless the latter includes health coverage. Refuge for the world's oppressed . . . as long as they stand in line.

Donald Trump stirred up all these contrarieties. He was an iconoclast who worshipped Wall Street, a renegade who lived in Trump Tower, an evangelist who never went to church. Trump was a Democrat at times, a Republican more often, but a fellow devoid of political discipline. He had the attention span of a gnat and no moral depth, but he appealed to seniors hooked on Fox News. Trump promised to drain the swamp but he dined with lobbyists. He wanted the unions to rebuild the roads even as he made the Supreme Court more ideological. Multitudes met their match in Donald Trump.

In many ways, though, the 2016 presidential campaign was fairly normal. Two establishment figures squared off, tempers were lost, outrageous statements made, and then it was over. All U.S. elections involve such soul-searching because identity is such a malleable thing in a nation housing roughly 330 million people, each with a short fuse. So Americans conduct a fresh introspection every four years: Truman populism, Nixon globalism, Carter moralizing, Reagan nationalism, Clinton progressivism, Bush belligerence, Trump protectionism. All these changes invited controversy.

But wasn't the 2016 presidential election especially dispiriting? Judged by conventional standards, perhaps so. In their book *Evaluating Campaign Quality*, Sandy Maisel, Darrell West, and Brett Clinton lay out a number of sensible criteria for judging a campaign's worth: Did it focus on fundamental issues? Did voters know what was going on? Was the discourse civil? Did the campaign inspire greater trust in government officials? Did the media referee the contest appropriately?[19]

Judged by these standards, the 2016 campaign did not measure up well. As ABC and the *Washington Post* reported in August of 2016, candidates Clinton and Trump were considered the most disliked candidates in the thirty years the poll had been conducted.[20] Each day, it seemed, a new low was reported in the press.

But as will be stressed throughout this book, the 2016 campaign is far too complicated – and far too important – to be dismissed easily. In many ways, it was a fine contest, especially when assessed via these standards:

- *Did the campaign expand communication networks?* Harry Truman's train trek in 1948; televising of the national conventions in 1952; live presidential debates in 1960; fresh political ads in 1972; satellite uplinks in 1980; digital canvasing in 2008.
- *Did the campaign foster partisan rumination?* The Goldwater revolution of 1964; the McCarthy and Perot challenges in 1968 and 1992; the emergence of "new Democrats" in 1992; "Reagan's third term" in 1988.
- *Did the campaign inspire serious moral interrogation?* Vietnam and civil rights in 1968; the Watergate purgation of 1976; women's rights in 1984; the Willie Horton ads of 1988; sexual impropriety in 1996.
- *Did the campaign expand the leadership pool?* An Army general in 1952; a movie actor in 1980; an African-American preacher in 1984;

a businessman in 1992; a female governor in 2008; a Mormon in 2012.

- *Did the campaign enfranchise new voters?* The Catholic voting bloc in 1960; McGovern's youth brigade in 1972; evangelical Republicans in 1980; African-American turnout in 2008.
- *Did the campaign widen the policy agenda?* The Soviet threat in 1956; the space race in 1960; the War on Poverty in 1964; Soviet decline in 1984; Middle East adventurism in 2000; national healthcare in 2008.
- *Did the campaign foster international rapprochement?* The possibility of the United Nations in 1944; postwar reconstruction in 1952; China and Nixon in 1972; the potential for Middle East accords in 1976; the prospect of NAFTA in 1992.
- *Did the campaign increase economic stability?* Strong post-election years: 1965, 1969, 1989, 1997, 2005; weak post-election years: 1949, 1957, 1981, 1993, 2001, 2009.

When examined via these criteria, the 2016 campaign looks rather good. For example, new ways of engaging the citizenry were found – cable channels got their share of the debates; stand-alone news sites (e.g., *Politico*, the *Drudge Report*, *HuffPost*) had some bite; vigorous social media outlets brought new consumers into the mix. In addition, partisan rumination starkly increased for both political parties, as Trump vanquished fifteen other Republicans and as Bernie Sanders gave Hillary Clinton a run for her money. Moral interrogation unquestionably took center stage for Republicans (Trump's treatment of women, the biases of "fake news," Russian interference in the election, the savaging of immigrants) and for Democrats (Benghazi, Hillary's emails, "baskets of deplorables," and the reemergence of Bill Clinton's liaisons).

The talent pool obviously expanded in 2016, as the first woman ever nominated by a major political party took on a corporate-titan-turned-TV-star. New voters were found in the Rust Belt by Republicans and in Texas and Georgia by Democrats, and new battleground states emerged (Virginia, Nevada, Colorado, West Virginia, and North Carolina). The campaign also brought old-but-new debates out into the open – healthcare, immigration, global trade, tax reform – but the campaign failed miserably when it came to furthering international rapprochement (largely because of Mr. Trump, a trend he continued once in office). In the economic short term, at least, GDP growth, unemployment levels, and the Dow all sent positive signals during 2017 and 2018.

In many ways, then, the 2016 campaign served the needs of democracy and did so surprisingly well. The women who marched wearing pink hats on January 21, 2017, the day after Donald Trump's inauguration, would have been otherwise occupied if Hillary Clinton had become president. Similarly, blue-collar workers who had been downsized and ostracized would not have turned out to vote unless Donald Trump had given them hope. As former White House advisor Eric Liu reports, the 2016 campaign triggered a "systemic immune response in the body politic, producing a surge in engagement among" Trump opponents.[21] Indeed, says Shaun Harper, then of the University of Pennsylvania's Center for Race and Equity in Education, one might even express a "painful gratitude" for Donald Trump's ability to galvanize a Democratic counter-force in 2018 and 2020 headed by young people, African-Americans, Hispanics, and other marginalized groups; the "gift of Trump," says Harper, has the capacity to change American politics for years to come.[22] Agreeing, columnist E. J. Dionne observes, "it's hard to imagine a president more likely to inspire Obama Nostalgia than Donald Trump."[23]

In short, the 2016 presidential election had considerable vitality. It inspired populist Republicans to rally against their establishment overseers and insurgent Democrats to question (via Bernie Sanders) their party's ideological homogeneity.[24] Presidential campaigns almost always energize the electorate, and the 2016 race was no exception. As this book was being written, most Americans were angry at something – at the President's detractors, at the aimlessness of the Democratic Party, at one of the cable news channels. These kinds of anger are the very stuff out of which democratic engagement has long been fashioned.

A Native Son?

Try as she might, Hillary Clinton rarely made it "above the fold" in the morning newspapers in 2016. That spot was almost always reserved for Donald Trump. This book asks why. What was it about Trump that so commanded the press's attention? Why did Candidate Clinton spend so much time attacking him personally rather than following her own game plan? Why were the elite media unable to resist his provocations and what does that say about current-day journalism? Trump's irresistibility, his insouciance, shed light on what ails the American people but also what exalts them. Although Donald Trump seems the least mysterious political candidate in human history, he tells a story far richer than himself.

Rhetorically speaking, there have been at least four types of American presidential candidate: (1) *Charismatics*, optimists who wandered onto the political scene largely unbidden (e.g., Eisenhower, Kennedy, Reagan, Bill Clinton, and Obama); *Designees*, establishment figures who worked their way through the system until it was their turn (Dewey, Stevenson, Nixon, Dole, Bush 43, McCain, etc.); *Legatees*, those who carried the torch of a popular predecessor (Truman, Johnson, Ford, Gore, Bush 41, etc.); and *Contrarians*, people who swam against the tide simply because they chose to do so (Goldwater, Wallace, McGovern, Carter, and Trump). Contrarians are the most interesting of the species because of their internal tensions: They want to control things by deconstructing things. They pose solutions to unclear problems but are fully in touch with their inner selves. Contrarians also want to command people's votes rather than solicit them and that, too, makes them interesting.

Some contrarians have a good sense of what ordinary people feel, and nobody was better at that than Donald Trump. Trump hates complexity and is filled with opinions, always in a hurry, and constantly ready for a fight – quintessentially American characteristics. Trump dislikes subtle distinctions, layered questions, or anything that circumscribes his personal freedom. Most Americans hate these things as well. Trump resents the landed gentry so he loves Twitter; Trump cannot abide fecklessness so he loves Twitter; Trump prizes spontaneity so he loves Twitter. The result: There is an obscene familiarity to Donald Trump, an inveigling invitation to better know ourselves by knowing him.

Despite his wealth, Trump is more plebeian than patrician. One has little trouble imagining him at tractor pulls or hot-dog-eating contests. During the campaign, Trump's wantonness attracted voters as did his braggadocio: "I'm speaking with myself, number one, because I have a very good brain and I've said a lot of things."[25] "If you do not get even," he once opined, "you are just a shmuck."[26] Trump is famously transactional – what can I get? what will it cost me? – and, like so many of his fellow citizens, is clumsily transactional. Trump likes neither poetry nor art (unless it is expensive), neither fine food nor fine music. He is more comfortable with opinions (especially his own) than with facts (especially those of others). He finds it hard to "rise above things" because doing so elevates him to an airy, undependable space. In these ways and more, Donald Trump is an American.

Many commentators disagree. Throughout the media and across the body politic, Trump is constantly exoticized. It has become popular to deem him a foreigner, dramatizing how he violates the conventions of logic, science, grammar, propriety, honesty, sociability, law, and morality, the same conventions most Americans violate each day. According to some observers, Trump exemplifies every human flaw, every personality tic:

- Trump is an example of how one man can ruin a country.[27]
- Trump is an example of someone who believes "the world began when I showed up."[28]
- Trump is an example of the wrong kind of assimilation.[29]
- Trump is an example of a traumatized child who refuses help.[30]
- Trump is an example of the stupid psychopath problem.[31]
- Trump is an example of an extreme narcissist.[32]
- Trump is an example of democratic extremism.[33]
- Trump is an example of an underlying caldron of hate making its way to the surface like a festering boil.[34]

Mixed metaphors aside, distancing oneself from Donald Trump has become a popular game as has infantilizing him (e.g., the "Angry Baby" balloon that stalked him throughout his visit to London in the summer of 2018). The more accurate charge, though, is that he is more an adolescent than a baby. Trump's moodiness, for example, often makes him an object of scorn. Like many adolescents, he has fears he cannot admit (his differential popularity, for example) and his opinions are often undermined by the surrounding facts. Like so many adolescents, Trump needs love but cannot admit it, feels tortured by bullies (e.g., the press), and resents established authorities (e.g., Congress, European leaders, etc.). Trump's emotions are raw, like those of any adolescent, and he lashes out in febrile ways. His speech is disconnected, filled with self-interruptions, and his thoughts disappear as soon as they appear. It is hard to be an adolescent and it is hard to be Donald Trump.

My argument in this book is that Donald Trump is one of us and ought not be dismissed as a cultural alien. Trump emanated from the land of reality television, for example, and that would be sinful if it were not for the fact that 52 percent of the American people watch such shows.[35] Trump has no sense of history, no aesthetic taste, and no moral complexity, sins committed from time to time by everyone we know. If Donald Trump was summoned from the gates of hell, then, he was summoned by us, I argue. And if Trump left the scene tomorrow, we would still have to sort out the *us* within him. To really understand the United States of America, we must make Donald Trump a question.

On February 27, 2017, Kellyanne Conway found herself kneeling on a couch in the Oval Office with her shoes pressed against the upholstery, distractedly scrolling through her smartphone as President Trump stood chatting with some thirty dignitaries from the nation's historically Black colleges. A photo of the scene went viral, a sure sign that something cultural was afoot. How dare Ms. Conway show such disrespect in the White House's sanctum sanctorum, taking a load off her feet, getting lost in social media, and acting as if she were just a person? Surely Ms. Conway – and her boss – had descended from some distant planet.

Donald Trump, with his oversized personality and legion insensitivities, makes it easy to dismiss him as an extraterrestrial. To do so, however, is to miss an opportunity to know how 62 million Americans helped him get where he got. Few would argue that Donald Trump is the best of the United States, but his grandiosity and shamelessness find him firmly rooted in the pugilistic, impatient culture that raised him. We need to know more about such matters.

A Responsible Electorate?

Most of the commentary about Donald Trump's 2016 campaign featured the candidate himself rather than his supporters. This book reverses that polarity. Instead of focusing on Trump-the-man, I feature Trump-the-empath, the fellow who turned emotional needs into votes. But a book entitled *Trump and Us* immediately prompts the question: Which *us* are you talking about? It inspires other questions as well: How could so many people vote for a serial adulterer-cum-New York hustler? Post-election, why did half of *us* find it so hard to be civil to the other half of *us*? Why did the campaign open up new wounds between men and women, Blacks and whites, churched and unchurched, documented and undocumented, young and old? Why did *they* put Trump in office? How could they have done that to *us*?

Using the first-person plural in the United States has always been problematic since few Americans identify with all Americans. "He's not my president," went the refrain in December of 2016, as if there were an alternative to that proposition. Donald Trump no doubt exacerbated the nation's tensions but he did not invent them. That deed was accomplished long ago by the American people themselves.

Pigeonholing Trump supporters has become a popular pastime in the United States. The characterizations have ranged from the benign (Trumpers are naïve, childlike) to the calamitous (Trumpers are xenophobic, unable to cope with their rapidly changing neighborhoods). Trumpers are said to be resentful of the "New Class" that emerged in the postwar United States, a class with more education, more wealth, and greater comfort with new technologies than their working-class brethren.[36] For yet others, Trumpers are outright totalitarians, protective of their station in life above all else. Trumpers are anti-Muslim, anti-media, anti-change, antediluvian. Voting for Donald Trump costs one one's humanity.

"People were scared to say they were voting for him" said Scottsdale hairstylist Audrey Katz. "They think 'Oh, so you must be a racist,' and that isn't true or fair."[37] "Virtually all of my friends or colleagues actively hate Mr. Trump," said Professor Philip Maymin, an academic with a Ph.D. from the University of Chicago. "We learn to stay quiet," he added.[38] "The greatest con of 2016 was not persuading a white laborer to vote for a nasty billionaire with soft hands," says author Sarah Smarsh. "It was persuading a watchdog press to cast every working-class American in the same mold."[39] Lifelong Republican Esther Valdés describes the "backhanded commentary" she received, "with the suggestion that I'm somehow disloyal to my race or to my profession." "It's never hurtful," she adds, somewhat unconvincingly, "because it's completely untruthful."[40]

There is a certain efficiency in presuming that all Trump admirers are either delusional or evil, but that seems preposterous given the breadth and depth of his support. As we will see throughout this book, Trump was successful because he listened to people who felt unheard. He also knew four things about them:

1. *Trump supporters like candor.* "Every time Trump opens his mouth it helps him," said veteran Anthony Holston. "I like that he's got

balls and he's willing to take a chance. Not taking a chance hasn't worked too well."[41] "He's a mouthy New Yorker," says Lenny Massumino of West Virginia, "and if you know anybody from New York, they all got a line of bullshit. That's the way they are."[42] "He grew up in the construction business and went to military school," said Billy Shreve of Frederick, Maryland; describing underdeveloped nations as shithole countries is "just common language. The snowflakes aren't used to it."[43] "In true Trump style," said former Boeing engineer Brad Pontious, "he spoke what he felt about Charlottesville. It might not be the political thing to say, but he was correct."[44] These commentators know that being frank has its downsides but that the truth sometimes demands it. A parent with an unruly child or a boss with an unresponsive subordinate accepts the costs of delivering unwanted news. But real candor is hard to find in politics so, as a result, it can become a craving for some. Donald Trump understood that.

2. *Trump supporters distinguish words from actions.* "Trump is arrogant and crass, I'll give you that," says former coal miner John Beatty, and "women don't like him much, other than the ones that sleep with him. I won't call him a bigot, but he's not too far from it. But I believe the way he thinks can do what has to be done."[45] "I have disrespect for Hillary for not doing more for herself, not standing up for herself with him," opines Palma Frable of Moscow, Pennsylvania, "that's more damaging than goofball words Trump came up with."[46] Such a sharp distinction between language and action drives elite reporters crazy but Trump's supporters hold firm: "The fact that Donald Trump is very blunt about it," says online contributor Carlos Rodriguez, "is not a surprise, this is just Trump being Trump."[47] Echoing poet Maya Angelou, Eric Johnson of Woodstock, Georgia, waxes philosophical: "People will always forget about what you say, forget what you do, but never forget how you make them feel." Johnson then goes all-out in defense of the President: "We said we needed a bulldog, someone who's going to fight for us, and he's our hired hand. It's kind of messy. He might make a mistake and hit the wrong person but I know he doesn't intend harm."[48]

3. *Trump supporters are as self-reflexive as anyone else.* "I'm guilty," says John Lusz of Milwaukee, "I employ illegals. Pay them cash. It's tough when it's there. I feel very guilty about it." But then Mr. Lusz

makes a Trumpian Turn: "It's just wrong. They don't pay in, but they want the stuff. Collecting social services with a cash-hustle on the side. They should learn English."[49] "I don't care if you're gay or any of that stuff," remarks Kris Wyrick of California. "I don't care if you're black, brown, yellow. I don't give a fuck. Just make your own money."[50] When first hearing about Mr. Trump's comments on Haiti, Danny Eapen of Oklahoma said he was "a bit skeptical" but then acknowledged "if it's true, then it's true. But at the same time, I would like to give him the benefit of the doubt."[51] "I still support my president," said Los Angeles' Angie Galvez, but he "should have more filters because he represents the United States." "We want him to look more professional," she concluded.[52] For Trump's opponents, this kind of double-thinking is maddening, especially when human dignity is at stake, but Trump's supporters have a ready retort: "The politically correct movement has no sense of humor. They cannot understand that the average person can see humor even in horrible things."[53] A Shakespearean thought, that.

4. *Trump supporters understand political dynamics.* A popular trope during the 2016 election was that Trump's supporters were either uninformed or incapable of reason. The established media were fans of that trope and often its progenitors: "If the media got together and wrote a script for Trump to read," said one Trumpian, "they would complain later that he was sending a different message because of his body language."[54] Said another online contributor: "President Trump could disavow all groups that promote racism [and] the media would still clutch their pearls and complain that wasn't good enough."[55] "Any Christian that watches CNN and the rest of the ilk," says a third observer, "are committing the sin of lust. They can't get enough of the Trump bashing."[56] These people see the landscape whole and many of them are rational actors, carefully weighing what they get with Donald Trump: "I'm hoping that he's as conservative as he says he is. He used to be liberal on a lot of things. That's life. Over the years, I've changed my mind about a lot of things. If I held the same viewpoints I did when I was younger, I'd be living in Colorado right now, rolling one fat one after another."[57]

We need to make questions out of Trump's supporters: Who are they? Why do they respond as they do? What explains their loyalty to the President? Trump voters may be imperfect but they hold fast to certain presuppositions: Truth is more important than propriety, the media are blind, people pick the facts they like, politicians can't be trusted, things aren't as simple as they seem, one must keep the Big Picture in mind. There is a bit of shamanism here but a bit of lay science as well.

Many Americans cannot understand how anyone could have voted for a dishonorable fellow like Donald Trump. But as Richard Dimery of Leander, Texas, observed, "In the Bible, prophets were generally despised but God had a purpose for them."[58] Trump did not assume, says Londa Chandler, that "because we're not all college professors we're worthless." Knowing she was swimming against the tide, Chandler nonetheless continued: Everybody but Trump "seemed to have this attitude that if you weren't part of the elite you didn't matter, and that whether you have a degree, a good job, raised wonderful families, you were worthless."[59] Sharon Ross adds another note: "You know exactly what [Trump's] thinking. You don't have to wonder what's going on."[60] Mr. Dimery, Ms. Chandler, and Ms. Ross somehow felt special because of Donald Trump. We need to know why they felt that way.

Conclusion

In a recent study of online commentary, Nicholas Subtirelu reports an interesting thing about Trump supporters: They are willing to work through Trump's words to find his true intentions.[61] That is a powerful gratuity. If Trump's remarks are off-kilter, or even deeply offensive, it can be seen as a verbal accident, not a sign of malevolence. Instead of calling Trump's supporters blind, then, we might call them doubly visioned – they look into his soul and then beyond to the future, excusing the linguistic middle. "It's like if someone tells a joke," says Florida's Wayne Lebnitsky, "one person might take it one way while someone else might take it another way. A lot of the things that are reported about him, whether bad or terrible, are probably taken out of context."[62] Here, intertextuality becomes an excuse but human psychology is available as well: "We need to keep our butts at home," says Ed Wiley of Coal Creek, West Virginia, and "stay out of these wars. That's the sort of thing you'd have to watch out with him – if he can keep himself calm, [maintain] control of his bipolar."[63]

It is tiring to be a Trump supporter. All of popular culture, much of media culture as well, repudiates everything the President says.

That sends many of his supporters into their shells or into moments of Fox News-watching or into conspiratorial conversations with like-minded friends. Emotions felt, emotions expressed, emotions denied.

Things are no easier for Trump haters. A simple question such as "What did He say today?" sends his detractors to their liquor cabinets. While anti-Trumpers can depend on late-night television to buoy up their spirits, doing so depends on two things: a taste for unbridled cynicism (which can itself be depressing) and a willingness to stay up past one's bedtime. For all Americans, then, the 2016 presidential campaign was, and continues to be, a nightmare.

Although this book focuses heavily on Donald Trump, he is not the only card in the nation's deck. Structural racism, institutional sexism, and a carnivorous right-wing media preceded him and continue to have their own, independent influence. Too, study after study shows declining political trust in the United States (trust in leaders, trust in fellow voters), trends from which Mr. Trump profited during the campaign.[64] He also aligned himself with a political party containing an increasing number of hard-bitten crusaders, many of whom rejected the bouquet of freedoms fashioned in the 1960s and 1970s and then institutionalized in the 1980s and 1990s. Donald Trump is very much the product of the country's recent political history.

For reasons such as these, it is tempting (a temptation to which many authors have succumbed) to treat Donald Trump as an outcropping of larger sociological and political tendencies – growing nationalism throughout the Western world, a renewed, testosteronal populism in the United States. Superb historical work has been done in this area, work showing a broad (and broadening) disenchantment of the white working class with all aspects of traditional democratic politics.[65] The mass media have played up such trends, trends often buoyed up only by randomly distributed and aggressively collected anecdotes. Perhaps there is more to Trump than Trump but it is too early to tell if that is true. As a result, I shall stick to what we can know for sure, focusing on the rhetorical facts available to us and leaving it to others to find the grand design to which Donald Trump is subordinate.

Instead of focusing on ideological matters, then, I will treat Trump as an emotional revolutionary, a person (1) who is proud of the feelings coursing within him, (2) who is unafraid to display them in public, (3) who treats his supporters' feelings with special reverence, and (4) who regards an unemotional politics as no politics at all. Trump is especially comfortable with real emotionality, including its herky-jerky repetitiveness, its bodily eccentricities, its aimlessness but also its earnestness. Trump feels what his supporters feel but, unlike them, he can attach words to those feelings. He says what some people say only in private and, for other Americans, he speaks their unspoken voice.

By focusing on Trump's emotions, I treat him not as an alien but as an American original. Trump may not be the best of us but he is one of us and we need to know what that means. We also need to know more about his supporters because they are emotionally complex and because they too are Americans. Toggling back and forth between what Trump says and how he is received gets us beyond the story of one election. It tells us who we are as a people and why US politics has become so clamorous. Within such self-understanding, I argue, virtue lies.

Notes

1 Hillary Rodham Clinton, *What Happened* (New York: Simon & Schuster, 2017), ch. 16. Examining the topics discussed in Clinton's chapter produces the following paragraph breakdown: Comey and emails (15.8 percent), economic distress (13.3 percent), racial resentment (13.3 percent), party deficiencies (12.5 percent), multiple factors (11.7 percent), Clinton shortcomings (10.0 percent), changing constituencies (8.3 percent), voter suppression (7.5 percent), and Russian interference (7.5 percent).
2 Ibid., pp. 407–08.
3 Ibid., p. 15.
4 Robert E. Pierre, "Civil War in Donald Trump's America: Conversations about Media and Mayhem on Main Street USA," in Robert E. Gutsche, Jr. (ed.), *The Trump Presidency, Journalism and Democracy* (New York: Routledge, 2018), p. 61.
5 Leonard Pitts, Jr., "Who Cares What's Wrong with Donald Trump? What's Wrong with Us," *Miami Herald*, July 14, 2017. Accessed at www.miamiherald.com/opinion/opn-columns-blogs/leonard-pitts-jr/article161473023.html.
6 "Anderson Cooper on Polls: What Did Everyone Get Wrong," CNN, November 9, 2016. Accessed at www.cnn.com/videos/politics/2016/11/09/election-night-anderson-cooper-what-did-everyone-get-wrong-sot.cnn.
7 Ibid.
8 Patrik Jonsson and Trevor Bach, "Trump and the Rise of the Extreme Right," *Christian Science Monitor*, February 27, 2017. Accessed at www.csmonitor.com/USA/Politics/2017/0227/Trump-and-the-rise-of-the-extreme-right.
9 Peter Grier, "The Year of Disruption: from Trump to 'Brexit' to Fury over Free Trade," *Christian Science Monitor*, December 24, 2016. Accessed at www.csmonitor.com/USA/Politics/2016/1224/The-Year-of-Disruption.
10 Jenna Johnson, "These Iowans Voted for Trump: Many of Them Are Already Disappointed, *Washington Post*, February 26, 2017. Accessed at www.washingtonpost.com/politics/these-iowans-voted-for-trump-many-of-them-are-already-disappointed/2017/02/26/18f86b86-fa8d-11e6-be05-1a3817ac21a5_story.html?utm_term=.6846f44751fa.

11 Susan Page, "Poll: Trump Has Not Yet Made Progress in Uniting USA," *USA Today*, December 21, 2016. Accessed at www.usatoday.com/story/news/politics/2016/12/21/poll-donald-trump-progress-uniting-usa/95667510/.

12 Thabiti Anyabwile, "I'm a Black Christian and Guess What? Donald Trump's America Is My America, Too," *Washington Post*, November 9, 2016. Accessed at www.washingtonpost.com/news/acts-of-faith/wp/2016/11/09/im-a-black-christian-and-guess-what-donald-trumps-america-is-my-america-too/?utm_term=.ac309354517a.

13 Manisha Sinha, "It Feels Like the Fall of Reconstruction," *Charleston Gazette-Mail*, December 4, 2016. Accessed at www.wvgazettemail.com/opinion/manisha-sinha-it-feels-like-the-fall-of-reconstruction/article_56d20169-26af-5a2d-a9a0-38045ab77aea.html.

14 Dan Farber, "Colin Powell: the America We Remember Is Back Again," *CBS News*, January 20, 2009. Accessed at www.cbsnews.com/news/colin-powell-the-america-we-remember-is-back-again/.

15 Kristi Keck, "Obama: Politician, Pop Icon – or Both?" *CNN.com*, January 18, 2009. Accessed at www.cnn.com/2009/POLITICS/01/18/obama.cool/index.html.

16 Vimal Patel, "'I Just Want to Be There,'" *Eagle*, January 18, 2009. Accessed at www.theeagle.com/news/local/i-just-want-to-be-there/article_e1f1bfab-8053-513b-a145-0456dc26dac6.html.

17 Kevin Coyne, "At Defining Moment, Stories of Injustice," *New York Times*, January 16, 2009. Accessed at www.nytimes.com/2009/01/18/nyregion/new-jersey/18colnj.html.

18 Pierre, "Civil War in Donald Trump's America," p. 75.

19 Sandy Maisel, Darrell West, and Brett Clinton, *Evaluating Campaign Quality: Can the Electoral Process Be Improved?* (New York: Cambridge University Press, 2009). Portions of the following argument have appeared in Roderick P. Hart, "Assessing Campaign Quality: Was the 2016 Election a Travesty?" *Presidential Studies Quarterly*, 49 (2019), 644–55.

20 Eliza Collins, "Poll: Clinton, Trump Most Unfavorable Candidates Ever," *USA Today*, August 31, 2016. Accessed at www.usatoday.com/story/news/politics/onpolitics/2016/08/31/poll-clinton-trump-most-unfavorable-candidates-ever/89644296/.

21 Eric Liu, "How Donald Trump Is Reviving American Democracy," *Atlantic*, March 8, 2017. Accessed at www.theatlantic.com/politics/archive/2017/03/how-donald-trump-is-reviving-our-democracy/518928/.

22 As quoted in Sarah Brown, "A Scholar of Racial Equity Describes His 'Painful Gratitude' for Donald Trump," *Chronicle of Higher Education*, January 10, 2017, A22.

23 E. J. Dionne, Jr., "The Good That Could Come from a Trump Presidency," *Washington Post*, December 28, 2016. Accessed at www.washingtonpost.com/opinions/the-good-that-could-come-from-a-trump-presidency/2016/12/28/63f5c82e-cd0e-11e6-a87f-b917067331bb_story.html?utm_term=.f76fe6129726.

24 Ross Douthat, "In Search of the American Center," *New York Times*, June 21, 2017. Accessed at www.nytimes.com/2017/06/21/opinion/in-search-of-the-american-center.html.

25 As quoted in Evan Osnos, "President Trump's First Term," *New Yorker*, September 26, 2016. Accessed at www.newyorker.com/magazine/2016/09/26/president-trumps-first-term.

26 Ibid.

27 Andhra Naidu, *News X Bureau*, February 6, 2017. Accessed at www.newsx.com/national/54985-andhra-cm-chandrababu-naidu-says-trump-is-an-example-of-how-one-man-can-ruin-a-country.

28 Dee Edington, *Facebook*, April 17, 2017. Accessed at www.facebook.com/dee.edington.

29 Andrew Anglin, *Daily Stormer*, April 1, 2017. Accessed at www.dailystormer.com/chinese-american-judge-suing-trump-is-an-example-of-the-wrong-kind-of-assimilation/.

30 Dr. Gabor Maté as quoted in Carolyn Baker, "Dr. Gabor Maté on Donald Trump, Traumaphobia, and Compassion," *CarolynBaker.Net*, May 15, 2018. Accessed at https://carolynbaker.net/2018/05/15/dr-gabor-mate-on-donald-trump-traumaphobia-and-compassion/.

31 Kevin Williamson, *National Review*, March 28, 2016. Accessed at www.nationalreview.com/2016/03/donald-trump-stupid-psychopath-ignorance-policy-complex-problems/.

32 Joseph Burgo, *Jewish Journal*, February 13, 2017. Accessed at http://jewishjournal.com/blogs/214944/trumps-mental-condition/.

33 Mark Triffitt, "A Growing Mistrust in Democracy Is Causing Extremism and Strongman Politics to Flourish," *The Conversation*, July 8, 2018. Accessed at http://theconversation.com/a-growing-mistrust-in-democracy-is-causing-extremism-and-strongman-politics-to-flourish-98621.

34 J. E. Jensen, *Hoodline*, January 31, 2017. Accessed at http://hoodline.com/2017/01/city-of-san-francisco-sues-trump-administration.

35 "Declines and Audience Shifts: The Unscripted Truth about Reality TV Viewership," *Civic Science*, April 4, 2017. Accessed at http://cs-marcomm.demandco.webfactional.com/wp-content/uploads/2015/03/Insight-Report-The-Unscripted-Truth-About-Reality-TV-Viewership-FINAL.pdf.

36 See, for example, Alvin W. Gouldner, *The Future of Intellectuals and the Rise of the New Class: a Frame of Reference, Theses, Conjectures, Arguments, and an Historical Perspective on the International Class Contest of the Modern Era* (New York: Palgrave, 1979).

37 As quoted in Mark Z. Barabak and Nigel Duara, "We're Called Redneck, Ignorant, Racist: That's Not True," *Los Angeles Times*, November 13, 2016. Accessed at www.latimes.com/politics/la-na-pol-donald-trump-american-voices-20161113-story.html.

38 Letter to the editor, *New York Times*, January 17, 2018. Accessed at www.nytimes.com/2018/01/17/opinion/trump-voters-supporters.html.

39 Sarah Smarsh, "Liberal Blind Spots Are Hiding the Truth about 'Trump Country,'" *New York Times*, July 19, 2018. Accessed at www.nytimes.com/2018/07/19/opinion/trump-corporations-white-working-class.html.

40 As quoted in Jenna Johnson, "What Trump's Address Sounded Like in Eight American Living Rooms," *Washington Post*, January 31, 2018. Accessed at www.washingtonpost.com/politics/what-trumps-address-sounded-like-in-eight-american-living-rooms/2018/01/31/d8890758-0536-11e8-8777-2a059f168dd2_story.html?utm_term=.ee4bcae2c455.

41 As quoted in Alexander Zaitchik, *The Gilded Rage: A Wild Ride through Donald Trump's America* (New York: Skyhorse Publishing, 2016), p. 17.

42 As quoted ibid., p. 81.

43 As quoted in Daniel Bush, "Trump's Supporters Dismiss S***hole Comments, Charges of Racism," *PBS Newshour*, January 12, 2018. Accessed at www.pbs.org/newshour/politics/trumps-supporters-dismiss-shole-comments-charges-of-racism.

44 As quoted in David Smith, "'He's Anti-Left, Anti-PC, Anti-Stupid': Trump Supporters in Their Own Words," *Guardian*, August 23, 2017. Accessed at www.theguardian.com/us-news/2017/aug/23/trump-supporter-interviews-phoenix-arizona-rally.

45 As quoted in Zaitchik, *The Gilded Rage*, p. 59.

46 As quoted in Emily Bazelon, "This Land in Trump's America – Pennsylvania," *New York Times Magazine*, November 20, 2016, 58.

47 Online comment regarding "Why Do Some of Donald Trump's Supporters Defend His References to Haiti and African Nations as 'Shithole' Countries?" *Quora*,

January 11, 2018. Accessed at www.quora.com/Why-do-some-of-Donald-Trumps-supporters-defend-his-references-to-Haiti-and-African-nations-as-shithole-countries.

48 Dakin Andone, "Trump Supporters React to His Derogatory Remark, in Their Own Words," *CNN*, January 12, 2018. Accessed at www.cnn.com/2018/01/12/politics/trump-supporters-react/index.html.

49 As quoted in Zaitchik, *The Gilded Rage*, p. 33.

50 As quoted ibid., p. 113.

51 As quoted in Andone, "Trump Supporters React to His Derogatory Remark, in Their Own Words," *CNN*.

52 As quoted ibid.

53 Kahnkeller's comment regarding Matt Vespa, "CNN's Epic Meltdown over Trump's 'S**thole Countries' Remark Was a Sight to Behold," *Townhall*, January 12, 2018. Accessed at townhall.com/tipsheet/mattvespa/2018/01/12/cnns-epic-meltdown-over-trumps-sthole-countries-remark-was-a-sight-to-behold-n2433476.

54 Online comment from Kingfish17 regarding Kyle Drennen, "Trump Remarks 'Didn't Do Enough,' 'Lowest Possible Bar,'" *MRC NewsBusters*, August 14, 2017. Accessed at www.newsbusters.org/blogs/nb/kyle-drennen/2017/08/14/msnbc-trumps-remarks-didnt-do-enough-lowest-possible-bar.

55 Online comment from Skeptical Shazaam regarding Joel Pollak, "Trump Was Right to Condemn Violence on 'Many Sides' in Charlottesville," *Breitbart News*, August 13, 2017. Accessed at www.breitbart.com/big-government/2017/08/13/charlottesville-donald-trump-right-condemn-violence-many-sides/.

56 Online comment from Rwmctrofholz regarding NB Staff, "Brent Bozell Incinerates Liberal Media over Ignoring Trump's Economy," *MRC NewsBusters*, January 12, 2018. Accessed at www.newsbusters.org/blogs/nb/nb-staff/2018/01/12/mrcs-brent-bozell-incinerates-liberal-media-over-ignoring-trumps.

57 Attributed to Mike from New Mexico by Zaitchik, *The Gilded Rage*, p. 94.

58 As quoted in Jonathan Tilove and Claire Osborn, "There's Joy in Texas Trumpland," *Austin American-Statesman*, February 5, 2017. Accessed at www.pressreader.com/usa/austin-american-statesman-sunday/20170205/281487866085466.

59 As quoted ibid.

60 As quoted ibid.

61 Nicholas Close Subtirelu, "Donald Trump Supporters and the Denial of Racism: an Analysis of Online Discourse in a Pro-Trump Community," *Journal of Language Aggression and Conflict*, 5:2 (2017), 323–346.

62 As quoted in Andone, "Trump Supporters React to His Derogatory Remark, in Their Own Words," *CNN*.

63 As quoted in Zaitchik, *The Gilded Rage*, p. 77.

64 Perhaps the two most definitive works in this area are Marc J. Hetherington and Thomas J. Rudolph, *Why Washington Won't Work: Polarization, Political Trust, and the Governing Crisis* (Chicago: University of Chicago Press, 2015); and Eric M. Uslaner (ed.), *The Oxford Handbook of Social and Political Trust* (New York: Oxford University Press, 2018).

65 For more on these matters, see Jefferson R. Cowie, *Stayin' Alive: the 1970s and the Last Days of the Working Class* (New York: New Press, 2010); Reece Peck, *Fox Populism: Branding Conservatism as Working Class* (Cambridge, UK: Cambridge University Press, 2018); and Benjamin Moffitt, *The Global Rise of Populism: Performance, Political Style, and Representation* (Stanford, CA: Stanford University Press, 2016).

Part II
FEELING IGNORED

2 TRUMP'S SIMPLICITY

In politics, words are never far from the action: How to describe the upcoming legislation? How to set the tone for the party's convention? How to address reporters when descending from Air Force One? "Word eruptions" – words about words about words – are a constant thing as a result and that was even truer when Donald Trump became president: One of his supporters, Roseanne Barr, lost her TV show after making racist allusions about an Obama staffer; Melania Trump wore a coat declaring "I really don't care. Do U?" which also caused a stir; comedian Michelle Wolf prayed that White House staffer Kellyanne Conway would be hit by a tree and also described Press Secretary Sarah Huckabee Sanders as "an Uncle Tom for white women"; Robert De Niro went on a rant against Trump at the Tony Awards; and Peter Fonda imagined ripping "Barron Trump from his mother" and putting him in a "cage with pedophiles."[1] Cruel words, incessant words, ineluctably political words.

The era of social media has dumped even more words onto the public stage. Consider, for example, how Donald Trump's odd habits of capitalization arrested the public imagination. Reading Trump's tweets, said @highfactdiet, is like "reading a flight analysis of a drunk turkey." "Dementia, definitely dementia," proclaimed @mjacobpgh. "How does capitalization work in Russia?" queried @twipdx23 conspiratorially. Trump "has adopted the unmistakable patois of a comic book villain," observed @Bauzerbaby. How to solve the mystery of the President's grammar? Perhaps we should "get the Unabomber guys on it," volunteered @PKMerlott.[2]

This sort of nonsense is fun for some but, for most people, it makes politics irrelevant. For them, the stuff of politics – protecting the nation, keeping the economy strong – vanishes beneath the weight of language. For them, politics is a game played by elites – speechwriters, journalists, advertising executives, academics, and comedians – people who do not have real jobs, jobs that make you perspire. Many Americans are logophobes as a result. If a politician says something is true, it must be false; otherwise the politician would have done something about it. Political campaigns only make things worse: Angry words, happy words; rousing words on TV, digital words in your pocket.

"Nothing is easier or more pathetic than being a critic," opined Donald Trump during his first college commencement speech as president, "the future belongs to the people who follow their heart."[3] "Don't listen to others' words," Trump seems to be saying; "just listen to me, for I will steer you truly." Trump is right, of course: Critics abound in politics. They do so because politics deals with incommensurate things (a *safe war*), even impossible things (*universal prosperity*). Political words rarely stand still (who is a *true conservative*, after all?) and the same word (*progressivism*) used by different people (e.g., Hillary Clinton and Bernie Sanders) means entirely different things. Some words (*tax cut*) sound fine when first uttered but then other words (*national deficit*) spoil the celebration. You cannot depend on politicians, people reason, and you surely cannot depend on their words.

Feelings like these paved the way for Donald Trump. He too used political words but he used them in unprecedented ways, ones that drew people to him. In this chapter, I lay out the basic features of his style and show why he was especially welcome to those who felt ignored. His voice had a sumptuous clarity to it. To be sure, he was artless, sometimes vulgar, a stark contrast to eight years of Barack Obama's immeasurable charm. Trump himself had an odd relationship with language. He produced words constantly, often without cortical processing, but he turned that flaw into a feature. Here, finally, was a man who would not be a tool of the Washington Word Machine.

This chapter, and the book itself, is the latest product of the Campaign Mapping Project, an ambitious effort begun at the University of Texas at Austin in 1995 that puts U.S. presidential campaigns in historical perspective. For example, Donald Trump seems similar to, but different from, Ross Perot, another business tycoon, but how, specifically, is that true? How can we be sure? The Project has, to date, produced 8 books and more than 200 journal articles, scholarly papers, and graduate theses and dissertations. The Project has resulted in a searchable textbase now housing some 70,000 speeches, debates, ads, print coverage, broadcast transcripts, letters to the editor, polling interviews, and social media exchanges between 1948 and the present, gathered throughout the United States. Given its size and consistency, the Project particularly lends itself to comparative content analysis using both human coders and automated language analysis. The database lets us "watch words move" – across time, across campaigns, across regions, across different media. The database helps us discipline the world of words and, given the torrent of words Donald Trump produces, that discipline is needed.[4]

To deal with such a great number of texts, computers come in handy. The results reported in this book have used three tools in particular. One is called DICTION 7.0, a program that uses more than fifty dictionaries (word lists) to take apart a verbal passage and then compare it to a set of preprocessed norms to see what makes that passage special (e.g., was Donald Trump nastier, or friendlier, in the early Republican debates than in the later exchanges?). To date, DICTION has produced some 700 scholarly studies across the social sciences – psychology, sociology, political science, communication, management, finance, etc. – and is especially good at finding rhetorical patterns the average person would never notice (but which might affect them profoundly). Another program, WordSmith, helped me track the use of individual words (e.g., do politicians talk more about *morality* today than they did thirty years ago?). A third program, AntConc, lets a researcher identify the *context* in which a word is used and so is especially useful for comparing different domains of discourse (e.g., do citizens talk more about *morality* than do mainstream reporters?).[5] Ultimately, of course, computer-based studies make sense only when political language is put back in context, so examples will be presented throughout this book.

Trump Essentials

For many Americans, national political campaigns have become a strategy-centered, personality-dominated, issueless fog. Donald Trump cut through the fog. That became clear to Representative Cheri Bustos of Illinois' 17th District when she encountered a retired farmer in

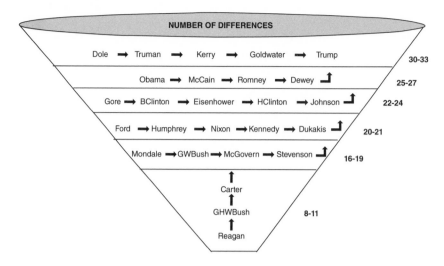

Figure 2.1 Distinctiveness of Lexicons for Presidential Candidates, 1948–2016
Note: Stacked in reverse order of statistically significant differences from the mean for each of sixty-three language variables.
Source: Data from Campaign Mapping Project.

a supermarket in 2018. She inquired what was on his mind and he said "I like Trump." She asked him why and he said "I like the way he talks." "My wife doesn't like him though," he continued; "she thinks he's crazy."[6]

Figure 2.1 explains both reactions. These data are based on analyses of 63 different language variables (e.g., Optimistic words, Concrete words, Angry words, etc.) generated from some 40,000 speech transcripts of major-party candidates between 1948 and 2016. The figure calculates how often each speaker deviates from the political norm. So, for example, Ronald Reagan clung to the middle-of-the-pack 87.3 percent of the time (fifty-five of the indices), with Bush 41 and Jimmy Carter also hovering near the mean. As one moves up the chart, the speakers become increasingly idiosyncratic until we get to Donald Trump, who conformed to the mean only 47.6 percent of the time (thirty of the sixty-three measures). Trump used more of everything, or less of everything, than anyone else.

Trump himself might have predicted these results. He prided himself on being his own man, telling voters he was not a politician and that that was good. He said that, unlike his rivals, he knew how to read a balance sheet, build a building, negotiate a contract, crown a beauty queen, dazzle a television audience, and raise kids correctly. He told them he did not want to be confused with traditional pols like Low-energy Jeb Bush, Lying Ted Cruz, Little Marco Rubio, Crooked Hillary Clinton, or Sleepy Joe Biden. He declared such sentiments in exactly these ways – crisply and forcefully. The farmers in Representative Bustos' district may have been shocked by the way he spoke but they had heard it all before. Just not from a politician.

Ronald Reagan's affability made people feel comfortable. It was as if he lived next door. Reagan never made people nervous (unless they examined his political worldview) and he told a great story, drawing on people's treasured memories simply and effortlessly. Donald Trump borrowed Reagan's slogan for his famous red baseball caps but the similarity ended there. Reagan was predictable while Trump was bizarre. Reagan's remarks were meant for the living room, Trump's for the nineteenth hole. Historians quote Reagan; the tabloids love Trump. They do so for three reasons:

1. *Simplicity.* Sometimes they say it harshly ("Donald Trump Talks Like a Third-Grader") and sometimes with faint admiration ("The Readability and Simplicity of Donald Trump's Language"), but commentator after commentator – some anecdotally, some scientifically – agree that Donald Trump likes little words and short sentences.[7] Table 2.1 shows the same thing but with a sizeable (and comparative) dataset. In addition, it shows that Trump is dead-last in his diversity of word choice; he hammers home the same points again and again and again. According to rhetoric scholar Orly Kayam, Hillary

Table 2.1 Trump's Basic Rhetorical Habits

Type	Token	Trump Rank (out of 26)	Highest	Lowest
Basic vocabulary	Word size	25	Eisenhower	Dole
	Word variety	26	Ford	Trump
	Words per speech	1	Trump	Gore
	Self-references	3	George H. W. Bush	Dewey

Note: Figures vs. all presidential candidates from 1948 to 2016.
Source: Data from Campaign Mapping Project.

Clinton's sentences were twice as long as Donald Trump's and, according to *Newsweek*'s Nina Burleigh, Barack Obama used twice as many unique words as Trump.[8] But who needs big words, Trump might ask, when one is a stable genius?

For Trump, little words, repeated words, will do quite nicely when it comes to immigration: "We're rounding 'em up in a very humane way, in a very nice way. And they're going to be happy because they want to be legalized. And, by the way, I know it doesn't sound nice, but not everything is nice." "I will build a great, great wall on our southern border," Trump famously declared, "and I will have Mexico pay for that wall. Mark my words." People marked his words and they marked these words too: "I have a great relationship with African-Americans, as you possibly have heard. I just have great respect for them. And they like me. I like them." People marked these words as well: "It's really cold outside [and] they are calling it a major freeze, weeks ahead of normal. Man, we could use a big fat dose of global warming!"[9] People had no trouble marking Donald Trump's words.

What does it mean to be incapable of rephrasing a thought, of turning it around in one's mind in fresh ways? What does it mean to use small words almost exclusively ("We're going to have very, very strong vetting. I call it extreme vetting, and we're going very strong on security")?[10] It means that people can understand you, that they do not become lost in the fog. It may also mean that one lacks perspicacity, the efficient use of beauty, but that sounds like an elite critique, and elites are not Donald Trump's people. Trump's people go to the movies. As we see in Table 2.2, they are comfortable with a guy who can out-Hollywood Hollywood by finding the smallest words possible to make the most memorable points.

When pressed to say something kind about Donald Trump, Hillary Clinton once said: "I have a new appreciation for the galvanizing power of big, simple ideas."[11] Many voters agree. According to political scientists Elizabeth Theiss-Morse and John Hibbing, the American people have developed a special distaste for democracy's messiness. "There's more to Trump's story than just uneducated, authoritarian, misogynist, angry, old racists," they observe.[12] "A quarter of the American electorate believes that governing is so easy that it should not be bogged down by discussion, compromise and understanding various points of view."[13]

Table 2.2 Complexity of Movie Quotations vs. Trump's Style

Quotation	Characters/word	Source
"Go ahead. Make my day."	3.4	Clint Eastwood as Harry Callahan in *Sudden Impact*
"Life moves pretty fast. If you don't stop and look around once in a while, you could miss it."	3.9	Matthew Broderick as Ferris Bueller in *Ferris Bueller's Day Off*
"We'll always have Paris."	5.0	Humphrey Bogart as Rick Blaine in *Casablanca*
"Where we're going, we don't need roads."	4.6	Christopher Lloyd as Dr. Emmett Brown in *Back to the Future*
"Well, it's not the men in your life that counts, it's the life in your men."	3.7	Mae West as Tira in *I'm No Angel*
"My Mama always said, 'Life was like a box of chocolates; you never know what you're gonna get.'"	4.2	Tom Hanks as Forrest Gump in *Forrest Gump*
"Get them to sign on the line that is dotted."	3.4	Alec Baldwin as Blake in *Glengarry Glen Ross*
"There's no crying in baseball."	5.0	Tom Hanks as Jimmy Dugan in *A League of Their Own*
"Keep your friends close but your enemies closer."	5.0	Al Pacino as Michael Corleone in *The Godfather: Part II*
"Love means never having to say you're sorry."	4.5	Ali MacGraw as Jennifer Cavilleri in *Love Story*
"You had me at hello."	3.0	Renée Zellweger as Dorothy Boyd in *Jerry Maguire*
"Calling it your job don't make it right, boss."	4.1	Paul Newman as Luke in *Cool Hand Luke*
"Hasta la vista, baby."	4.3	Arnold Schwarzenegger as T-800 in *Terminator 2*
Mean for movie quotations	4.5	
Mean for Trump in debates	4.1	

Source: Data from Campaign Mapping Project.

Donald Trump is more than happy to oblige. As "a man of the people," Michael Kranish and Marc Fisher report, Trump is "more interested in the praise of cabdrivers and construction workers than in accolades from the rich and powerful."[14] It doesn't take big words to reach such people. It just takes the right words and Trump consistently finds them. "The day I realized it can be smart to be shallow was, for me, a deep experience," he once reported.[15] Academics blanch when hearing such stuff but Trumpers lean forward.

2. *Energy*. Donald Trump, it seems, cannot stop talking. As Table 2.1 reports, he fills his formal addresses with more words than anyone who has run for president during the past seventy years. In statistical terms, his words-per-speech average is more than two standard deviations from the political mean. He became even more voluble during the Republican primary debates, taking a total of 783 turns-of-speech compared to Ben Carson's 131, Jeb Bush's 272, and Ted Cruz's 344. Even chatterbox Marco Rubio got only 388 swings at the pitch. During Hillary Clinton's general election debates with Trump, and even though she produced 58 speech segments to Trump's 56, Clinton only uttered a total of 2,830 words while Trump hit the 3,589 mark.

These differences may reflect regional variations (New Yorkers are more talkative than Midwesterners), but gender may also be a variable. As Yale's Victoria Brescoll reports, a U.S. senator's relative power in Congress is directly tied to their volubility – unless they are women, in which case they are often punished for being too talkative. What is true in Washington is also true in Los Angeles, reports the Signal Analysis and Interpretation Lab at USC. In a study of 1,000 popular film scripts, male characters produced 37,000 turns-of-speech compared to women's 15,000. It is not surprising, then, that the "Clinton cackle" was linked by some to an uncooperative persona and by others to nagging.[16] In contrast, Trump's freewheeling style was linked to his irrepressible energy, a desire to start solving the nation's problems.

Volubility sends a number of other signals as well. It suggests, for example, that Trump holds nothing back, that he cares enough about people to take them into his confidence *even while thinking his way through a problem*. Such apparent openness was particularly appealing to those who felt shut out of the political process. People who already felt included, in contrast, were attracted to the prepared, analytical Hillary Clinton. But each time Clinton paused while speaking, each time she tried to make the most cogent response possible, she was seen as too calculating by many voters.

Trump's volubility meant he was often his own worst leaker. That, too, impressed people on the outside even though it drove his staffers crazy. Trump's freewheeling style, say reporters John Wagner and Matt Zapotosky, "is a large part of his appeal and has kept him in good stead with his political base."[17] Was there nothing Trump would not say? Was there no way of shutting him up? To ask such questions is to miss the Trump Phenomenon. Anyone can edit, his supporters felt, but it takes a real man to forsake editing altogether. The political world had never seen anything like Donald Trump.[18]

Volubility also signals relentlessness – Trump-the-salesman. Trump's "burlesque" personality, filled as it was with gross over-statements and self-promotion, took Americans by surprise.[19] His instinct for moment-to-moment invention, of interrupting everyone (including himself), would drive a defense lawyer crazy when pre-paring a client for a deposition. But with Trump it meant folding a bunch of adjectives into a money-back guarantee:

- I know the details of taxes better than anybody. Better than the greatest CPA (December 28, 2017).
- ISIS is in retreat, our economy is booming, investments and jobs are pouring back into the country, and so much more! (January 17, 2018).
- This is our new American moment. There has never been a better time to start living the American dream (January 26, 2018).
- The people that like me best are the people, the workers. They're the people I understand the best. Those are the people I grew up with (November 29, 2017).[20]

Classicist W. Robert Connor notes that, historically speaking, politicians have mostly lived by the Demosthenesean principle that "the scale of discourse should correspond to the mag-nitude of the achievement or the depravity under discussion."[21] Demosthenes never met Donald Trump and he certainly never heard of "truthful hyperbole." "People may not always think big them-selves," Trump declared in *The Art of the Deal*, "but they can still get very excited by those who do."[22] When Connor confronted a

Trump admirer with one of The Donald's misstatements, she replied "Oh sure, it is extreme, but I think I know what he means." "Her tone of voice," observed Connor, "resembled that of a mother coming to the defense of a wayward child."[23] The metaphors are thick here: Trump the salesman asking voters to adopt him so he, the child, can lead them to the Promised Land. That child is now the forty-fifth president of the United States.

3. *Dominance.* With Trump, anything can happen at any time. Such an approach shows great trust in an audience. As anthropologist Richard Wilson notes, it also forces them to listen more closely.[24] Trump's style is filled with "that wild supplement," a "sense of pure presence" that journalists often dismiss because of its logical short-comings, says the University of Chicago's William Mazzarella.[25] In these ways, says author Michael Wolff, Trump resembles William Jennings Bryan, a turn-of-the-twentieth-century stem-winder. Following Bryan, Trump's rhetoric was "part hortatory, part personal testimony, part barstool blowhard, a rambling, disjointed, digressive, what-me-worry approach that combined aspects of cable television rage, big-tent religious revivalism, Borscht Belt tummler, motivational speaking, and YouTube vlogging."[26]

All politicians have an ego, but none more than Donald Trump. One need not listen to him for long to note the me-me-me-ness of his rap. Trump has a "self-sufficient personality," notes Ricardo Casañ-Pitarch, and his beliefs are self-validating as a result.[27] As we see in Table 2.1, Trump's self-references drive his discourse. *His* experience, *his* belief system, *his* loathings predominate.[28] When celebrating Black History Month in 2017, for example, Trump used the occasion to tell Black leaders in the Roosevelt Room how reporters were persecuting him. Martin Luther King Jr.'s martyrdom, says the *New York Times'* Ben Wiseman, became Trump's martyrdom. "Trump's analysis of people and situations," says Wiseman, "hinges on whether they exalt him. A news organization that challenges him is inevitably 'failing.' A politician who pushes back at him is invariably a loser. Middle-school cliques have more moral discernment."[29]

Trump's self-absorption would normally have turned off the good folks in middle America but, for some reason in 2016, it did not. Not this: "I will be the greatest president God ever created." Not this: "I'm really rich." And not this: "Nobody out-thinks me."[30]

Trump's 2007 emasculation of rival wrestling promoter Vince McMahon (which saw Trump shave McMahon's head in a televised extravaganza) foreshadowed his ego-driven capacity for abuse. "You wouldn't need Jane Goodall or Sigmund Freud," notes writer James Fallows, "to see in this spectacle every ritual of dominance, emasculation, ridicule, and humiliation." "Once I had seen that video," Fallows reports, "it replayed in my mind every time Trump stepped onto a debate stage."[31]

Another piece of telling data: When Trump's extemporaneous statements were compared to his prepared remarks I found that his Self-references were off the scale, as was his Tenacity ("I am," "you are," "she is") and Negativity (use of denial words).[32] In other words, Trump's spontaneity released his inner demons, baring his ego needs. But still people listened and still they approved. "People walk away from Trump feeling as though he were casually talking to them," notes Tara Golshan, "allowing them to finish his thoughts."[33]

Trump's confidence, his willingness to wander from point to point, is unique in politics. While doing so, Trump tries out thoughts he had never thought before, building a kind of spontaneous intimacy with his audience. When he starts on one of his excursions, one is almost compelled to ride along, in part because the trip is so weirdly exciting and in part because it might end in a brilliant, multi-car accident:

> My uncle was a great professor and scientist and engineer, Dr. John Trump at MIT; good genes, very good genes, okay, very smart, the Wharton School of Finance, very good, very smart – you know, if you're a conservative Republican, if I were a liberal, if, like, okay, if I ran as a liberal Democrat, they would say I'm one of the smartest people anywhere in the world – it's true! – but when you're a conservative Republican they try – oh, do they do a number – that's why I always start off: *Went to Wharton, was a good student, went there, went there, did this, built a fortune –* you know I have to give my, like, credentials all the time, because we're a little disadvantaged – but you look at the nuclear deal, the thing that really bothers me – it would have been so easy, and it's not as important as these lives are

(nuclear is powerful; my uncle explained that to me many, many years ago, the power and that was 35 years ago; he would explain the power of what's going to happen and he was right – who would have thought?), but when you look at what's going on with the four prisoners – now it used to be three, now it's four – but when it was three and even now, I would have said it's all in the messenger; fellas, and it is fellas because, you know, they don't, they haven't figured that the women are smarter right now than the men, so, you know, it's gonna take them about another 150 years – but the Persians are great negotiators, the Iranians are great negotiators, so, and they, they just killed, they just killed us.[34]

Simplicity, energy, and dominance do not travel Trump's road alone. They intersect constantly to produce a sparkling ingenuity but also a capacity for menace. "Look, we are worse than the lions in the jungle," Trump once observed, "worse than any predator. Lions hunt for food, to live. We hunt for sport. Our hunting involves doing lots of bad things to other people, whether it's stealing their money or whatever. People are bad, they really are."[35] Given Trump's reveries and his kill-or-be-killed mentality, his election is all the more surprising. But elected he was and that, I believe, shows the danger of letting people feel ignored. Despite her gold-plated resumé and unquestionable sense of duty, many felt forgotten by Hillary Clinton and her establishment coterie. Donald Trump ignored nobody. He attacked his opponents vigorously and he embraced his supporters vigorously. Bizarre though he was, many could not resist him.

Trump Assessments

Donald Trump is not a literary man. Once in the White House, he did everything he could to avoid reading, causing his military advisors to make colorful PowerPoint charts when preparing briefs for him. "Expecting a man who has always preferred chatting and watching television to the printed word to become a reader at 71 would be foolish," observes the *Atlantic*'s David Graham.[36] Donald Trump is "an idiot surrounded by clowns," said his former chief economic advisor Gary Cohn. "Trump won't read anything – not one-page memos, not brief policy papers; nothing. He gets up halfway through meetings with world leaders because he is bored. And his staff is no better."[37]

"The president's inability to use the English language is really without precedent in American politics," says Boston University's Andrew Bacevich.[38] "Trump is a reductive force," says journalist Peter Ross. "He wants everything to be as small and mean as his own heart, and he has made a start with words."[39] "Trump does have a way with words," says historian Michael Winship. "Unfortunately, it's a gruesome way. His way is to use them as a blunt instrument to bully and belittle opponents. The rest of the time – when he's not reading prepared remarks from a teleprompter – his way with English is fumbling, incoherent, reckless."[40]

These are the remarks of rhetorical fundamentalists, people for whom words are sacred – academics and journalists primarily. For them, language reveals the soul. Therefore, when confronted with a slacker like Donald Trump, the rhetorical fundamentalists become lyrical in their denunciations: Trump produces an "incessant flow of hyperbolic, polarizing, contradictory statements," according to the *Washington Post*'s Nichole Russell and Patrick A. Stewart.[41] When it comes to Trump's language, says columnist Derek Thompson, he "evinces not a Midas touch, but a Moses touch – an extraordinary talent for planting a stake in the ground and dividing the landscape before him."[42] "Trump comes from a place where words are cheap," says CNN's Fareed Zakaria, "and he's spending them like a drunk in a casino."[43]

Trump would think such a critique odd. "Words have no monetary value," he might declare. "They're purely utilitarian. With things changing so fast in the business world, you need to stay flexible." "The only time words are important," he would add, "is when you find them in a legal contract and, even then, you can always fudge things." Given Trump's feelings about the weightlessness of words, dialogues like the following were predestined:

REPORTER:	"The President repeated this claim in the Oval Office today, saying we're the highest taxed nation in the world. Why does the President keep saying this? It's not true, overall."
SARAH HUCKABEE SANDERS:	"We are the highest taxed corporate tax in the developed economy. That's a fact."

REPORTER:	"But that's not what the President said."
SARAH HUCKABEE SANDERS:	"That's what he's talking about. We are the highest corporate taxed country in the developed economies across the globe."
REPORTER:	"Sarah, so that's accurate. But the President keeps repeating the claim that we're the highest taxed nation."
SARAH HUCKABEE SANDERS:	"We are the highest taxed corporate nation."
REPORTER:	"But that's not what he said. He said we're the highest taxed nation in the world."
SARAH HUCKABEE SANDERS:	"The highest taxed corporate nation – it seems pretty consistent to me. Sorry, we're just going to have to agree to disagree."[44]

There is almost something comical in this exchange as words are parsed and reparsed. But there is something serious as well – a growing *institutional* chasm between those who love words and those who do not. "Most previous White Houses I've covered," said CBS's Major Garrett, "had a sense of fear" about such exchanges. "I don't think this White House has that fear," he concluded.[45] "Don't you think that it's kind of surreal," asked CNN's Anderson Cooper, "that we are in a place now in our country where we're like, 'Oh, don't listen to the president,' like he's a crazy person on a park bench with an onion tied to his belt, just mumbling incoherently?"[46]

Given Trump's attitudes toward language, the White House was awash in "secondary speech" after he became president. Press secretary-for-a-time Sean Spicer was marched out in May of 2017 to explain Trump's use of the word *covfefe* in one of his tweets. Spicer resolutely assured the press corps that "the president and a small group of people know exactly what he meant."[47] Similarly, White House Counsel Donald McGahn was brought in to clarify what Trump had in mind when (falsely) accusing Barack Obama of wiretapping Trump Tower prior to the 2016 election. Vice President Mike Pence was delegated to clarify the President's remarks about NATO, Chief of Staff John Kelly to explain Trump's "evolution" on the border wall controversy, and the plucky Sarah Sanders to explore what Trump's "calm before the storm" remark meant vis-à-vis North Korea. It took a village to clean up after Donald Trump.

Given Trump's wayward use of language, how did he establish credibility for vast segments of the populace? Why did the press's deconstructions of his remarks so often fall on deaf ears? Journalists are mystified – and enraged – by these questions. Even more enraging is Trump supporters' *self-consciousness* about such matters. Many of his backers realize that the President misrepresents reality, contradicts himself, and makes up evidence on the fly. They know he declares things to be true only because he wants them to be true. They surely know that he talks too much:

- He's full of himself and he talks a lot and he wants praise. I think we can accomplish these other things without all that type of fanfare (Everett Pannier, Morrison, Illinois).
- You can't accomplish anything if you're making everybody mad as a president. He should just stop talking for a while and be a president (Chris Underwood, Gays Mills, Wisconsin).
- I think you can accept Donald Trump as president while disagreeing with his positions or his rhetoric or his comments as it relates to certain issues (Andrew Chesney, Freeport, Illinois).
- He's not going along with the agenda. He's a wild card. In America, we have freedom of speech. You don't have to agree with it (Meryl Fischer, Long Island, New York).[48]

People like these do not live in a world of words. They do things for a living – make cars, cook meals, read water meters – and hence sharply distinguish between language and action. "The reality is," says one former White House official, that "more Americans speak like President Trump than speak like [CNN's] Jim Acosta."[49] Such Americans are uncomfortable with abstractions (*federal deficit, nuclear disarmament, racial resentment*) and often feel funny about eloquence itself, treating it as a faintly European thing. Words are easy going down, they reason, but one quickly feels empty when things do not work out as predicted.

As a result, many Americans are rhetorical apostates, embracing such beliefs as these: (1) *overstatements are part of the human condition* ("ISIS is honoring President Obama. He is the founder of ISIS"); (2) *conflictual situations back people into a corner* ("You could see there was blood coming out of her eyes, blood coming out of her wherever"); (3) *words can miss the mark even when well-intended* (e.g., "Look at my African American over here!"); (4) *the media unfairly reprise people's remarks* ("Look at that face! Would anyone *vote* for that? Can you imagine that, the face of our next president?"); (5) *words are ephemeral and conditions can change* ("Just heard Foreign Minister of North Korea speak at UN. If he echoes thoughts of Little Rocket Man, they won't be around much longer!"); (6) *words are often the products of emotion and hence can be forgiven* (e.g., "John McCain was a war hero because he was captured"); (7) *people often brag too much* (e.g., "I know words. I have the best words"); and (8) *we all sound irredeemably dumb from time to time* ("Two Corinthians, right?").[50]

Many Americans have routinely extended these gratuities to Donald Trump. Are they wrong for having done so? Should they have held a president to higher rhetorical standards? Should they have resisted the force of his overweening personality, the shimmering glitz of all things Trump? Should they have treated him not as one of their own (how many billionaires did they know, after all?) and kept him at a distance, as the press did? Should they have *read* his words rather than watched clips of him on TV? Should they have regarded his tweets as the mindless products of someone who sleeps poorly at night?

In much of the United States, words are not worshipped. Donald Trump capitalized on those feelings. For him, words are best when spoken. In face-to-face encounters with others, he reasons, you get a sense of the crowd. Spoken words move through time, not space (as with writing), so you can revise things as you move along, doubling down when the moment seems right. In contrast, journalists and lawyers – Trump's sworn enemies – like their words printed so they can go over them again and again. Such people are ontologically dishonest, Trump reasons, by letting old events (his gaffes, his temper tantrums) reappear on the nightly news. It is better, he reasons, to reinvent the world each morning, seeking out new audiences whose histories have not yet been written. "I'm not proud of my locker room talk," he declared in October of 2016, "but this world has serious problems. We need serious leaders."[51] Case closed; pivot made; tomorrow is another day.

Conclusion

Recent U.S. presidents have ranged from the eloquent (John Kennedy, Barack Obama) to the plain-spoken (Harry Truman, Jerry Ford), but Donald Trump is something else entirely. Trump says things in public that even an earthy fellow like Lyndon Johnson would say only in private. Trump's standby words are single-syllabled (*rich*, *great*, *huge*, *win*) as are his ideological words (*coal*, *wall*, *guns*, *God*). Trump strings small words together to express his disdain (*drain the swamp*, *witch hunt*, *fake news*) as well as his delights (*tax cuts*, *more jobs*, *Fox News*). While he is fond of a few multi-syllable words (*American*, *military*, *corporations*), he hates most of them: *Obamacare*, *immigrants*, *regulations*, *diversity*, *collusion*.

Not all voters who felt ignored in 2016 appreciated Donald Trump, but many did. Trump opened doors normally closed to ultra-rich Republicans with no governmental experience. His style had an accessible, I-hear-you quality that caused many Americans to proudly wear their MAGA hats. The press, of course, hated Trump's style but even they could not resist it. "Trump's intelligence," says CNN commentator Michael D'Antonio, "lies in using the right word in the right way, knowing how the media will do the rest of the work for him."[52] Trump's Republican rivals in 2015–16 also hated his style and for the same reason: "I don't think Trump had any idea what he was going to say until he said it," observes former Marco Rubio advisor, Alex Conant. "All you could be certain of is that if he said something funny or outlandish, that would dominate the news and you'd be even further behind."[53]

Academics especially hate Trump's language. His reductionism, his reliance on hearsay and anecdotes, they argue, irredeemably ignores relevant facts and standards of accountability.[54] "Trump's personality and charisma," says political historian Richard Wolin, render voters "consistently willing to engage in a worrisome suspension of disbelief, waving the evidentiary claims that voters traditionally rely on to evaluate a candidate's trustworthiness and viability."[55] Trump's grandiosity, says another team of social scientists, actively causes voters to misunderstand what they are voting for.[56]

There is another downside to Trump's rhetoric: Because his style is so accessible it can become contagious. As the Trump administration wore on, for example, media reports of citizens' overt racism multiplied daily. While it is hard to know if such occurrences were in fact more plentiful or if the media were just exploiting the ones they did find, Donald Trump's presidency called greater attention to them.[57] So, for example, systems administrator Estebán Guzman reports how his mother was upbraided by the neighbor of a woman whose house she was cleaning. "She came out of her home to yell at my mom, 'Go back to Mexico.'" "Why do you hate us?" Guzman asked the woman. "Because you're Mexican," the neighbor replied. "We're honest people," Guzman retorted, to which the neighbor replied "Ha, ha. Yeah, rapists ... animals." "She's quoting the president right now!" Guzman thought to himself.[58]

Clearly, these are things to worry about. But we also need to know how people insulate themselves from such criticisms. Consider, for example, how some reacted when tape recordings of Trump's sexist remarks to Billy Bush (of *Access Hollywood* fame) were released on election eve in 2016. Although most Americans were appalled by what they heard, not all were. "I like men who are successful and know what they want," tweeted @DeplorableAnne. "I am offended by people who sit during the national anthem, not by what Trump said," declared @Lisa3682. "He was talking to another man about women. It was wrong, but how many do that?" argued @DianeSymons. "Anyone who is appalled by what Trump said must have a really boring sex life," concluded @BarbieKeleigh.[59]

Major Garrett met such folks on the campaign trail. "Always, I would talk to Trump supporters at these rallies," he recalled, "and I would have this conversation about things that he would say that were manifestly untrue." "And what I would hear back repetitively," Garrett continues, "was 'Yes, but you're missing the point. He's right about the larger truth.'"[60] It may be deplorable, and it is certainly remarkable, that 62 million Americans were able to find larger truths in Donald Trump. But they did so because they felt unnoticed. Whether or not their feelings were justified is a question only they can answer, although the rest of us will no doubt chime in.

Notes

1 See Michael M. Grynbaum, "Michelle Wolf Sets Off a Furor at White House Correspondents' Dinner," *New York Times*, April 29, 2018. Accessed at www.nytimes.com/2018/04/29/business/media/michelle-wolfs-routine-sets-off-a-furor-at-an-annual-washington-dinner.html; and Caitlyn Hitt, "Who Is Peter Fonda? Actor Who Said Barron Trump Should be Taken from Melania Revealed," *Daily Mail.com*, June 20, 2018. Accessed at www.dailymail.co.uk/news/article-5867311/Who-Peter-Fonda-Actor-said-Barron-Trump-taken-Melania-revealed.html.

2 Preceding comments submitted to @NateSilver538 on *Twitter*, May 7, 2018. Accessed at https://twitter.com/natesilver538.

3 As quoted in Kevin Dolak and John Verhovek, *ABC News*, "Trump Slams 'Critics' in His First Commencement Address as President," May 13, 2017. Accessed at

https://abcnews.go.com/Politics/president-trump-deliver-commencement-address-lib
erty-university/story?id=47380501.

4 For more information about the Campaign Mapping Project, see https://moody
.utexas.edu/centers/strauss/campaign-mapping-project.

5 For more information about these programs, see the following: DICTION: www
.dictionsoftware.com/; WordSmith: www.lexically.net/wordsmith/; AntConc: www
.laurenceanthony.net/software/antconc/.

6 As quoted in Dan Balz, "Loyalty, Unease in Trump's Midwest," *Washington Post*,
May 20, 2018. Accessed at www.washingtonpost.com/graphics/2018/national/
trump-voters/?utm_term=.60050a618891.

7 Jack Shafer, "Donald Trump Talks Like a Third-Grader," *Politico*, August 13, 2015.
Accessed at www.politico.com/magazine/story/2015/08/donald-trump-talks-like-a-
third-grader-121340; Orly Kayam, "The Readability and Simplicity of Donald
Trump's Language," *Political Studies Review*, 16:1, 2017, 1–16.

8 Kayam, "The Readability and Simplicity of Donald Trump's Language," 11;
Nina Burleigh, "Trump Speaks at Fourth-Grade Level, Lowest of Last Fifteen U.S.
Presidents, New Analysis Finds," *Newsweek*, January 8, 2018. Accessed at www
.newsweek.com/trump-fire-and-fury-smart-genius-obama-774169.

9 Quotations from, respectively, *60 Minutes*, November 11, 2015; Campaign
announcement, June 16, 2015; *Anderson Cooper 360*, July 22, 2015; *Twitter*,
October 19, 2015. Handily archived at "The Fifty Most Ridiculous Trump Quotes,"
ShortList. Accessed on July 29, 2018 at www.shortlist.com/news/the-50-most-ridicu
lous-trump-quotes-ever/54443.

10 Donald Trump interview on *60 Minutes*, July 17, 2016, and discussed in www
.nbcnews.com/politics/2016-election/donald-trump-shifts-muslim-ban-calls-extreme-
vetting-n611276.

11 Hillary Rodham Clinton, *What Happened* (New York: Simon & Schuster, 2017),
p. 234.

12 Elizabeth Theiss-Morse and John R. Hibbing, "A Surprising Number of Americans
Dislike How Messy Democracy Is; They Like Trump," *Washington Post*, May 2,
2016. Accessed at www.washingtonpost.com/news/monkey-cage/wp/2016/05/02/a-
surprising-number-of-americans-dislike-how-messy-democracy-is-they-like-trump/?
utm_term=.27de95eb9732.

13 Ibid.

14 Michael Kranish and Marc Fisher, *Trump Revealed: The Definitive Biography of the
45th President* (New York: Scribner, 2016), p. 4.

15 As quoted ibid., p. 168.

16 See Caryl Rivers and Rosalind C. Barnett, "Why Hillary Clinton Gets in Trouble
When She Talks," *Chicago Tribune*, September 30, 2015. Accessed at www
.chicagotribune.com/news/nationworld/ct-hillary-clinton-bill-presidency-speech-talk-
obama-perspec-1001-jm-20150930-story.html.

17 John Wagner and Matt Zapotosky, "Trump and His Advisers Can't Keep Quiet –
and It's Becoming a Real Problem," *Washington Post*, March 16, 2017. Accessed at
www.washingtonpost.com/politics/trump-and-his-advisers-cant-keep-quiet–and-its-
becoming-a-real-problem/2017/03/16/157d2100-0a63-11e7-93dc-00f9bdd74ed1_
story.html?utm_term=.c5f96edb0a38.

18 Christina Grigoryan notes that Trump's creative and unpredictable style often leads
him to combine elements from entirely different cognitive domains (e.g., family and
business, identity and crime, trust and finance, etc.). See "Metaphors We Choose By:
the Role of Conceptualization in Donald Trump's Success," occasional paper
accessed at www.academia.edu/34664015/moscow_article.docx.

19 As quoted in Edward C. Appel, "Burlesque, Tragedy, and a (Potentially) 'Yuuge Breaking of Frame': Donald Trump's Rhetoric as 'Early Warning,'" *Communication Quarterly*, 66:2 (2018), 157–75.

20 A handy compilation of Trump's best lines is provided by Karen Yourish and Denise Lu Jan, "Trump as Optimist, Salesman or Bully: Mixing Messages in His First Year," *New York Times*, January 31, 2018. Accessed at www.nytimes.com/interactive/2018/01/31/us/politics/many-sides-of-trump.html.

21 W. Robert Connor, "Hyperbole in Political Discourse, Ancient and Modern," August 2017, occasional paper, 6, Accessed at www.wrobertconnor.com/uploads/3/3/5/8/3358534/hyperbole_august_2017.pdf.

22 Donald J. Trump and Tony Schwartz, *Trump: The Art of the Deal* (New York: Ballantine, 2015), p. 58.

23 Connor, "Hyperbole in Political Discourse, Ancient and Modern," 8.

24 As paraphrased in Olivia Goldhill, "Rhetoric Scholars Pinpoint Why Trump's Inarticulate Speaking Style Is So Persuasive," *Quartz*, April 22, 2017. Accessed at https://qz.com/965004/rhetoric-scholars-pinpoint-why-trumps-inarticulate-speaking-style-is-so-persuasive/.

25 William T. S. Mazzarella, "Brand(ish)ing the Name, or Why Is Trump So Enjoyable?," occasional paper, 6, available at www.academia.edu/35333795/Brand_ish_ing_the_Name_or_Why_is_Trump_So_Enjoyable.

26 Michael Wolff, *Fire and Fury: Inside the Trump White House* (New York: Henry Holt and Co., 2018), pp. 45–46.

27 Ricardo Casañ-Pitarch, "'Mr. President, Discourse Matters': a Contrastive Analysis of Donald Trump and Barack Obama's Discourse," *Journal of Language Studies, Semiotics, and Semantics*, 9:1 (2018), 173–85.

28 For more on Trump's use of self-references, see Jacques Savoy, "Analysis of the Style and Rhetoric of the 2016 U.S. Presidential Primaries," *Digital Scholarship in the Humanities*, 33:1 (2018), 143–59.

29 Ben Wiseman, "Me, Me, Me, Me, Me," *New York Times*, February 4, 2017. Accessed at www.nytimes.com/2017/02/04/opinion/me-me-me-me-me.html.

30 As quoted in Appel, "Burlesque, Tragedy and a (Potentially) 'Yuuge Breaking of Frame,'" 164.

31 James Fallows, "When Donald Meets Hillary," *Atlantic*, April 12, 2017. Accessed at www.theatlantic.com/press-releases/archive/2016/09/who-will-win-the-debates-and-the-election-james-fallows-on-the-cover-of-the-atlantics-october-issue/499751/.

32 Statistical patterns for Self-references: prepared texts = 9.6774; spontaneous texts = 18.3983; $F_{[1, 440]} = 117.483$, $p < 0.000$; for Tenacity scores: prepared texts = 34.1697; spontaneous texts = 48.2294; $F_{[1, 440]} = 213.497$, $p < 0.000$; for Denial words: prepared texts = 5.9895; spontaneous texts = 9.8875; $F_{[1, 440]} = 102.434$, $p < 0.000$.

33 Tara Golshan, "Donald Trump's Unique Speaking Style, Explained by Linguists," *Vox*, January 11, 2017. Accessed at www.vox.com/policy-and-politics/2017/1/11/14238274/trumps-speaking-style-press-conference-linguists-explain.

34 Donald Trump, South Carolina campaign rally, July 21, 2015, as quoted ibid.

35 As quoted in George Beahm, *Trump on Trump: Understanding Donald Trump through His Own Words* (London: Cassell Octopus, 2016), pp. 146–47.

36 David A. Graham, "The President Who Doesn't Read: Trump's Allergy to the Written Word and His Reliance on Oral Communication Have Proven Liabilities in Office," *Atlantic*, January 5, 2018. Accessed at www.theatlantic.com/politics/archive/2018/01/americas-first-post-text-president/549794/.

37 As quoted in Joe Scarborough, "I Asked Trump a Blunt Question: Do You Read?" *Washington Post*, January 4, 2018. Accessed at www.washingtonpost.com/opinions/can-you-read/2018/01/04/46d967a2-f18c-11e7-b3bf-ab90a706e175_story.html?utm_term=.efdcd293b1ff.

38 As quoted in Michael Winship, "For Trump, Words Are Stupid Things," *BillMoyers.com*, October 27, 2017. Accessed at https://billmoyers.com/story/trump-language-words-are-stupid-things/.

39 As quoted in Winship, "For Trump, Words are Stupid Things," *BillMoyers.com*.

40 Ibid.

41 Nichole Russell and Patrick A. Stewart, "Why Do We Care about Trump's Body Language? It's More Honest Than His Words," *Washington Post*, April 26, 2018. Accessed at www.washingtonpost.com/outlook/why-do-we-care-about-trumps-body-language-its-more-honest-than-his-words/2018/04/26/5114e26c-4963-11e8-827e-190efaf1f1ee_story.html?utm_term=.8a3f23cdf0d4.

42 Derek Thompson, "Donald Trump's Language Is Reshaping American Politics," *Atlantic*, February 15, 2018. Accessed at www.theatlantic.com/politics/archive/2018/02/donald-trumps-language-is-reshaping-american-politics/553349/.

43 Fareed Zakaria, *GPS on CNN*, April 5, 2017. Accessed at www.cnn.com/videos/politics.

44 Press briefing with Sarah Huckabee Sanders, *White House*, October 17, 2017. Accessed at www.presidency.ucsb.edu/ws/index.php?pid=128492.

45 Transcript from NPR's *On Point*, December 3, 2017. Accessed at www.npr.org/programs/on-point/2017/12/03/568357267.

46 As quoted in Ed Mazza, "Anderson Cooper Shreds 'Incoherent' Trump: 'Like a Crazy Person on a Park Bench,'" *HuffPost*, April 27, 2018. Accessed at www.huffingtonpost.com/entry/anderson-cooper-donald-trump-park-bench_us_5ae2881 2e4b02baed1b88f70.

47 Jessica Estepa, "Sean Spicer Says 'Covfefe' Wasn't a Typo: Trump Knew 'Exactly What He Meant,'" *USA Today*, May 31, 2017. Accessed at www.usatoday.com/story/news/politics/onpolitics/2017/05/31/sean-spicer-says-covfefe-wasnt-typo-trump-knew-exactly-what-he-meant/102355728/.

48 As quoted in Balz, "Loyalty, Unease in Trump's Midwest," *Washington Post*; John Verhovek, Dylan Wells, and Saisha Talwar, "Poll Respondents Explain Their Support for Trump's Response to Charlottesville," *ABC News*, August 23, 2017. Accessed at https://abcnews.go.com/Politics/poll-respondents-explain-support-trumps-response-charlottesville/story?id=49376403.

49 Jonathan Easley, "Trump Allies See 'S—hole' Controversy as Overblown," *TheHill.com*, January 13, 2018. Accessed at http://thehill.com/homenews/administration/368816-trump-allies-say-shithole-controversy-as-overblown.

50 These and other Trump miscues can be found at Michael Kruse and Taylor Gee, "The Thirty-Seven Fatal Gaffes That Didn't Kill Donald Trump," *Politico*, September 25, 2016. Accessed at www.politico.com/magazine/story/2016/09/trump-biggest-fatal-gaffes-mistakes-offensive-214289.

51 Donald J. Trump, *Twitter*, October 9, 2016. Accessed at https://twitter.com/realdonaldtrump/status/785286990153543681?lang=en.

52 Michael D'Antonio, "The Cynical Brilliance of Donald Trump," *CNN Opinion*, October 28, 2017. Accessed at www.cnn.com/2017/10/27/opinions/trumps-cynical-intelligence-dantonio-opinion/index.html.

53 As quoted in James Fallows, "When Donald Meets Hillary," April 12, 2017. Accessed at www.theatlantic.com/magazine/archive/2016/10/who-will-win/497561/.

54 For a fuller dissection of Trump's rhetorical impertinences, see Kathleen Hall Jamieson and Doron Taussig, "Disruption, Demonization, Deliverance, and Norm Destruction: the Rhetorical Signature of Donald J. Trump," *Political Science Quarterly*, 20:20 (2017), 1–32.

55 Richard Wolin, "Our 'Prophet of Deceit': WWII-Era Social Scientists Explained Trump's Appeal," *Chronicle Review*, November 4, 2016, B9.

56 Sara Ahmadian, Sara Azarshahi, and Delroy L. Paulhus, "Explaining Donald Trump via Communication Style: Grandiosity, Informality, and Dynamism," *Personality and Individual Differences*, 107 (2017), 49–53.

57 The most exhaustive study completed to date on this matter finds "no persistent increase in hate speech or white nationalist language either over the course of the [2016] campaign or in the aftermath of Trump's election," a finding that will surely be questioned by many. See Alexandra Siegel, Evgenii Nikitin, Pablo Barbera, Joanna Sterling, Bethany Pullen, Richard Bonneau, Jonathan Nagler, and Joshua A. Tucker, "Trumping Hate on Twitter?: Online Hate in the 2016 US Election and its Aftermath," working paper, Social Media and Political Participation (SmaPP) Laboratory, New York University. March 6, 2019. Accessed at https://smappnyu .org/wp-content/uploads/2019/04/US_Election_Hate_Speech_2019_03_website.pdf.

58 Avi Selk, "'Rapist!' She Yelled at a Hispanic Man. 'She's Quoting the President,' He Thought," *Washington Post*, June 27, 2018. Accessed at www.washingtonpost.com/ news/post-nation/wp/2018/06/26/rapist-she-yelled-at-a-hispanic-man-shes-quoting-the-president-he-thought/?utm_term=.54b58d44e262.

59 Excerpted from Jacob Geers, "These People Applauding Donald Trump's 'Grab 'Em' by the Pussy' Comments Prove Deplorables Are Real," *Thought Catalog*, October 8, 2016. Accessed at https://thoughtcatalog.com/jacob-geers/2016/10/here's-all-the-people-applauding-donald-trumps-vulgar-grab-em-by-the-pussy-remarks/.

60 See NPR's *On Point*, December 3, 2017.

3 TRUMP'S POPULISM

Although football has stood for quintessential American values – competition, sportsmanship, teamwork – and afforded prized cultural bounties, including pageantry, tradition, celebrity, etc., things have gone poorly in the Age of Trump. "Sports fans should never condone players who do not stand proud for their National Anthem or their Country," Trump tweeted in September of 2017. "NFL should change policy," he commanded.[1] The President was referring to the mini-revolution begun by San Francisco 49ers quarterback Colin Kaepernick on August 14, 2016, when he remained seated during the anthem to protest police brutality. "People of color have been targeted by police," Kaepernick explained, and "they are put in place by the government. So that's something that this country has to change."[2]

Other players soon joined the fray, producing a variety of semiotic displays: taking-a-knee, heads-respectfully-bowed, arms-locked-in-solidarity, staying-in-the-dressing-room. The rhetoric increased too. Said Julius Thomas of the Miami Dolphins: "I'm not OK with somebody trying to prevent someone from standing up for what they think is important." Baltimore Colts owner Jim Isray agreed: "I am troubled by the president's recent comments about our league and our players." Dallas Cowboys owner, Jerry Jones, in contrast, declared that his players would stand respectfully on the sidelines during the anthem, a decision that resonated with at least one NFL fan on Twitter: "Our anthem has always been a sign of respect and pride for freedom. Interesting that privileged millionaires #TakeTheKnee to disrespect it."[3]

Politicians of every stripe joined the chorus, from Representative Steve King on the Right to former attorney general Eric Holder on the Left. NASCAR driver Richard Petty suggested that nonstanders be deported, while singer Stevie Wonder took both knees, although the exact purpose of his prayer was unclear. "I'm a Republican who voted for [Trump] but I think this is a battle he doesn't need to get into," said New York Jets season ticket-holder Greg Zaccaria, while New Orleans Saints quarterback Drew Brees hedged his bets: "I disagree with what the president said and how he said it," but "I will always feel that if you are an American that the national anthem is the opportunity for us all to stand together, to be unified and to show respect for our country."[4]

When it became obvious that football was becoming a fault line, President Trump did some backtracking: "I'm going to ask all of those people to recommend to me, because that's what they're protesting, people that they think were unfairly treated by the justice system . . . and if I find, and my committee finds, that they're unfairly treated, we will pardon them, or at least let them out."[5] But why would the leader of the free world waste his time thinking about grown men running around in pads and hitting one another with abandon? "Because I'm a populist," the President would declare.

But what does it mean to be a populist in the twenty-first century, and what does it mean, especially, for a billionaire to be a populist? Apparently, according to Pierre Bourdieu, *the people* is an elastic concept whose meanings are a function of time and circumstance.[6] Sometimes populists are found on the left, complaining how moneyed interests subvert workers, while populists on the right decry the "deep state's" suppression of individual liberties. Sometimes, populism grows out of national chauvinism buttressed by history, family, culture, and religion, but there are other forms of populism instigated by charismatics (as has often occurred in Latin America).

But who are "the people"? Everyone living in a given nation-state or just its legal residents? Must "the people" be active civil participants or can they live quietly and retain their peoplehood? Can the disaffected and the downtrodden be counted among "the people"? Which sacred norms, what key traditions, must "the people" respect to be legitimate? And do "the people" have a voice of their own? If so, what does it sound like? "The people as a source of action and authority," says political theorist Margaret Canovan, "is more often potential than actual, haunting the political imagination."[7]

But can any leader be a true populist? By standing apart from the people, that is, does not one inevitably stand above them? Given the hard work of politics and the ebb and flow of power, can any leader be a 24-hour populist? Indeed, might populism be just a rhetorical invention deployed when favor must be curried and votes solicited? Can a populist live in Trump Tower and still love the people?

This chapter explores Donald Trump's unique brand of populism, a populism that inspired, and alienated, half the nation. Sometimes, it seemed, the 2016 campaign was pitting all the people against all the other people. Trump attacked the nation's revered truths throughout the campaign – open elections, free trade, civil rights, an independent press. What sort of populist does that?[8] Also, while it took several hundred years to create two viable grassroots parties in the United States, Donald Trump – a party standard-bearer – seemed to be running against both of them. What sort of populist does that? Mr. Trump told the people they could become wealthier while hating elites, better educated by distrusting expertise, and truer Americans by turning their backs on the downtrodden.[9] What sort of populist says that?

Rhetorically, at least, Donald Trump was indeed a populist. As we see in Table 3.1, he was outdistanced only by Harry Truman in his use of *people* references. When Trump's campaign discourse was probed with a broader research tool, his use of Human Interest words – 150 relational terms including *brother, aunt, friend, children, folks,* etc. – outdid all other candidates running for the presidency since 1948. Figure 3.1 takes a broader look at Trump's rhetoric, showing that he mentioned *people* twice as often as his predecessors on the campaign trail and even out-peopled the people themselves (i.e., those who wrote letters to the editor). He also generated four times more references than those working for the mainstream press.[10]

Other data paint the same picture: (1) although there had been a fairly consistent use of *people* references between 1948 and 2012, the 2016 election was entirely different – both Trump and his rival, Hillary Clinton, dramatically upped the ante; (2) during the last phase of the campaign (October 15th through election day), Trump used three times as many Human Interest words as he had prior to that time (a strategic move Clinton did not make); (3) his *people* references were equally plentiful across campaign genres – news conferences, campaign speeches, press interviews, and political ads; (4) while he made slightly fewer *people* references in the general election than during the

Table 3.1 Trump's Populism vs. Other Presidential Candidates, 1948–2016

Type	Token	Trump Rank (out of 26)	Highest	Lowest
Interpersonal language	People references	2	Truman	Kerry
	Human Interest terms	1	Trump	Stevenson
Ceremonial language	Religious terms	21	Dewey	Truman
	Patriotic terms	22	Goldwater	Truman
	Moral terms	15	Kerry	Truman
	Inspirational terms	26	Gore	Trump
	Praise terms	4	Dewey	McGovern

Source: Data from Campaign Mapping Project.

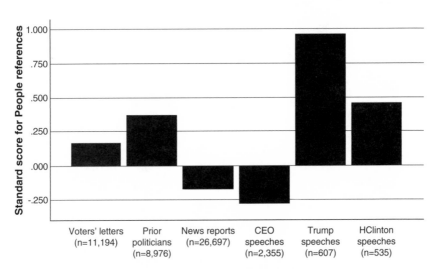

Figure 3.1 People References by Type of Speaker
Source: Data from Campaign Mapping Project.

primaries, he still surpassed Hillary Clinton. Trump's *people* references sent a consistent meta-message: I am one of you. Journalists called it pandering but as one-time Trump aide Steve Bannon said, the "opposition party" – members of the press – "don't understand this country.

They still do not understand why Donald Trump is the president of the United States."[11]

Raw numbers like these are important but they do not tell us everything, so this chapter looks at *how* Donald Trump embraced the people. Football is part of that story, so even when a twelve-year-old says something, you listen: "I do not think it is a bad thing for people to kneel, they are showing what their rights are," said Alex Jackson of Loves Park, Illinois. Hearing such sentiments, Donald Trump began making concessions: "Standing with locked arms is good, kneeling is not acceptable." And then he added a Trumpian afterthought, warning the NFL of the worst fate he could imagine: "Bad ratings!"[12]

In adding his postscript, Trump unveiled the first of what I shall argue are four key components of his populism. These components do not fit together in a particularly logical way, which is to say they are wholly owned by Donald J. Trump. Complicated though Trump's populism is, it says this to his followers: "I know you're there and you're important to me." For individuals who had felt ignored, that was a welcome message. Finally, acknowledgment.

Monetary Populism

Donald Trump proves both the strengths and weaknesses of getting an undergraduate degree in business and then entering the corporate world for the rest of your life. Whenever he speaks in public, that personal history abides, making his populism fundamentally trans-actional: (1) a person's worth must be calculable for it to be meaningful; (2) capital acquisition is the surest sign of citizenship; (3) a polity is an economy. While the late Hugo Chavez of Venezuela – like many populists – specialized in "abrasive ... anti-establishment, anti-elite messages" and "constructed himself as the ultimate outsider, a sort of anti-political superhero," Trump is a wannabe populist, a trickle-down populist.[13] Said he in his first speech as president:

> For too long, a small group in our nation's Capital has reaped the rewards of government while the people have borne the cost. Washington flourished – but the people did not share in its wealth. Politicians prospered – but the jobs left, and the factories closed. The establishment protected itself, but not the citizens of our country. Their victories have not been your

victories; their triumphs have not been your triumphs; and while they celebrated in our nation's capital, there was little to celebrate for struggling families all across our land. That all changes – starting right here, and right now, because this moment is your moment: it belongs to you.[14]

Here, Trump sounds like a conventional, supply-and-demand Republican but he is more than that. Any action that fails to "materially benefit the United States, either through resource acquisition or financial recompense," is forsaken by Trump, according to Charlie Laderman and Brandon Simms.[15] "Politically," they argue, Trump "is a Bourbon who has learned and forgotten nothing over the past three decades."[16] Is Japan paying us enough for its defense? Are we getting the "right kind" of migrants? What sort of real American needs a German automobile?

Trump's transactionalism is so fully integrated within him that it intrudes in the strangest ways. Said Mr. Trump on the stump in North Carolina: "Jobs will return, incomes will rise, and new factories will come rushing onto our shore. Once more we will have a government of, by, and for the people."[17] Note here the seamlessness between Trump's first and second sentences, as people's rights and incomes are conflated. Note, too, the lack of transition when Mr. Trump moved from his personal life to his corporate life in his acceptance speech: "To my sisters Mary Anne and Elizabeth, my brother Robert and my late brother Fred. I will always give you my love; you are most special to me. I have loved my life in business."[18]

Consider also the *first words* Trump spoke when addressing the civil unrest in Charlottesville in August of 2017. Given the turmoil in Virginia, how should he begin his remarks? By reminding the nation of its storied history of civil rights? Its commitments to civility? Its laws protecting lawful assemblage and free speech? All were possible, but Mr. Trump took another route: "I'm in Washington today to meet with my economic team about trade policy and major tax cuts and reform. We are renegotiating trade deals and making them good for the American worker. And it's about time."[19]

There is a kind of casual empiricism in Donald Trump's populism. Although he was educated at Wharton prior to the Age of Business Metrics, he quickly caught up with it. "The people love me," he declares, "and I can prove it." And prove it he does, tracking wins and losses at the oddest times, such as at the Washington Mall on January 22, 2017. Six hundred thousand attendees at the Trump inaugural was not good enough for him: "It looked like a million, million and a half people," he estimated.[20] "Polls are fake, just like everything else," he said in Tampa during the campaign, but then later in that same speech he crowed: "They just came out with a poll – the most popular person in the history of the Republican Party is Trump! Can you believe that?"[21]

Data are sacred to Trump. Imagined data are also sacred to Trump: "I would've won the popular vote if I was campaigning for the popular vote, I would've gone to California where I didn't go at all."[22] "Thank you for all the nice compliments and reviews on the State of the Union speech. 45.6 million watched, the highest number in history."[23]

All politicians want to be loved but few as much as Donald Trump. All politicians want to savage their enemies but few as punctiliously as Donald Trump: "NBC News is firing sleep eyes Chuck Todd in that his ratings on *Meet the Press* are setting record lows."[24] "Charles Krauthammer is a totally overrated person who really dislikes me personally."[25] "Ross Perot isn't successful like me. Romney – I have a Gucci store that's worth more than Romney."[26] "The failing *New York Times* writes total fiction concerning me. They have gotten it wrong for two years, and now are making up stories & sources!"[27] "Everyone is talking about the fact that the White House Correspondents Dinner was a very big, boring bust. The so-called comedian really 'bombed.'"[28] "I was so happy when I heard that *Politico*, one of the most dishonest political outlets, is losing a fortune. Pure scum."[29]

All populists need a bogeyman and Trump has an army of them – intellectuals, globalists, Mexicans, the Vatican. "We reject the bigotry of Hillary Clinton which panders and talks down to communities of color," he told an African-American audience.[30] "It is time for rule by the people, not rule by the special interests. Every insider, getting rich off of our broken system, is throwing money at Hillary Clinton. The hedge fund managers, the Wall Street investors, the professional political class."[31] There is a circular conferral of authority here, says Massimiliano Demata, wherein Trump calls on the people to call on him.[32] "It's hard to square his rhetoric," says columnist Michael Grunwald, "with his hires of Goldman Sachs alumni or his calls for more high-end tax cuts," but many Americans square it anyway.[33] They do so because Donald Trump acknowledges their existence. It was time someone did, they reason.

Needy Populism

Trump completes himself in others and people sense that. Such vulnerability would normally be seen as a weakness in a politician but it became Trump's badge of honor. It also flattered his supporters, allowing a second level of reciprocity to develop: One of the richest men in the world acknowledges me. "You want to know what total recognition is?" Trump once asked. "I'll tell you how you know you've got it. When the Nigerians on the street corners who don't speak a word of English, who have no clue, who're selling watches for some guy in New Jersey – when you walk by and those guys say 'Trump! Trump!' That's total recognition."[34]

Professor Tom Nichols of the U.S. Naval War College nicely captures the psychological roots of Trump's populism: "I think Trump comes from an aspirational background where no matter how rich he gets, no matter how many skyscrapers he gets, he still has that annoying sense of insecurity about being from Queens ... a nose-pressed-up-to-the-glass feeling."[35] Trump's supporters sense that dynamic. Larry Laughlin, a retired businessman from Minneapolis, once compared Trump to a high school senior who could "walk up to the table with the jocks and the cheerleaders and put them in their place." That is something, says Laughlin, that the "nerds and the losers, whose dads are unemployed and moms are working in the cafeteria," could never do. "The guys who wouldn't like me wouldn't like Trump," Laughlin concluded. "The guys who were condescending to him were condescending to me."[36]

Via such victimhood appeals, Trump converts "issues of policy into issues of identity."[37] "My opponent asks her supporters to recite a three-word loyalty pledge," said Mr. Trump. "It reads: 'I'm with her.' I choose to recite a different pledge. My pledge reads: I'm with you."[38] Trump's commitment is to flesh-and-blood people here, not to an abstract cluster of values. Such an approach was particularly attractive to older voters, evangelicals, and veterans, struggling farmers and factory workers too. That was especially true when Trump spoke off the cuff, trusting people with his unabashed openness.[39]

For Trump, love must be measurable or it is nothing. "As you know, I have millions of people on Facebook and Twitter," he once boasted. "Wow, the ratings for 60 Minutes last night were their biggest in a year – very nice!" "I have always liked the *New York Post* but they have really lied when they covered me in Iowa. Packed house. Standing O. Best speech!"[40] Trump's paratactic and subjective style, says linguist John McWhorter, marks a clear bid for authenticity.[41] Who could vouchsafe a man with nothing left to hide? Even after being in the spotlight for many years, Hillary Clinton rarely evoked such feelings.

Benjamin Enke of the National Bureau of Economic Research found that while Clinton stressed "individualizing values" during the 2016 campaign, Trump emphasized "communal values" and did so more often than any Republican in recent years. "The working class outside of the urban centers," says Enke, have historically exhibited a high demand for such values, and that was especially true in 2016.[42] Trump presented himself as more agent than leader, often referring to himself in the third person (e.g., "Nobody would be tougher on ISIS than Donald Trump"), as if he had been anointed by some celestial being.[43] Trump asked to be led so he could lead. "I have joined the political arena so that the powerful can no longer beat up on people that cannot defend themselves," Trump declared in his 2016 acceptance speech. "Nobody knows the system better than me, which is why I alone can fix it."[44]

Presidential candidates rarely speak of love but Donald Trump did. "Do you like me?" he queried a crowd. After the cheering subsided, Trump vowed "I like you too. I love you."[45] "Look, they dismiss you as poorly educated," he told another audience, "but I'm with you. I love you and I am your only hope for being accounted as American citizens with the right to a better future."[46] What was good for the candidate was good for the voter: "I know when he's waiting to come out his heart is pounding because he's coming to a field of love," said Gene Huber, a former used car salesman; "the rallies fuel him up."[47] "West Virginia could not have dreamed a president would come back to us," observed Lynette McQuain, a retail merchandiser; "West Virginians are always overlooked but he hasn't overlooked us. The people love him: he connects with the average American."[48]

Populism is normally associated with anger, not love. As we will see in Chapter 6, Donald Trump was something of an artist when it came to anger, but his appeals to love cannot be ignored. Nobody, of course, will ever know the fullness of Trump's heart. As a businessman, he was as pitiless as Cornelius Vanderbilt, but as a politician he displayed real emotional needs and, remarkably, seemed unembarrassed by them. His was a populism not seen before.[49]

Banal Populism

Some years ago, rhetoric scholar Carroll Arnold identified what he called an omnipresent tension between transcendent and empirical themes in American public discourse. U.S. politicians are compelled, Arnold noted, to observe two different, contradictory commandments: (1) do the will of God and (2) do business.[50] According to Arnold, these duties are imposed on all who would lead the American people, even though the emphasis on one or the other may change from time to time. "There's no danger that we'll feel inferior to Trump when he speaks," observes MacMurray College's Allan Metcalf, "but maybe that's what makes him a good salesman. He puts us at ease with his talk."[51]

Then came Charlottesville, a test that Donald Trump failed miserably. "I think there is blame on both sides," the President declared, "you had a group on one side that was bad. You had a group on the other side that was also very violent."[52] Arguably, there was some truth to Trump's observation since (1) there were indeed two sides and (2) both fought viciously. Video evidence easily substantiates both claims. But that, of course, is not the point. Trump's legalisms and his attempts to imply moral equivalence between the contending parties were universally decried.

Somehow, it seems, Mr. Trump had failed to mention that it was *white supremacists* who started the turmoil in Charlottesville, a fact that registered even with financier Anthony Scaramucci: "With the moral authority of the presidency, you have to call that stuff out."[53] Campbell Soup CEO Denise Morrison argued that racism and murder "are not morally equivalent to anything else that happened in Charlottesville."[54] JP Morgan Chase's Jamie Dimon echoed Morrison, noting that "constructive economic and regulatory policies are not enough and will not matter if we do not address the divisions in our country."[55] General Electric's Jeff Immelt, Merck's Ken Frazier, Johnson & Johnson's Alex Gorsky, and many others left the White House's Manufacturing Council rather than countenance the President's failed rhetoric. As important as business is, the CEOs reasoned, transcendence has its demands.

"While not every president manages to offer extraordinarily memorable rhetoric at moments of national crisis," says Penn State's Mary Stuckey, "it's difficult to recall one who did not at least make an attempt."[56] Then came Donald Trump. It is not as if the nation had not been warned, however. As we see in Table 3.1, Trump's campaign rhetoric steadfastly avoided the language of values. While he spread Praise words around like any good salesman, he ranked dead last in his use of Inspirational terms and largely avoided Religious and Patriotic terms as well. All of this happened on the campaign trail, so one might have expected something different in the White House. 'Twas not to be. While Trump's use of Religious and Inspirational terms increased slightly, his Patriotic terms barely moved and his use of Moral terms shifted not an iota.[57] Donald Trump got a new job but the citizenry did not get a new Donald Trump.

The irony, of course, is that Trump followed Barack Obama, a person who blended language and emotion with exquisite sensitivity. When he visited Israel's Yad Vashem Holocaust memorial, for example, Obama proclaimed "we are blessed to have such a powerful reminder of man's potential for great evil, but also our capacity to rise up from tragedy and remake our world."[58] Presented with that same opportunity, Mr. Trump gushed, "It is a great honor to be here with all of my friends. So amazing. Will never forget!"[59] During this moment Trump reveals his essence: He got trained in college, not educated, so he finds soliciting easy, presiding difficult. He has no sense of poetry, no moral vocabulary.

In an earlier work, I described a "rhetorical contract" between Church and State in the United States that keeps them from one another's throats.[60] The contract demands that both entities share a language of transcendence and also confess to their interdependence. Policy matters, in contrast, are considered best left to the State. While this contract is constantly being challenged in a cantankerous nation beset by arguments over abortion rights, capital punishment, hate crimes, etc., the contract has largely held for officialdom. Church officials tip their hats to the State on the Fourth of July and during state funerals; elected officials bow their heads at the inauguration and during the Christmas blessing. Otherwise, the contenders retreat to their own corners – moral entreaties from the Church, binding legislation from the State.

Donald Trump came to the White House with none – none – of the requisite ceremonial skills, and that has cost him dearly. His crudeness at Yad Vashem and his tone-deafness about Charlottesville are but two examples. Trump habitually violates form as well as substance – speaking at the wrong time, talking too much, nurturing irrelevancies, violating the rules of etiquette. He also lacks graciousness – the capacity to reveal the grace within himself and to find it in others.

Because Trump lives in the moment, he has no sense for what T. S. Eliot called the "pastness of the past" and how it can become a new and vital present. For Trump, political institutions are about people, not principles, about Lincoln-the-politician, not the Emancipation Proclamation. Trump's inaugural address, says political scientist Julia Azari, showed no "linkage with the founders or the founding texts" nor did it show "a clear grounding in long-term traditions."[61] Grand narratives, sacred myths, revered traditions – Donald Trump avoids them all.

Trump's history with the lowest art form known to humankind – reality TV – and his nonstop "victory rallies" three years after the 2016 campaign, show him to be an immersive populist. Consequently, he stumbles over words like *justice* but speaks readily of criminals; he decries immigrants but is silent about the *freedoms* they seek. For Trump, churches are buildings that house voters, not places where *righteousness* and *repentance* can be found. Living in the moment as he does, Trump cannot speak meaningfully of a future time. As a result, although Trump-the-businessman became Trump-the-candidate, he has not yet become a real president and rhetoric is part of that story. "We should call evil by its name," said Senator Orrin Hatch. "My brother didn't give his life fighting Hitler for Nazi ideas to go unchallenged here at home."[62] This is how a leader talks but it is not how Donald Trump talks.

Table 3.2 contains a partial list of abstractions to be found in Trump's speeches. The terms on the left, Trump's preferred terms, point to real problems and real people; those on the right identify ideals to be achieved. Trump speaks easily of the former but is uncomfortable with the latter. Voters notice the difference. Polls show that Trump is rated highly for being competitive, intense, and enthusiastic but poorly for being inspiring, caring, or visionary.[63] Such reactions may cost him in the long run since it is a president's job to tell a nation what it is and what it might become. Thus far, Donald Trump does not tell the stories presidents tell.

In short, there are liabilities associated with putting a populist in the White House. For some voters that was a risk worth taking. Ivar Kalins, the grandson of World War II refugees and a staunch Trump supporter, can do without the poetry. "All these grandiose speeches"

Table 3.2 Abstractions Used by Trump in 2015–2016

Heavily used		Less heavily used	
Security	172	Respect	86
Policy	143	History	82
Law	139	Justice	44
Interests	105	Truth	42
Crime	103	Freedom	26
Terrorism	102	Rights	25
Disaster	101	Tolerance	16
Choice	94	Liberty	9

Source: Data from Campaign Mapping Project.

that make politicians sound like politicians, Kalins says, are passé in the Age of Trump. "Even Bush, who wanted to be the aw-shucks guy, it was all in there, a nice half-hour speech saying absolutely nothing."[64] Donald Trump, in contrast, always says something, often too much. He is not in the moral business; he is in the business business. Voters like Mr. Kalins appreciate that.

While Trump's monetary populism may have put him in the White House, it cannot sustain his presidency if history is our guide. Speaking beyond the moment, calling on universal truths when needed, is what presidents have done since the time of Washington. Donald Trump must get beyond himself to follow in their footsteps.

Divisive Populism

A fourth dimension of Trump's populism is its saddest. He has exploited the nation's fault lines, turning them into a Dadaist art form: *To native Americans:* "You were here long before any of us were here ... although we have a representative in Congress who they say was here a long time ago, they call her 'Pocahontas.'" *On criminals:* "When you see these thugs being thrown into the back of a paddy wagon," Trump declared to the Suffolk County Police Department, "you just see them thrown in, rough – I said please don't be too nice." *To the press:* "You, The *New York Times*, are an icon. I'm a New York icon, you're a New York icon. And the only difference is, I still own my buildings." *On young people:* "We were talking about the Dreamers and quite honestly, Democrats can fantasize all they want about winning in 2020 ... those are the dreamers."[65]

According to columnist Jett Heer, Trump's acerbic humor owes "much to the tradition of insult comedy which flourished after the Second World War and was best exemplified by figures like Don Rickles and Joan Rivers."[66] Although insult comedy has diminished in popularity in the Age of Identity, Trump has aggressively pursued the genre. He has done so because he is pugilistic by nature but also because it builds both a constituency and an unconstituency. Trump intuitively understood that "many people dislike group-based claims of structural disadvantage and the norms obligating their public recognition."[67] His use of group-against-group humor, then, was quite intentional.

While it is easy to conceive of vertical populism in which an underclass is held down by oligarchs (e.g., Bernie Sanders' populism), Trump's is a lateral populism – people no better than me are sabotaging my attempts to get ahead. Such an approach works well when the alleged rivals – journalists, the impoverished, college professors, refugees, low-level bureaucrats – cannot possibly affect society's financial wellbeing. In boxing, they call Trump's approach a "cinch fight," whereby a boxer sharpens his skills by sparring with someone having no ability to rearrange his face.

My studies show that during the 2016 campaign, out of some 250,000 words used, Trump referred to *people* 2,112 times and, in a similar-sized dataset, Clinton mentioned the term only 1,212 times. More interestingly, Clinton referred to *America* 706 times while Trump mentioned *Americans* 684 times: the totemic nation (Clinton's) vs. the inhabited nation (Trump's). Clinton the coalescer vs. Trump the divider; Clinton's village vs. Trump's tribe. His was a nostalgic rhetoric hearkening back to a time when everyone was white and everyone spoke English, a dynamic that Benjamin Krämer calls "talk radio populism," whereby anonymous callers habitually savage those living in someone else's neighborhood.[68]

Donald Trump did not invent the divisions he exploited. He inherited them. Along with Trump, says rhetoric scholar Ira Allen, all of us must assume "collective ownership" of Trump's white supremacism, recognizing it "not as aberrant but as thoroughly American."[69] Trump's discourse, says Indiana University's Robert Terrill, "closes us down" to one another, making islands where a land mass should be. By not acknowledging racial disparities in the United States and by *selectively* identifying economically distraught communities, says Terrill, Trump made *American* the only socially acceptable label.[70]

Trump's anti-immigrant rhetoric let him escape charges of invidiousness. Real Americans were not creating the problems, he warned; non-Americans were doing that. Trump's logic resonated with many in the middle class. Communities harboring the unemployed and the undocumented – not those in the heartland struggling with opioid abuse – were easy targets for all the usual reasons: they were outnumbered, they had neither discretionary income nor discretionary time, and their rhetorical defenses were easily breached. As the Brookings Institution's William Galston says, "no issue has done more than immigration to feed populism."[71]

How to counteract an internecine populism? Heroes must be found. The world of professional basketball offered up one such candidate – San Antonio Spurs coach Gregg Popovich. Popovich began by affirming that all Americans want the President to be successful. "It's our country," says Popovich, "we don't want it to go down the drain." Popovich continues: "But that does not take away the fact that he [Trump] used that fear-mongering and all the comments from day one ... I'm a rich white guy and I'm sick to my stomach thinking about it. I can't imagine being a Muslim right now, or a woman, or an African-American, a Hispanic, a handicapped person, how disenfranchised they might feel."[72]

Long-time Spurs fan Cassandra Casanova was having none of it. "After all those years supporting the team," she declared, "and now I have no interest. Popovich really messed up." "It ruined my basketball life," Casanova said, "I took it personally. I was such a loyal fan and he insulted me. Why would you start attacking the people who had been so loyal?"[73] Why indeed? Perhaps because American politics has been a vertical–lateral struggle right from the start. Donald Trump learned its lessons well.

Conclusion

What kind of populist is Donald Trump? He is a Trumpian Populist, the only one of its breed. He knows that the people are oppressed and he offers them succor, even while offering the business world absolution-by-omission. Trump is a populist because it completes him, because his need for adulation is more powerful than any particular ideology. Trump avoids the moral universe because it requires grand abstractions and Donald Trump knows nothing of abstractions. He knows profit and he knows losses and he owns a personal calculator. Finally, Trump's populism embraces the people but not all of them. Those he leaves out become the targets of his ire; if Muslims had not existed, Trump would have had to invent them.

Before becoming a functioning populist, Trump-the-billionaire "bragged about how he had been able to make vast sums of money while paying his workers as little as possible," says rhetoric scholar Robert Rowland.[74] In so many ways, then, populism is at least in part a *performance* for Trump, a way of being with the world. "Trump does not speak to history except in extremely rare cases," says the *New York Times*' Charles Homans. Instead, "he is always speaking to a proximate audience; unlike other presidents, the speaking, not the speech, is the point ... To be a member of his audience is to feel valued, part of an immediate and privileged 'you' defined in relation to some broader population."[75] Trump is constantly aware of being seen and he is even aware of his awareness. After winning the primaries, for example, Trump figured, "Well, the one thing good is now I'll get good press [but] it got worse ... it actually, in my opinion, got more nasty."[76] Is that any way to treat a certified man of the people? Mr. Trump thought not.

Trump's lateral populism opened up wounds during the campaign, still more wounds when he took office. There is a "perverse," game-like aspect to Trump's populism, says Joshua Gunn, one that lets people participate in an alternate reality in which barbs are directed at the politically correct and the insufferably smart.[77] The game mixes insult politics with insult humor, staving off the worst of all postmodern fates: intense boredom.[78] The game also has utilitarian value, with Trump tweeting at three or four in the morning "knowing that if he says something outrageous, it will be on the morning news shows."[79]

To describe Donald Trump as a mere politainer, however, insults a great many Americans who voted for him, thinking they were advancing the national project by so doing. Quirky though it was, Trump's populism framed a core issue – underemployment stoked by advancing globalism – for those feeling the lash of its unfairness.[80] A few citizens may have voted for Trump because they liked his reality

TV moves but those people, too, must not be dismissed. Reality TV, after all, showcases unpolished citizens making unfiltered remarks and then doing something outlandish in an attempt to outdo their opponents. Donald Trump took that formula on the road, mowing down his rivals in the process. As Michael Wolff has observed, Trump took the wonk out of politics.[81] To be sure, his act consistently went overboard but it sent the message he wanted sent – I hear you; we are one. Many listened.

Notes

1 Donald J. Trump, *Twitter*, September 24, 2017. Accessed at https://twitter.com/ realdonaldtrump/status/912080538755846144?lang=en.

2 As quoted by Matt Maloco, "Kaepernick Made Prior Statement with Police-as-Pigs Socks," *NBC Sports*, September 1, 2016. Accessed at www.nbcsports.com/bayarea/ 49ers/kaepernick-made-prior-statement-police-pigs-socks.

3 All of the preceding commentary can be found in Benjamin Hoffman, Victor Mather, and Jacey Fortin, "After Trump Blasts NFL, Players Kneel and Lock Arms in Solidarity," *New York Times*, September 24, 2017. Accessed at www.nytimes.com/ 2017/09/24/sports/nfl-trump-anthem-protests.html.

4 Ibid.

5 As quoted in Scott Davis, "Trump Says He Wants to Meet with NFL Players Who Protest During the National Anthem to Get Recommendations for More Pardons," *Business Insider*, June 8, 2018. Accessed at www.businessinsider.com/trump-nfl-players-protesting-during-anthem-pardon-recommendations-2018-6.

6 Pierre Bourdieu, "The Social Space and the Genesis of Groups," *Theory and Society*, 14:6 (1985), 723–744.

7 Margaret Canovan, *The People* (Cambridge: Polity Press, 2005), p. 9.

8 For a fine discussion of Trump's unique kind of nationalism, see Robert Lieberman, Suzanne Mettler, Thomas B. Pepinsky, Kenneth M. Roberts, and Richard Valelly, "Trumpism and American Democracy: History, Comparison, and the Predicament of Liberal Democracy in the United States," occasional paper, *SSRN*, August 31, 2017. Accessed at https://papers.ssrn.com/sol3/papers.cfm?abstract_id=3028990.

9 For more on this triad of beliefs, see J. Eric Oliver and Wendy M. Rahn, "Rise of the Trumpenvolk: Populism in the 2016 Election," *ANNALS of the American Academy of Political and Social Science*, 667:1 (2016), 189–206.

10 Statistical patterns for *people* references: voters' letters = 0.1738, prior politicians = 0.3733, news reports = -0.1718, CEO speeches = -0.2809, Trump speeches = 0.9643, HClinton speeches = 0.4589; $F [5, 50357] = 668.880$, $p < 0.000$. When Human Interest words were compared across genre, the same patterns shown in Figure 3.1 appeared. To wit: voters' letters = 0.1299, prior politicians = 0.4299, news reports = -0.2707, CEO speeches = -0.2246, Trump speeches = 0.190695, HClinton speeches = 0.8081; $F [5, 51480] = 1180.255$, $p < 0.000$.

11 As quoted in John Cassidy, "Steve Bannon's War on the Press," *New Yorker*, January 27, 2017. Accessed at www.newyorker.com/news/john-cassidy/steve-bannons-war-on-the-press.

12 All of the above can be found in Hoffman, Mather, and Fortin, "After Trump Blasts NFL, Players Kneel and Lock Arms in Solidarity," *New York Times*.

13 Elena Block and Ralph Negrine, "The Populist Communication Style: Toward a Critical Framework," *International Journal of Communication*, 1 (2017), 186.

14 Donald J. Trump, "Inaugural Address: Trump's Full Speech," *CNN*, January 21, 2017. Accessed at www.cnn.com/2017/01/20/politics/trump-inaugural-address/index.html.

15 Charlie Laderman and Brandon Simms, *Donald Trump: The Making of a World View* (London: Endeavor Press, 2017), p. 82. For more on this matter, see Jason A. Edwards, "Make America Great Again: Donald Trump and Redefining the U.S. Role in the World," *Communication Quarterly*, 66:2 (2018), 176–95.

16 Laderman and Simms, *Donald Trump: The Making of a World View*, p. 77.

17 Donald J. Trump, "Campaign Speech in High Point, North Carolina," September 20, 2016. Accessed at www.presidency.ucsb.edu/2016_election_speeches.php?candidate=45&campaign=2016TRUMP&doctype=5000.

18 Donald J. Trump, "Victory Speech," *CNN*, November 9, 2016. Accessed at www.cnn.com/2016/11/09/politics/donald-trump-victory-speech/index.html.

19 Donald J. Trump, "President Trump Speaks about Charlottesville," *New York Times*, November 14, 2017. Accessed at www.nytimes.com/2017/08/14/us/politics/transcript-and-video-president-trump-speaks-about-charlottesville.html.

20 As quoted in Timothy B. Lee, "Trump Claims 1.5 Million People Came to His Inauguration: Here's What the Evidence Shows," *Vox*, January 23, 2017. Accessed at www.vox.com/policy-and-politics/2017/1/21/14347298/trump-inauguration-crowd-size.

21 As quoted in Emily Birnbaum, "Trump Says 'Polls are Fake' before Bragging about Polls Showing His Popularity," *The Hill*, July 31, 2018. Accessed at http://thehill.com/homenews/administration/399808-trump-says-polls-are-fake-before-bragging-about-poll-that-shows-he-is.

22 As quoted in Aaron Bandler, "Nine Times Trump Talked About His Popularity with ABC News," *Daily Wire*, January 26, 2017. Accessed at www.dailywire.com/news/12843/11-times-trump-talked-about-his-popularity-abc-aaron-bandler.

23 Donald J. Trump, *Twitter*, February 1, 2018. Accessed at https://twitter.com/realdonaldtrump/status/959034299222843394?lang=en.

24 As quoted in George Beahm, *Trump Talk: Donald Trump In His Own Words* (Avon, MA: Adams Media, 2016), p. 133.

25 As quoted ibid., p. 81.

26 As quoted ibid., p. 104.

27 Donald J. Trump, *Twitter*, February 6, 2017. Accessed at https://twitter.com/realdonaldtrump/status/828642511698669569?lang=en.

28 Donald J. Trump, *Twitter*, April 29, 2018. Accessed at https://twitter.com/realDonaldTrump/status/990557728752926725?ref_src=twsrc%5Etfw%7Ctwcamp%5Etweetembed%7Ctwterm%5E990557728752926725&ref_url=http%3A%2F%2Fwww.foxnews.com%2Fpolitics%2F2018%2F04%2F29%2Ftrump-rips-white-house-correspondents-dinner-as-boring-bust.html.

29 As quoted in Beahm, *Trump Talk*, p. 157.

30 Donald J. Trump, "Full Text: Donald Trump Campaign Speech in Wisconsin," *Politico*, August 17, 2016. Accessed at www.politico.com/story/2016/08/full-text-donald-trumps-speech-on-227095.

31 Ibid.

32 Massimiliano Demata, "'A Great and Beautiful Wall': Donald Trump's Populist Discourse on Immigration," *Journal of Language Aggression and Conflict*, 5:2 (2017), 274–294.

33 Michael Grunwald, "From Obama to Trump: No Ordinary Lurch," *Politico*, January 20, 2017. Accessed at www.politico.com/magazine/story/2017/01/donald-trump-inauguration-barack-obama-214671.

34 As quoted in Beahm, *Trump Talk*, p. 136.

35 As stated in an interview with Chauncey DeVega, "Author Tom Nichols on How Trump Won," *Salon*, July 30, 2017. Accessed at www.salon.com/2017/07/30/author-tom-nichols-on-how-trump-won-people-looked-up-from-their-phones-and-said-wheres-my-money/.

36 As quoted in Sabrina Tavernise, "A Deal Breaker for Trump's Supporters? Nope. Not This Time, Either," *New York Times*, August 19, 2017. Accessed at www.nytimes.com/2017/08/19/us/politics/trump-supporters.html.

37 Michael J. Steudeman, "Demagoguery and the Donald's Duplicitous Victimhood," in Ryan Skinnell (ed.), *Faking the News: What Rhetoric Can Teach Us about Donald J. Trump* (Exeter, UK: Imprint-Academic, 2018), p. 11.

38 Donald J. Trump, "Acceptance Speech at the Republican National Convention," Cleveland, OH, *Politico*, July 21, 2016. Accessed at www.politico.com/story/2016/07/full-transcript-donald-trump-nomination-acceptance-speech-at-rnc-225974.

39 For more on this, see Anna M. Young, "Rhetoric of Fear and Loathing: Donald Trump's Populist Style," in Skinnell (ed.), *Faking the News*, pp. 21–38.

40 The foregoing can be found in Beahm, *Trump Talk*, pp. 101, 156, 134 respectively.

41 John McWhorter, "What Trump's Speech Says about His Mental Fitness," *New York Times*, February 6, 2018. Accessed at www.nytimes.com/interactive/2018/02/06/opinion/trump-speech-mental-capacity.html.

42 Benjamin Enke, "Moral Values and Voting: Trump and Beyond," working paper, January 2018, p. 34. Accessed at www.nber.org/papers/w24268.

43 See Katelyn Guichelaar and Ksristin Du Mex, "Donald Trump and Hillary Clinton, by Their Words," *Patheos*, July 28, 2018. Accessed at www.patheos.com/blogs/anxiousbench/2016/07/donald-trump-and-hillary-clinton-by-their-words/.

44 Trump, "Acceptance Speech at the Republican National Convention," *Politico*.

45 As quoted in Michael A. Cohen, "Trump Loves His Supporters, But Why Do They Love Him?" *Boston Globe*, March 13, 2018. Accessed at www.bostonglobe.com/opinion/2018/03/13/trump-loves-his-supporters-but-why-they-love-him/dfGRhzooH9JgbzaGDAbAhO/story.html.

46 As quoted in "'I Love the Poorly Educated' – Read Donald Trump's Full Nevada Victory Speech," *Quartz*, February 24, 2016. Accessed at https://qz.com/623640/i-love-the-poorly-educated-read-donald-trumps-full-nevada-victory-speech/.

47 As quoted in David Smith, "Why Trump Still Needs the Love of the Crowd: 'This Is Like Medicine to Him,'" *Guardian*, August 6, 2017. Accessed at www.theguardian.com/us-news/2017/aug/05/donald-trump-rallies-supporters-west-virginia.

48 As quoted ibid.

49 For more on the emotional dimensions of populism, see Matthew Levinger, "Love, Fear, Anger: the Emotional Arc of Populist Rhetoric," *Narrative and Conflict: Explorations of Theory and Practice,*" Fall/Winter 2017. Accessed at https://journals.gmu.edu/NandC/article/download/1954/1378.

50 Carroll C. Arnold, "Reflections on American Public Discourse," *Communication Quarterly*, 28:2 (1977), 73–85.

51 Allan Metcalf, "Trump: Down to Earth But Not Dignified," *Chronicle of Higher Education*, May 4, 2017. Accessed at www.chronicle.com/blogs/linguafranca/2017/05/04/trump-down-to-earth-but-not-dignified/.

52 As quoted in Michael D. Shear and Maggie Haberman, "Trump Defends Initial Remarks on Charlottesville; Again Blames 'Both Sides,'" *New York Times*, August 15, 2017. Accessed at www.nytimes.com/2017/08/15/us/politics/trump-press-conference-charlottesville.html.

53 As quoted in Meghan Keneally, "Scaramucci Criticizes Trump's Reaction to Char-lottesville Violence," *ABC News*, August 13, 2017. Accessed at https://abcnews.go.com/Politics/scaramucci-criticizes-trumps-reaction-charlottesville-violence/story?id=49055043.

54 As quoted in Damian Paletta and Jena McGregor, "Trump's Advisory Councils Disband as CEOs Abandon President over Charlottesville Views," *Washington Post*, August 16, 2017. Accessed at www.washingtonpost.com/news/on-leadership/wp/2017/08/16/after-wave-of-ceo-departures-trump-ends-business-and-manufacturing-councils/?utm_term=.2e5504d45964.

55 As quoted ibid.

56 Mary E. Stuckey, "Unlike Trump, Most Presidents Emphasize Our Common Ideals," *Washington Post*, August 25, 2017. Accessed at www.washingtonpost.com/news/monkey-cage/wp/2017/08/25/unlike-trump-most-presidents-try-to-unite-americans-around-our-common-ideals-in-their-speeches/?utm_term=.91180538cfc9.

57 Statistical patterns for Religious terms: as campaigner = 0.9782, as president = 2.7474; $F_{[1, 1139]} = 31.906$, $p < 0.000$; for Patriotic terms: as campaigner = 2.4524, as president = 3.1558; $F_{[1, 1139]} = 4.906$, $p < 0.027$; for Moral terms: as campaigner = 1.7981, as president = 1.9983; $F_{[1, 1139]} = 2.237$, $p < 0.135$; for Inspirational terms: as campaigner = 3.2988, as president = 4.5944; $F_{[1, 1139]} = 25.788$, $p < 0.000$; for Praise terms: as campaigner = 8.5246, as president = 10.0765; $F_{[1, 1139]} = 14.793$, $p < 0.000$.

58 As quoted in Max Bearak, "The Huge Contrast Between Obama's and Trump's Visit to Israel's Holocaust Memorial," *New York Times*, May 23, 2017. Accessed at www.washingtonpost.com/news/worldviews/wp/2017/05/23/the-huge-contrast-between-obama-and-trumps-visits-to-israels-holocaust-memorial/?utm_term=.0af2bd9412c0.

59 Ibid.

60 Roderick P. Hart, *The Political Pulpit* (West Lafayette: Purdue University Press, 1977).

61 Julia Azari, "Populism Is Not What It Seems," *New York Times*, January 20, 2017. Accessed at www.nytimes.com/interactive/projects/cp/opinion/presidential-inauguration-2017/trump-populism-is-not-what-it-seems.

62 As quoted in Eli Blumenthal, "Trump's Remarks on Charlottesville Draw Strong Reactions Across Political Spectrum," *USA Today*, August 13, 2017. Accessed at www.usatoday.com/story/news/2017/08/12/the-latest-trumps-remarks-on-clashes-draw-strong-reactions/104540810/.

63 Polling results are detailed in Frank Newport, "More Insight on Support for Trump Actions, Leadership Style," *Gallup*, October 16, 2017. Accessed at https://news.gallup.com/opinion/polling-matters/220565/insight-support-trump-actions-leadership-style.aspx.

64 As quoted in Karl Vick, "American Values," *Time*, July 2, 2018, 30.

65 As quoted in Philip Bump, "While Honoring Native American Veterans, Trump Lobs His Favorite Native American Insult," *Washington Post*, November 27, 2017. Accessed at www.washingtonpost.com/news/politics/wp/2017/11/27/while-honoring-native-american-veterans-trump-lobs-his-favorite-native-american-insult/?utm_term=.6f581e534eb2; Devan Cole, "Trump's Top Jokes from the Gridiron Dinner," *CNN*, March 4, 2018. Accessed at www.cnn.com/2018/03/04/politics/trump-best-jokes-gridiron-dinner/index.html. For more on Trump's divisiveness, see Marnie Lawler McDonough, "The Evolution of Demagoguery: An Updated Understanding of Demagogic Rhetoric as Interactive and Ongoing," *Communication Quarterly*, 66:2 (2018), 138–56.

66 Jett Heer, "Donald Trump Comedic Genius," *New Republic*, September 8, 2015. Accessed at https://newrepublic.com/article/122738/donald-trumps-comedic-genius.

67 Matt Grossman, "Racial Attitudes and Political Correctness in the 2016 Presidential Election," *Niskanen Center*, May 10, 2018. Accessed at https://niskanencenter.org/blog/racial-attitudes-and-political-correctness-in-the-2016-presidential-election/.

68 Benjamin Krämer, "Media Populism: A Conceptual Clarification and Some Theses on Its Effects," *Communication Theory*, 24 (2014), 50. For more on the nativist aspects of Trump's populism, see Corina Lacatus, "Populism and the 2016 American Election: Evidence from Official Press Releases and Twitter," *PS: Political Science and Politics*, 52:2 (2019), 223–28.

69 Ira J. Allen, "Who Owns Donald Trump's Antisemitism?" in Skinnell (ed.), *Faking the News*, p. 68.

70 Robert E. Terrill, "The Post-Racial and Post-Ethical Discourse of Donald J. Trump," *Rhetoric and Public Affairs*, 20:3 (2017), 493–510.

71 William A. Galston, "Populism's Challenge to Democracy," *Wall Street Journal*, March 16, 2018. Accessed at www.wsj.com/articles/populisms-challenge-to-democracy-1521239697.

72 As quoted in Alysha Tsuji, "Gregg Popovich Goes on Passionate Tirade in Wake of Trump Election: 'We Are Rome,'" *USA Today*, November 11, 2016. Accessed at https://ftw.usatoday.com/2016/11/san-antonio-gregg-popovich-trump-election-rant-we-are-rome.

73 As quoted in "Longtime Spurs Fans 'Turned Off' by Coach Gregg Popovich's Anti-Trump Comments, Report Says," *Fox News*, April 17, 2017. Accessed at www.foxnews.com/sports/2018/04/17/longtime-spurs-fans-turned-off-by-coach-gregg-popovichs-anti-trump-comments-report-says.html.

74 Robert Rowland, "Donald Trump and the Rejection of the Norms of American Politics and Rhetoric," in Benjamin R. Warner, Dianne G. Bystrom, Mitchell S. McKinney, and Mary C. Banwart (eds.), *An Unprecedented Election: Media, Communication, and the Electorate in the 2016 Campaign* (Santa Barbara, CA: Praeger, 2018), p. 191.

75 Charles Homans, "The Post-Campaign Campaign of Donald Trump," *New York Times Magazine*, April 9, 2018. Accessed at www.nytimes.com/2018/04/09/magazine/donald-trump-rallies-campaigning-president.html. For a fine article on how Trump also makes conservatism a performance, see Michael Lee, "Considering Political Identity: Conservatives, Republicans, and Donald Trump," *Rhetoric and Public Affairs*, 20:4 (2017), 719–30.

76 As quoted in Callum Borchers, "'When I Won,' Trump Thought, 'Now I'll Get Good Press,'" *Washington Post*, April 24, 2017. Accessed at www.washingtonpost.com/news/the-fix/wp/2017/04/24/when-i-won-trump-thought-now-ill-get-good-press/?utm_term=.01c53d4a0e49.

77 Joshua Gunn, "On Political Perversion," *Rhetoric Society Quarterly*, 48:2 (2018), 161–86.

78 See Thomas Lynch, "President Donald Trump: A Case Study of Spectacular Power," *Political Quarterly*, 88:4 (2017), 612–621. See also Oscar Winberg, "Insult Politics: Donald Trump, Right-Wing Populism, and Incendiary Language," *European Journal of American Studies*, 12:2 (2017). Accessed at https://journals.openedition.org/ejas/12132.

79 Kelly Field, "What Reality TV Taught Trump, According to Professors Who Study It," *Chronicle of Higher Education*, February 15, 2017. Accessed at www.chronicle.com/article/What-Reality-TV-Taught-Trump/239200. See also Olivia Goldhill, "Five Reality TV Show Strategies Donald Trump Has Used Throughout His Campaign," *Quartz*, November 6, 2016. Accessed at https://qz.com/828700/2016-

presidential-election-donald-trump-has-used-reality-tv-strategies-throughout-his-cam
paign/.

80 For more on populism as a framing strategy, see Bart Bonikowski and Noam Girdon,
"The Populist Style in American Politics: Presidential Campaign Discourse,
1952–1996," *Social Forces*, 94:4 (2015), 1593–1621.

81 Michael Wolff, *Siege: Trump Under Fire* (New York: Henry Holt and Co., 2019),
p. 23.

Part III
FEELING TRAPPED

4 TRUMP'S PASSIONS

Donald Trump became president because some Americans felt trapped – no economic freedom, too much political correctness, a dubious future time. People in Homer, Alaska, especially felt that way in February of 2017 when a group of citizens proposed a resolution welcoming immigrants to "The Halibut Fishing Capital of the World," a city sitting at the end of a spit on the Kenai Peninsula, making it the least accessible destination in the United States for any would-be traveler, immigrant or not. When National Public Radio producer Brian Reed asked people in Homer if they had ever encountered an undocumented immigrant, they said they had not. Chief of Police Mark Robel backed up their story.[1]

Nonetheless, when the welcoming resolution came before the City Council, everyone in town turned out. Before the meeting, half of Homerites were enraged by the proposal and half supported it. At the end of the meeting, everyone was upset. Although the City Council eventually turned down the proposal, they quickly faced a recall petition for having agreed to discuss the matter in the first place. Eventually, the American Civil Liberties Union stepped in, the pastors started preaching, the resolution failed, and then everyone in Homer hated their neighbors.

"Why do you have to legislate something or mention something that we're already doing just fine?" asked Homer resident Christina Partridge. "It's very sad that they're bringing this up and causing all this strife in the community."[2] In many ways, Ms. Partridge captured what many Americans felt during the 2016 presidential election – too many rules of decorum; too much forced liberalism; too little room for individuality; too many strangers in town. The United States' famed openness – openness to others, yes, but openness to blazing one's own trail as well – was being challenged on every front.

In 2016, said Hillary Clinton in retrospect, the American people "wanted a candidate to be as angry as they were and they wanted someone to blame."[3] Even worse, says Clinton, Donald Trump wore his feelings on his sleeve and did so brazenly, making debate prep hard for a cognitive person like herself. Trump "was rarely linear in his thinking or speaking," observed Clinton. "He digressed into nonsense and then digressed even more. There was no point in refuting his arguments like it was a normal debate – it was almost impossible to identify what his arguments were, especially since they changed minute to minute."[4] Trump's mind, Trump's magic, were surfeited with emotion.

This chapter examines how Trump reached those who felt trapped. The old American standbys – filled churches on Sundays, baseball players with pronounceable names – were ceding ground to government-approved lesson plans in the schools and a list of approved doctors at the clinic. Things were that way on the job too. Scott Adams, creator of the *Dilbert* comic strip, understands the world of work but he also knows the world of politics. "If you see voters as rational you'll be a terrible politician," Adams writes in his blog. "People are not wired to be rational. Our brains simply evolved to keep us alive. Brains did not evolve to give us truth. Brains merely give us the movies in our minds that keep us sane and motivated."[5] Trump gorged himself on emotional events. For him, nothing important happened quietly.

A considerable amount of research documents the importance of political emotions. A classic study by George Marcus and Michael MacKuen, for example, notes that people pay more attention to issues, open up their minds, and get more politically involved if they are emotionally aroused. "When politics makes people anxious," Marcus and MacKuen report, "they sharpen their eyes and pay careful attention."[6] Emotion can also detach people from party oligarchies and constrictive ways of thinking.[7] Emotions help people identify with like-minded others, causing them to lean into political involvement.[8] Television has been especially influential in such matters, says Robert Frank, giving people sharp, clear pictures of alternative lifestyles.[9]

Anger and fear – two of the emotions discussed in this chapter – are especially important political stimuli, although they do different kinds of work. Anger decreases our perceptions of risk, say the University of Michigan's Stuart Soroka and his colleagues, while fear does the opposite, making us more timid and self-protective.[10] So, for example, anxious voters were less likely to support the war in Iraq while angry voters were more hawkish.[11] Making people afraid sometimes has short-term benefits, causing citizens to rally round a father figure. On the other hand, too much fear can have the opposite effect, shutting people's eyes to a world grown too scary.[12] Still, say Cenzig Erisen and José Villalobos, American presidents are especially drawn to emotional appeals when addressing foreign policy matters, proving that feelings rarely stop at the water's edge.[13]

"The presidency is much more than an institution," said Duke's James David Barber in 1992, "it is a focus of feelings."[14] Barber's observations still ring true. "We have seen the rise of more postmodern worldviews which emphasize other-than-rational ways of knowing," says cultural researcher Annick de Witt, "such as moral, emotional, and artistic ones, as well as values beyond the material, such as creativity, self-expression, and imagination."[15] Donald Trump, the master of all things expressive, is part of that trend. A year after Trump took office, says columnist Jack Hunter, the President's supporters were even more passionate about him than on election day; the other half of the country continued to despise him.[16]

Such intense feelings normally recede at campaign's end as folks get back to their Scrabble games and rounds of golf. But as the 2020 presidential election came into view, the emotions of 2016 were still raw, although there were a few exceptions. Lisa Kirchner, a liberal feminist, found herself falling in love with a cute guy with a good sense of humor, a fellow named Paul who worried about her health, enjoyed furniture shopping, liked Frank Sinatra records, and was willing to cede space in their apartment for her yoga exercises.[17] But then came a key disclosure: Paul had voted for Donald Trump. Could young love survive? Must Lisa and Paul return to swiping left and swiping right until a proper match could be found? But here is the real question: Why did the *Huffington Post* allot precious digital space to such a banal story? The answer: We live in the Age of Trump. Political emotions rule the day.

Trump Listens

It wasn't supposed to be this way. A bloated and inefficient government, displacement of the work force, millennial stagnation, income inequality, indecipherable rap lyrics, Ellen cavorting shamelessly on television. The 1950s, after all, had promised a roaring economy and social conformity; the 1970s had promised an end to American adventurism abroad; the 1980s, especially as interpreted by Ronald Reagan, had promised self-determination for all. Now, thirty years later, women-on-the-job was a requirement, not an option; computers were out-manufacturing an army of union members; bowling leagues were declining and the Boy Scouts were admitting girls; college professors spewed out endless deconstructions of longstanding cultural truths; Hollywood lampooned all things bourgeois. It was enough to make a person vote for Donald Trump.

Heaven Engle, twenty years old, and her boyfriend, Venson Heim, were among those who felt trapped in 2016. Engle and Heim worked at the Bell & Evans plant in Fredericksburg, Pennsylvania, processing poultry, he on the first shift, she on the second. The job's monotony did not bother Heaven (she got benefits, after all) and, having no interest in going to college, she figured she could process chickens for a while. It was not the smell of the chicken juice that spilled on her face one day that bothered her. It was that she had nobody to talk to about it. Heaven spoke English; everyone else in the plant spoke Spanish.

The demographics of Lebanon County, Pennsylvania, were rapidly changing, as hundreds of Dominican families came to work in the low-paying but available jobs. But Heaven's plight was hardly the end of reporter Terrence McCoy's *Washington Post* story.[18] Almost immediately after the story was published, McCoy himself became an object of scorn. His narrative resembles a "John Hughes teen angst film gone haywire with deeply-rooted xenophobia," said a group of Hispanic journalists. "McCoy does nothing to humanize anyone else in his story except for Engle and Heim ... presenting the Latino workers in the story as dangerous, distant, cliquey and yes, threatening."[19] The fact that Engle and Heim felt trapped, they argued, has been a perennial problem in the United States: New people keep showing up; things change; you adjust.

Donald Trump could have easily coauthored McCoy's story and, in many senses, he did, channeling what many Americans felt

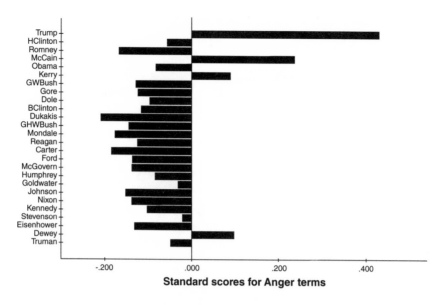

Figure 4.1 Use of Anger Terms by Presidential Candidates, 1948–2016
Source: Data from Campaign Mapping Project.

during the 2016 presidential election. Figure 4.1 shows how dramatically Trump changed the norms of political discourse. These data are provided by DICTION-based analyses of some 6,500 campaign speeches and are guided by specially built dictionaries tapping Anger, Fear, Hurt, and Joy.[20] During the campaign, Trump consistently talked about the Anger Americans were feeling and, by so doing, he added to it. His combination of Hurt and Anger was especially deft, helping him identify with those who felt trapped but also letting him set things right. His use of both appeals increased linearly during the campaign and he mentioned Anger four times more often than Hillary Clinton. Trump even edged out Clinton on Hurt, countervailing what should have been a "nurturance edge" for a female, Democratic candidate.[21]

Also interesting is what Trump did *not* do. When it came to Fear, he ranked twenty-first of the twenty-six major-party candidates running for office between 1948 and 2016. To acknowledge fear, Trump reasoned, was to risk being overwhelmed by it and that was not his style. Implicitly, perhaps, he knew that giving in to Fear was a loser's strategy, which is exactly what my studies have found.[22] Trump also seemed to understand other research: (1) Voters who feel Angry are more likely to vote in elections and to do volunteer work; (2) Angry voters make political decisions more quickly, even at the cost of being less deliberative; (3) Angry voters discuss things with like-minded individuals, a phenomenon amplified at Trump's campaign rallies; (4) Angry voters are more willing to take risks, a special advantage for an outside-the-box candidate like Trump.[23]

Appealing to Anger also resonated with the inner Trump. According to his sometime-advisor, Steve Bannon, Trump was a "fundamentally emotional man" and "the deepest part of him was angry and dark."[24] In January of 2016, South Carolina governor Nikki Haley warned Republicans not to listen to the "siren calls" of her party's "angriest voices," but Trump still gave her a bear hug when he saw her. "She did say there was anger," Trump explained, and "I'm very angry because our country is being run horribly," so "I will gladly accept the mantle of anger."[25]

"Donald Trump Talks Like a Woman" said *Politico* in October of 2016, quoting research showing that the female style is "more socially oriented, expressive and dynamic, whereas masculine language is more impersonal, long-winded, and unemotional."[26] With the exception of long-windedness, there is some truth in *Politico*'s report but Trump's relationship with emotion is more complicated than that. True, as some studies show, Trump's speech is both intuitive and unanalytical.[27] But Trump also relishes conflict. When a protester was being removed from one of his rallies, Trump blurted out, "Try not to hurt him. If you do, I'll defend you in court." On another occasion, Trump mused: "There's a guy totally disruptive, throwing punches. We're not allowed to punch back anymore. I love the old days. You know what they used to do to guys like that when they were in a place like this? They'd be carried out on a stretcher, folks."[28]

Trump often portrays himself as a reluctant provocateur, one who jerks back with his left what he throws with his right. "I was going to say 'dummy' Bush, I won't say it. I won't say it." "I refuse to call Megyn Kelly a bimbo, because that would not be politically correct." "Unlike others, I've never attacked dopey Jon Stewart for his phony last name. Would never do that!" "I promised I would not say that she [Carly Fiorina] ran Hewlett-Packard into the ground . . . I said I will not say it, so I will not say it."[29] As seen here, Trump exorcizes his inner demons and then immediately re-recruits them.

Trump is both primal and puritanical, keenly aware of what disgusts him – Hillary Clinton's bathroom breaks, Marco Rubio's perspiring under the klieg lights, John Kasich's eating habits. "Bodies," says scholar Michael Richardson of Trump, "are what disgust him most: women's bodies above all, but those of men too. Sweating, seeping, leaking, excreting, lactating, masticating – the body-ness of bodies."[30] Trump often performs his disgust, with "body jerking, pursed lips, face contracting and relaxing in vaudevillian style."[31]

Because he is so emotional, Trump is one of the most watched politicians in human history. Reporters and voters cannot take their eyes off of him because of his unpredictability. For these same reasons, Trump opens himself up to parody. Said one faux Trump ad: "I have heard a phone call where Hillary says ... that she enjoys watching illegal immigrants stab your wives and daughters. Rape, too. Only Donald Trump can prevent you from being raped by an illegal immigrant." Or this: "Crooked Hillary is going to shut all the hospitals and let Syrian refugees live there for free. I've seen the plan. On the campaign trail, where I beat 17 people very badly, beat them like dogs, I met many dying grandmothers. Sorry, Grandma. Can't go to the hospital. That's where Mohammad and his 12 children live."[32]

According to one group of scholars, Trump traffics "in desire and fantasy," giving "suffering a public cause, anger a target, and aspiration a horizon."[33] He gives his supporters a kind of affective freedom, letting them entertain their wildest fears but doing so within his gentle embrace.[34] The truth he offers is what communication scholar Jayson Harsin calls "emo-truth." Even though Trump's comments are often "bafflingly untranslatable," he reaches people by endorsing "feeling as knowing."[35] Societies have usually been governed by formal authority (the State) and moral authority (the Church) but in an age of celebrity, says Dov Seidman, they can also be governed by emotional authority: You feel what I feel and so I trust you.[36] In such an age, the right emotions can transcend all factual conditions, all doctrinal assertions, all interpersonal expectancies.

The result is that Trump has turned the rant into an art form. Desultory though they are, rants are also (1) deliciously spontaneous ("anything can happen"), (2) self-consciously inappropriate ("let us sin together"), (3) endlessly repetitious ("lock her up!"), (4) overwhelmingly bombastic ("billions and billions of dollars"), and (5) self-authenticating ("what you see is not what's happening"). Like radio provocateur Michael Savage, Trump's rants become "a kind of talk show scat, jumping from a mini-lecture about the Khmer Rouge, to a rave about barbecue chicken, to a warning that he feels a bit manic, which mean's he'll be depressed for tomorrow's show."[37] Whereas Savage celebrates his depression, Trump stays up late tweeting.

Nighttime is also a time for dreaming and Donald Trump is good at that too – "Mexico will pay for the wall," "The GDP will go up 5 or 6 percent," "No cuts to Medicare or Medicaid," "We'll bring back waterboarding," "'Merry Christmas' at every store." For Trump, it is *the promising*, not the promises, that best supports those who feel trapped. His approach rests on a curious logic – to imagine a thing is to make it plausible; to want a thing is to make it manifest. In such a world, consistencies are irrelevant, giving rise to a popular internet meme: "Trump didn't say that. And if he did, he didn't mean that. And if he did, you didn't understand it. And if you did, it's not a big deal. And if it is, others have said worse."

An emotional logic easily transcends facts such as indictments, guilty pleas, and convictions: *On Paul Manafort*: "He is a good man. He was with Ronald Reagan." *On Michael Flynn*: "A wonderful man. I think he has been treated very, very unfairly." *On Joe Arpaio*: "He's done a great job for the people of Arizona. He's very strong on borders." *On Michael Cohen*: "A fine person with a wonderful family ... who I have always liked and respected."[38]

While the press scoffs at such manipulations, everyday people – those whose fathers have disappointed them or who have promiscuous daughters – know that, ultimately, family is family. That rings truest during liminal moments – when the imperfect father dies, when the licentious daughter needs shelter once again. For these reasons, Trump's emotional logic resonates strongly for people as, for example, when he called for a "total and complete shutdown of Muslims entering the United States" at a rally in South Carolina:

> The roar came when Trump read his press statement aloud. It was a long, full-bodied roar – hands clapping, fists stabbing the air. The roar you give when things that you and your family and your friends have long believed are suddenly utterable on what is arguably the greatest stage on earth: the American presidential election. It was a roar of relief: These were no longer notions that had to be muttered under your breath. Trump wasn't just "saying what he means," in that phrase so often used by pundits to explain his success. He, the freest of men, was saying what *they* meant.[39]

My studies show that Donald Trump acknowledged his supporters' fears but never dwelled on them. Anger was his game and for good reason: The fifty counties with the highest anxiety ratings in the United States showed a 9 percent increase in turnout in 2016.[40] Angry people are generally more motivated to vote and that was truer of Trump's supporters than Clinton's.[41] Communication scholars Dan Schill and Rita Kirk conducted a number of focus groups during the election and found that Trump's supporters sounded eerily similar to one another – and to the candidate himself. "Trump's recognition of their anger," Schill and Kirk report, "allowed voters to feel heard."[42]

Trump supporters felt heard because the candidate himself was such a fine listener. Here is what he heard: New technologies have sidelined my well-honed skills; there's a political elite in this country and I'm not part of it; I'm white but feel outnumbered, a church-goer sitting amidst empty pews; I went to a community college but that's not enough. Feelings like these were widespread in 2016, and Donald Trump seized on them. In losing to him, Hillary Clinton lost to an avalanche of emotions.

The People Join In

A phrase like "Donald Trump feels what I feel" can mean at least two things: (1) Trump and I share certain attitudes (e.g., "the United States is admitting too many immigrants") or (2) Trump understands my inner self (e.g., "I'm losing my place in the world"). The Trump phenomenon was of the latter sort, making the 2016 race the most emotional campaign since 1948.[43] Policy issues were important, of course, but it was Trump's volatility that drew voters to him (and also made him one of the most loathed candidates in U.S. history).

Political scientists Eric Oliver and Thomas Wood have argued that the nation has become riven between Rationalists (those committed to science and reason) and Intuitionists (those who embrace conspiracy theories and who distrust experts and the media).[44] While both strains of thought have long existed in the United States, Oliver and Wood find evidence that Intuitionists are especially active today and that many of them are Trumpians. My studies provide some corroborating evidence for that notion.

Figure 4.2 compares the language of Anger found in campaign speeches to that found in letters to the editor written during presidential

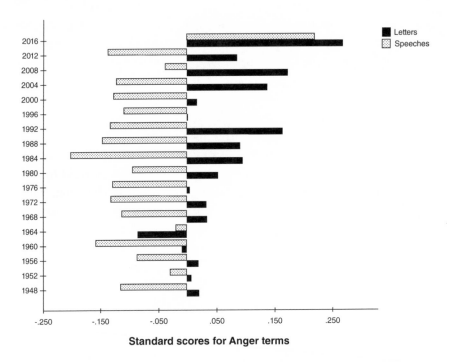

Figure 4.2 Use of Anger Terms in Speeches vs. Letters to the Editor
Source: Data from Campaign Mapping Project.

elections in twelve mid-sized American cities between 1948 and the present. The cities chosen ranged from coast to coast and from north to south, and are largely blue-collar places, not especially distinctive politically. The newspapers publish roughly 90 percent of the letters submitted to them because free content is better than no content and because letters to the editor are so heavily read. My book, *Civic Hope: How Ordinary Americans Keep Democracy Alive*, offers an exhaustive analysis of 10,000 such letters, but Figure 4.2 captures its essence: Letter writers are universally unhappy with how things are going, and they say so lustily.[45] Political candidates, in contrast, are more reliably drawn to arrant possibilities.

All of that changed in 2016, with the letter writers being angrier than normal and with the candidates (especially Trump) joining their chorus. These data parallel the overall increase in political polarization that researchers have documented in recent years. Writing during the 2016 election, UCLA's Lynn Vavreck noted that "Americans are angry. That's the sentiment that many believe is driving the 2016 election.

They are angry because the rich are getting richer, the average guy is struggling and the government in Washington hasn't done anything to stop the trend." "But it may not be that simple," Vavreck continues, because "Americans aren't annoyed only by the economy; they're annoyed with one another."[46]

Partisan polarization is part of this story, with Congress having been slowed to a halt in recent years. Republicans and Democrats find it hard to do business with one another and now they do not even use the same language: *estate tax* vs. *death tax*; *right to choose* vs. *right to life*; *tax breaks* vs. *tax relief*. Party demographics are also changing, with Democrats becoming less white and less religious, considerably younger, and better educated than before, and with Republicans becoming more male than female and more economically diverse. As the Pew Center reports, all of this results in "two coalitions moving further apart."[47]

The 2016 campaign brought these matters to a head, with Trump appealing to voters pining for reestablishment of the "correct hierarchies."[48] Such voters have a "social dominance orientation," said one group of researchers, nurturing the hope that Mr. Trump would repudiate the creeping egalitarianism of the Obama years (in many ways, they got their wish).[49] On the other hand, both Democrats and Republicans now seek out news that reaffirms rather than questions their values.[50] Not surprisingly, strong Ds and strong Rs have become especially receptive to candidates stressing "existential threats," worries about life and death vs. mere dollars and cents.[51] As political scientists Andrew Gelman and Julia Azari report, "weak parties and strong partisanship tell much of the story of the 2016 race."[52]

Candidates and their supporters colluded at the emotional level during that campaign. "I'm not voting for [Trump] to be my pastor," said Kathy Rehberg of Grand Junction, Colorado; "I'm voting for him to be my president. If I have rats in my basement, I'm going to try to find the best rat killer out there. I don't care if he's ugly or if he's sociable."[53] Said Matt Patterson, also of Grand Junction: "I've never been this emotionally invested in a political leader in my life. "The more they hate him, the more I want him to succeed. Because what they hate about him is what they hate about me."[54] Trump voters wanted a businessman, said the *New Yorker*'s Peter Hessler, but they also wanted to "feel a certain way."[55]

The more outrageous Trump became in 2016, the more he spilled his guts, the more attractive he became to "threat-sensitive" voters, says the University of Nebraska's John Hibbing. Such people gravitate toward candidates who "will protect them from threats posed by out-groups and in-group norm violators." "People who are less threat-sensitive," says Hibbing, "are mystified by the allure of these same policies and candidates. And so feelings intensify, battle lines harden, tribal conflicts clarify, political stalemate descends, the social fabric frays."[56]

Because so much of Trump's support came from people who were "energized by his bombast and his animus more than any actual accomplishments," they remained strongly committed to him a year after the election.[57] Indeed, says *Politico*'s Michael Kruse, for many citizens, support for Trump became completely untethered to issues. As long as Trump stayed "increasingly angry on their behalf," says Kruse, his supporters remained protective of the President.[58] Restoring manufacturing in Johnstown, Pennsylvania? "You're never going to get those steel mills back," said Maggie Frear. No wall on the southern border? "I don't give a shit," Frear declared. No repeal of Obamacare? "That's Congress," she observed. The scourge of drugs in western Pennsylvania? "It's not going to improve for a long time until people learn, which they won't," said Ms. Frear.[59] For voters like this, says Kruse, "Trump is their megaphone. He is their scriptwriter. He is a singularly effective, intuitive creator of a limitless loop of grievance and discontent that keeps them in absolute lockstep."[60]

As we saw in Figure 4.2, those who wrote letters to the editor in 2016 more than matched Mr. Trump's (and to a lesser extent Mrs. Clinton's) anger. But when reading the letters closely, one finds something deeply cultural about the letters supporting Trump. It is as if the writers' lifestyles, their very beings, hung in the balance. Consider, for example, a meandering letter written in a contradictory, staccato style by Judy Reams of Iowa Park, Texas. DICTION rated Ms. Reams' letter the highest on emotionality of all 1,208 letters analyzed in 2016. Policy issues are mentioned in the letter but more compelling is its sense of ambient loss. Said Ms. Reams in her "Apology Letter to My Grandchildren":

> I'm sorry you will only feel safe with a gun in your home because my generation disrespected and even killed police officers who protected us and now nobody wants to be one. I'm sorry you never said the Pledge of Allegiance or heard a public

prayer over the loud speaker in school or sporting events. I'm sorry you never learned cursive so you can read the Constitution.

I'm sorry when there is a tragedy in America, you have to see fellow Americans burn buildings and hurt innocent people. I'm sorry you don't see the Ten Commandments displayed publicly anymore. I'm sorry your school has to be locked at all times for fear of a shooting inside. I'm sorry your child can't go to a public restroom for fear of the opposite sex being there.

I'm sorry you will have to support people in our country who are not supposed to be here in the first place. I'm sorry you have never seen a confederate flag. I'm sorry when you get sick, you will have no say in which doctor treats you. I'm sorry you have to question the reference "Black Lives Matter" when ALL lives matter. I'm sorry there is a group called ISIS that hates you. They are bad people.

I'm sorry your children will not be allowed to hug teachers or co-workers for fear of sexual harassment. I'm sorry you can buy marijuana everywhere. I'm sorry you cannot watch a movie or TV without hearing curse words. I'm sorry you see Americans disrespect the National Anthem at a public event you pay to attend. I'm sorry you never hear Merry Christmas publicly anymore.

You see, my precious grandchildren, this country was once a proud place to live. Many in my generation tried, but failed you. We have the opportunity to vote the next person to help change and make our country great again. If that person is not chosen, it will continue to get worse. For that, I'm so sorry. We failed you once again.

I love you, Nanna.[61]

Ms. Reams' letter is a lament for a world fallen apart and opens up a bevy of questions. What sorts of people live in a perpetual state of anger? Why does anger wax and wane for others? How do the privileged justify their anger? How do the meek avoid it? When does anger become dangerous? When does it promote social goods? Why are some forms of anger righteous, others self-indulgent? What makes people like Donald Trump aficionados of anger? Can politics exist without anger? In 2016, at least, the answer to the last question was no.

The Press Pays Attention

The Campaign Mapping Project now contains some 22,000 news stories produced in eight national and supra-regional newspapers between 1948 and the present. DICTION analysis shows an uptick in Anger in such publications during the 2016 campaign.[62] While modest, these changes are noteworthy because reporters (especially print reporters) are so heavily constrained by norms of objectivity. But the story of the 2016 race goes beyond simple word counts. To get a more nuanced understanding, I probed the Lexis-Nexis database of news coverage in a variety of ways, noting when the words *Trump* or *Clinton* appeared adjacent to a variety of emotional tokens. I repeated these observations for print coverage during primary vs. general election seasons, for all major-party candidates between 1948 and 2012, and for first-year presidents vs. campaigners. In addition, I calculated the extent to which the press focused on (1) emotions vs. actions, (2) issues vs. values, and (3) positive vs. negative emotions. The overall result: The press operated differently when Donald Trump entered the picture.

Historically, Trump has had a love/hate relationship with the press, but he has also become addicted to its ministrations, sensing that no publicity is bad publicity and that bad publicity is a license to make a scene. He brought those attitudes into the 2016 campaign, making the press a hobgoblin whenever possible. In August of 2018, he broadened his critique to Google, tweeting thusly:

> Google search results for "Trump News" shows only the viewing/reporting of Fake News Media. In other words, they have it RIGGED, for me & others, so that almost all stories & news is BAD. Fake CNN is prominent. Republican/Conservative & Fair Media is shut out. Illegal?[63]

Mr. Trump was both right and wrong. He did indeed receive a lot of bad coverage but that is only because he received so much coverage. Searches show (in Table 4.1) that Trump generated twice as much coverage as Hillary Clinton during the general election when the Lexis-Nexis database was examined for Policies (*healthcare, trade, terrorism, crime,* etc.), Principles (*faith, liberty, progress, justice,* etc.), and the Horserace (*polls, strategy, votes, opinions,* etc.). That ratio almost doubled for Positive emotions (*like, admire, appreciate, enjoy,* etc.) and Negative emotions (*hurt, denounce, hate, dislike,* etc.). The

Table 4.1 News Coverage Ratios for Donald Trump vs. Hillary Clinton

| News domain | General election coverage | |
	Search tokens (no. of hits)	Trump/Clinton ratio
General matters	Policy terms (n = 3,716)	2.62
	Horserace terms (n = 2,303)	2.03
	Principled terms (n = 1,302)	2.50
	Positive emotions (n = 2,393)	3.68
	Negative emotions (n = 1,546)	3.86
	Moral values (n = 651)	4.42
Specific matters	Financial issues (n = 403)	1.13
	Social net (n = 1,713)	0.61
	Immigration (n = 272)	23.73
	Social diversity (n = 671)	6.29
	Global threats (n = 485)	2.73
	Domestic threats (n = 172)	1.05

Source: Data gathered via guided Lexis-Nexis searches for 2016 news coverage.

ratio increased once again for Morals (*honesty, reputation, conscience, character,* etc.), with Trump generating over four times as much value-based coverage as Clinton between August 15th and election day.

The mathematics here are impressive but the news text is even more intriguing, as we see in one of the press's most-prized tropes – the person-on-the-street interview. Everyone, it seemed, had an opinion about Donald Trump in 2016 and the press offered them a platform:

> When Donald Trump challenged Hillary Clinton's stamina on the debate stage, Pennsylvania voter Patricia Bennett said she heard a "dog whistle" that smacked of unmistakable sexism. "Why doesn't he just say that she needs more testosterone?" said Bennett.[64]

Aaron Regunberg ... said he was "surprised and concerned" that the race is so tight. "I still think we are likely to win, but I think anyone who's not concerned about a bigoted, KKK-endorsed sociopath being this close right now in the polls is not living in reality."[65]

The first lady, exasperated and angry, said video of Trump bragging about leveraging his stardom to force himself on women "has shaken me to my core." Although careful never to mention Trump by name, Obama sternly admonished him for behavior she called "cruel," "sick," and devoid of basic human decency.[66]

At times, the press seemed aware of its penchant for drama. "Anyone who can break through the media chatter," said *Washington Post* blogger Jennifer Rubin, "make an emotional connection with voters, and project competence and empathy can capture the public, regardless of the ideological content they are peddling."[67] Donald Trump typically shifted the blame. When a homeless Latino man was beat up by perpetrators using the candidate's own words as justification, Trump responded, "I will say that people who are following me are very passionate ... they have anger. They love this country. It's a beautiful thing."[68] For Donald Trump, anger had its own aesthetic.

As we see in Table 4.2, the Lexis-Nexis database has expanded considerably over the years, with more and more online sources being added and with news stories being constantly updated. To correct for the database's burgeoning size, comparisons between the Trump administration and its predecessors are presented here as proportional data. The results are clear: When Positive emotions (*enjoy, love, admire, like, cheer*, etc.) are compared to Negative emotions (*fear, criticize, dislike, despise, ignore*, etc.), the ratios remain high for first-year presidents until we get to the Trump administration, where it drops off dramatically. Table 4.2 also shows that presidential feelings have increasingly dominated presidential actions (*came, made, took, used, went*, etc.), a trend that is especially apparent in Trump's case. Similarly, Trump's statements (*claim, declare, said, tell, propose*, etc.) share equal time with his emotions, something that was not as true for his predecessors.

"Donald Trump has ushered in an emotional regime of anger," says Karin Wahl-Jorgensen, and that anger has become contagious, instinctual, for many Americans.[69] The press has been part of that story,

Table 4.2 News Coverage Ratios for First-Year Presidents

Chief executive (no. of hits)	News coverage		
	Positive/ negative ratio	Action/feeling ratio	Action/speech ratio
G. H. W. Bush (n = 24,869)	2.42	10.3	1.55
Bill Clinton (n = 47,710)	2.12	6.67	1.15
George W. Bush (n = 57,044)	2.60	7.65	1.34
Barack Obama (n = 97,876)	2.53	4.74	1.30
Donald Trump (n = 216,378)	1.18	3.70	1.04

Source: Data gathered via guided Lexis-Nexis searches for 2016 news coverage.

in part because so many reporters despise Trump: "Trump is the epitome of the 'ugly American,'" says the *Bismarck Tribune*. "Trump is the epitome of rape culture," reports the *Washington Post*. Trump is "the epitome of a one-percenter," says the *Mississauga News*. "Trump is the epitome of not suave; even grade school children couldn't miss that he's a clown," says the *Los Angeles Times*. "Trump is the epitome of vulgarity," says the *New York Times*, of "the bad poet," says the *Irish Times*.[70] If you feel anything, if you feel everything, Donald Trump is your man, a man for all feelings.[71]

Conclusion

For those who felt trapped in the fall of 2016, Donald Trump was just the ticket. He bodied forth their sentiments, addressing their frustrations directly, often cruelly. He sought out voters such as Cindy (no last name provided) of Russell, Kansas, who had spotted an imminent Muslim invasion: "it's just a matter of time when someone gives the signal and we're all going to be beheaded."[72] Such talk was deeply unsettling to Veronica Escobar of El Paso, Texas, who saw pro-Trump, anti-immigrant messages posted throughout her city. "How did America get that way?" she asked.[73] How indeed?

The politics of the 2016 election were so polarizing, says Virginia psychotherapist Toni Coleman, "that people are getting mad at each other ... even if they voted the same way."[74] Not surprisingly, Emily Holmes Hahn, the founder of LastFirst Matchmaking, reports that "the political situation has absolutely made it harder to match people."[75] Meanwhile, at Fresno State University, history lecturer Lars Maischak risked his job by posting a tweet recommending, "Trump must hang."[76] "We are inundated by rage," says Senator John Danforth of Missouri; "it's not just practicing politicians. It's the demand from the base of the two parties, and it is in large part encouraged by the media."[77] As if to prove the point, one tweeter threatened to shoot Representative Martha McSally in the head; another tried to run Representative David Kustoff off the road with her car; a third grievously wounded Representative Steve Scalise at a baseball game. "I wouldn't rent to you if you were the last person on Earth; one word says it all – Asian," said an Airbnb host to a prospective guest during a vicious snowstorm.[78] America, the land of unbridled emotions.

Trump "needs to say something about this," says Ivet Lolham of San Francisco, who had just been accosted on the subway by a stranger who, after hearing Lolham's Assyrian accent, declared "you are an ugly, mean, evil little pig who might get deported and I pray that you do."[79] A Nazi billboard adorned with Trump's picture in Phoenix, Arizona. A KKK banner proudly displayed in Dahlonega, Georgia. A vandalized car of a (Puerto Rican) Army veteran in San Jose replete with the scrawled words "Trump" and "Go home."[80] "I was there for the riots and what happened to Dr. King," said B. J. Middleton of Fairhope, Alabama, "and I'll tell you, it feels like we're building toward something again."[81]

Tracing the causal arrow is not easy, however. As the data presented in this chapter show, Donald Trump rode to 1600 Pennsylvania Avenue in a limousine of anger but he was not alone. In many ways, he reproduced what he had picked up in his trips to the heartland. Hillary Clinton trafficked in anger as well, most of it directed at Donald Trump personally. Ordinary Americans writing letters to the editor joined in, as did the press. When the off-year elections of 2018 rolled around, there were enough emotions available for all persons for all purposes.

"Before the [2016] election," said Hillary Clinton, "it felt as if half the people were angry and resentful, while the other half was still fundamentally hopeful. Now pretty much everyone is mad about something."[82] Perhaps. But the United States has been through all this before: the civil rights and anti-war protesters of the 1960s, the angry feminists of the 1970s, the gay activists of the 1980s, and the environmentalists of the 1990s. But while these movements focused on policy clashes and basic human freedoms, the Trump Era is about something else entirely – people's identities in an age of unforgiving globalization. "We think of ourselves as people with an inner self ... that is denigrated, ignored, not listened to," says Francis Fukuyama, and "a great deal of modern politics is about the demand of that inner self to be uncovered, publicly claimed, and recognized by the political system."[83] Given U.S. diversity, this will be a tall order to fill. Save a land war or two, however, there is time.

Notes

1 "Fear and Loathing in Homer and Rockville," *NPR*, July 21, 2017. Accessed at www.thisamericanlife.org/621/fear-and-loathing-in-homer-and-rockville.

2 As quoted in Becky Bohrer, "Inclusivity Measure Stirs Debate in Homer," *JuneauEmpire.com*, February 27, 2017. Accessed at http://juneauempire.com/state/2017-02-27/inclusivity-measure-stirs-debate-homer.

3 Hillary Rodham Clinton, *What Happened* (New York: Simon & Schuster, 2017), p. 272.

4 Ibid., p. 105.

5 As quoted in Michael Cavna, "Donald Trump Will Win in a Landslide: the Mind Behind Dilbert Explains Why," *Washington Post*, March 21, 2016. Accessed at www.washingtonpost.com/news/comic-riffs/wp/2016/03/21/donald-trump-will-win-in-a-landslide-the-mind-behind-dilbert-explains-why/?noredirect=on&utm_term=.943647b4c10e.

6 George Marcus and Michael B. MacKuen, "Anxiety, Enthusiasm, and the Vote: the Emotional Underpinnings of Learning and Involvement during Presidential Campaigns," *American Political Science Review*, 87:3 (1993), 672–85. For more on the effects of emotions on rational decision-making, see Martyn Griffin, "Deliberative Democracy and Emotional Intelligence: an Internal Mechanism to Regulate the Emotions," *Studies in Philosophy and Education*, 31:6 (2012), 517–38.

7 See for example Ted Brader, "Striking a Responsive Chord: How Political Ads Motivate and Persuade Voters by Appealing to Emotions," *American Journal of Political Science*, 49:2 (2005), 388–405; Barry Richards, "The Emotional Deficit in Political Communication," *Political Communication*, 21:3 (2004), 339–52.

8 See Jennifer S. Lerner and Dachner Keltner, "Fear, Anger, and Risk," *Journal of Personality and Social Psychology*, 81:1 (2001), 146–59.

9 Robert H. Frank, *Passions within Reason: the Strategic Role of the Emotions* (New York: Norton, 1981).

10 Stuart Soroka, Lori Young, and Meital Balmas, "Bad News or Mad News? Sentiment Scoring of Negativity, Fear, and Anger in News Content," *ANNALS of the American Academy of Political and Social Science*, 650 (2015), 108–21.

11 Leonie Huddy and Nayda Terkildsen, "Gender Stereotypes and the Perception of Male and Female Candidates," *American Journal of Political Science*, 37:1 (1993), 119–47.

12 Krista De Castella, Craig McGarty, and Luke Musgrove, "Fear Appeals in Political Rhetoric about Terrorism: an Analysis of Speeches by Australian Prime Minister Howard," *Political Psychology*, 30:1 (2009), 1–26; Krista De Castella and Craig McGarty, "Two Leaders, Two Wars: a Psychological Analysis of Fear and Anger Content in Political Rhetoric about Terrorism," *Analyses of Social Issues and Public Policy*, 11:1 (2011), 180–200.

13 Cengiz Erisen and José D. Villalobos, "Exploring the Invocation of Emotion in Presidential Speeches," *Contemporary Politics*, 20:4 (2014), 460–88.

14 James David Barber, *The Presidential Character: Predicting Performance in the White House* (Englewood Cliffs, NJ: Prentice-Hall, 1992), p. 270. See also Lynn Ragsdale, "Strong Feelings: Emotional Responses to Presidents," *Political Behavior*, 13:1 (1991), 33–65.

15 Annick de Witt, "Understanding Our Polarized Political Landscape Requires a Long, Deep Look at Our Worldviews," *Scientific American*, June 28, 2016. Accessed at www.scientificamerican.com/author/annick-de-witt/.

16 Jack Hunter, "Americans Are More Emotional about Trump Than Ever," *Austin American-Statesman*, January 2, 2018. Accessed at www.mystatesman.com/news/opinion/jack-hunter-americans-are-more-emotional-about-trump-than-ever/OAGus qhLkdleULzSz1GInM/.

17 See Lisa L. Kirchner, "I'm a Liberal Feminist and Next Month I'm Marrying a Trump Voter," *Huffington Post*, April 6, 2018. Accessed at www.huffingtonpost.com/entry/liberal-feminist-marrying-a-trump-voter_us_5ac3cc81e4b00fa46f874949.

18 Terrence McCoy, "White, and in the Minority: She Speaks English. Her Co-workers Don't. Inside a Rural Chicken Plant, Whites Struggle to Fit In," *Washington Post*, July 30, 2018. Accessed at www.washingtonpost.com/news/local/wp/2018/07/30/feature/majority-minority-white-workers-at-this-pennsylvania-chicken-plant-now-struggle-to-fit-in/?utm_term=.3e800f615a16.

19 Latino Rebels, "Why the *Washington Post*'s 'White, and in the Minority' Story Is So Damn Dangerous," *Latino Rebels*, August 1, 2018. Accessed at www.latinorebels.com/2018/08/01/washingtonpostswhiteandintheminority/.

20 The Anger dictionary (61 base terms) includes such tokens as *bad, bitter, disgusting, hate, insulting, mad*, etc., while the Fear dictionary (50 base terms) includes *afraid, frantic, panic, scared, terrified*, etc. and their cognates. Hurt (97 base terms) was tapped by uses of *alone, depressed, desolate, disappointed, helpless, sad*, etc., while Joy (92 base terms) was signaled by *blessed, cheerful, delighted, eager, hopeful, love, pleased*, etc. For more on content analysis and emotions, see Christelle Gilloz, Johnny R. J. Fontaine, Cristina Soriano, and Klaus R. Scherer, "Mapping Emotion Terms into Affective Space: Further Evidence for a Four-Dimensional Structure," *Swiss Journal of Psychology*, 75:3 (2016), 141–48; Thomas Hoffmann, "'Too Many Americans are Trapped in Fear, Violence, and Poverty': a Psychology-Informed Sentiment Analysis of Campaign Speeches from the 2016 U.S. Presidential Election," *Linguistics Vanguard*, January 2018. Accessed at www.researchgate.net/publication/322479904_Too_many_Americans_are_trapped_in_fear_violence_and_poverty_a_psychology-informed_sentiment_analysis_of_campaign_speeches_from_the_2016_US_Presidential_Election.

21 Statistical patterns for Anger terms: Hillary Clinton = 0.2517; Donald Trump = 0.8340; $F_{[1, 950]} = 46.552$, $p < 0.000$; for Hurt terms: Hillary Clinton = 0.4334; Donald Trump = 0.6611; $F_{[1, 950]} = 9.514$, $p < 0.000$. For more of Trump's ability to co-opt both Republican and Democratic themes, see Robert J. Gonzalez, "Hacking the Citizenry: Personality Profiling, 'Big Data' and the Election of Donald

Trump," *Anthropology Today*, June 2017. Accessed at onlinelibrary.wiley.com/doi/pdf/10.1111/1467-8322.12348.

22 Statistical patterns for Fear terms: winning candidates = 0.2050; Losing candidates = 0.3406; F [1, 950] = 30.437, p < 0.000.

23 See Christopher Weber, "Emotions, Campaigns and Political Participation," *Political Research Quarterly*, 66:2 (2012), 414–28; Nicholas A. Valentino, Vincent L. Hutchings, Antoine J. Banks, and Anne K. Davis, "Is a Worried Citizen a Good Citizen? Emotions, Political Information Seeking, and Learning via the Internet," *Political Psychology*, 29:2 (2008), 247–73; Jaeho Cho, "Campaign Tone, Political Affect, and Communicative Engagement," *Journal of Communication*, 63:6 (2013), 1130–52; Jennifer Jerit, "Survival of the Fittest: Rhetoric during the Course of an Election Campaign," *Political Psychology*, 25:4 (2004), 563–75.

24 As quoted in Michael Wolff, *Fire and Fury: Inside the Trump White House* (New York: Henry Holt and Co., 2018), p. 181.

25 As quoted in Michelle Hackman, "Donald Trump: 'I Will Gladly Accept the Mantle of Anger,'" *Vox*, January 14, 2016. Accessed at www.vox.com/2016/1/14/10773784/trump-debate-anger.

26 Julie Sevivy, "Donald Trump Talks Like a Woman," *Politico*, October 25, 2016. Accessed at www.politico.com/magazine/story/2016/10/trump-feminine-speaking-style-214391. Social class adds yet another dimension to the gender-based differences in speech patterns. See, for example, James Milroy and Lesley Milroy, "Mechanisms of Change in Urban Dialects: The Role of Class, Social Network and Gender," *International Journal of Applied Linguistics*, 3:1 (1993), 57–77.

27 Kayla N. Jordan and James W. Pennebaker, "The Exception or the Rule: Using Words to Assess Analytic Thinking, Donald Trump, and the American Presidency," *Translational Issues in Psychological Science*, 3:3 (2017), 312–16.

28 These examples are recounted in Samira Saramo, "The Meta-Violence of Trumpism," *European Journal of American Studies*, 12:2 (2017). Accessed at https://journals.openedition.org/ejas/12129.

29 Examples provided by Joe Romm, "Donald Trump May Sound Like a Clown, But He Is a Rhetoric Pro like Cicero," *ThinkProgress*, March 28, 2016. Accessed at https://thinkprogress.org/donald-trump-may-sound-like-a-clown-but-he-is-a-rhetoric-pro-like-cicero-ac40fd1cda79/.

30 Michael Richardson, "The Disgust of Donald Trump," *Continuum: Journal of Media and Cultural Studies*, 31:6 (2017), 747.

31 Ibid., 750.

32 "Transcript [sic] of Donald J. Trump's Acceptance Speech at the RNC," *Thoughts on the Dead*, July 23, 2016. Accessed at www.thoughtsonthedead.com/transcript-of-donald-j-trumps-acceptance-speech-at-the-rnc/.

33 Alyson Cole and George Shulman, "Donald Trump, the TV Show: Michael Rogin Redux," *Theory and Event*, 21:2 (2018), 350.

34 For more on this, see John Street, "What Is Donald Trump? Forms of 'Celebrity' in Celebrity Politics," *Political Studies Review* (May 2017), 1–11. Accessed at http://journals.sagepub.com/doi/pdf/10.1177/1478929918772995.

35 Jayson Harsin, "Trump l'Oeil: Is Trump's Post-Truth Communication Translatable?" *Contemporary French and Francophone Studies*, 21:5 (2017), 513, 517.

36 Dov Seidman, *How: Why How We Do Anything Means Everything* (New York: Wiley, 2011).

37 David Segal, "Call It Ludacris: the Kinship between Talk Radio and Rap," *New York Times*, September 19, 2009. Accessed at www.nytimes.com/2009/09/20/week inreview/20segal.html.

38 "Trump Calls Manafort 'Good Man' after Former Campaign Chairman Found Guilty on Eight Counts in Fraud Trial," *CBS Philly*, August 21, 2018. Accessed at https://philadelphia.cbslocal.com/2018/08/21/paul-manafort-jury-ver dict/; Tessa Berenson, "'I Don't Think He Did Anything Wrong'; Five Times President Trump Defended Michael Flynn," *Time*, December 1, 2017. Accessed at http://time.com/5045158/donald-trump-michael-flynn-quotes/; Kevin Liptak, "Trump Defends Arpaio Pardon, Says Timing Was Intended to Draw Attention," *CNN*, August 28, 2017. Accessed at www.cnn.com/2017/08/28/politics/donald-trump-joe-arpaio-pardon/index.html; Rebecca Ballhaus and Janet Hook, "Trump Denies Directing Cohen to Break Campaign-Finance Laws," *Wall Street Journal*, August 22, 2018. Accessed at www.wsj.com/articles/trump-attacks-michael-cohen-says-hes-a-poor-lawyer-1534943248.

39 Anand Giridharadas, "Trumpism after Trump," *New York Times*, December 11, 2015. Accessed at www.nytimes.com/2015/12/11/magazine/trumpism-after-trump .html.

40 Martin Obschonka, Michael Stuetzer, Peter J. Rentfrow, Neil Lee, Jeff Potter, and Samuel D. Gosling, "Fear, Populism, and the Geopolitical Landscape: the 'Sleeper Effect' of Neurotic Personality Traits on Regional Voting Behavior in the 2016 Brexit and Trump Elections," *Social Psychological and Personality Science*, 9:3 (2018), 285–98.

41 Soren Jordan and Danielle C. Wong, "Affect towards Politics and the Success of Donald Trump," Paper presented at the annual meeting of the Midwest Political Science Association, April 2018, Chicago; Dilin Liu and Lei Lei, "The Appeal to Political Sentiment: an Analysis of Donald Trump's and Hillary Clinton's Speech Themes and Discourse Strategies in the 2016 U.S. Presidential Election," *Discourse, Context and Media*, May 2018. Accessed at www.researchgate.net/publication/325030488_The_appeal_to_political_sentiment_An_analysis_of_Donald_Trump%27s_and_Hillary_Clinton%27s_speech_themes_and_discourse_strategies_in_the_2016_US_presidential_election.

42 Dan Schill and Rita Kirk, "Angry, Passionate, and Divided: Undecided Voters and the 2016 Presidential Elections," *American Behavioral Scientist*, 61:9 (2017), 1063.

43 Hillary Clinton was also part of this trend. She ranked sixth of twenty-six candidates on Anger and seventh on Hurt. Unlike Trump, who ranked quite low on the use of Fear appeals (twenty-first of twenty-six), Clinton was a bit higher (ranking fourteenth).

44 J. Eric Oliver and Thomas J. Wood, *Enchanted America: How Intuition and Reason Divide Our Politics* (Chicago: University of Chicago Press, 2018).

45 Roderick P. Hart, *Civic Hope: How Ordinary Americans Keep Democracy Alive* (New York: Cambridge University Press, 2018).

46 Lynn Vavreck, "American Anger: It's Not the Economy. It's the Other Party," *New York Times: The Upshot*, April 2, 2016. Accessed at www.nytimes.com/2016/04/03/upshot/american-anger-its-not-the-economy-its-the-other-party.html.

47 "The Parties on the Eve of the 2016 Election: Two Coalitions, Moving Further Apart," *People-Press.Org–Pew Research Center*, September 13, 2016. Accessed at www.people-press.org/2016/09/13/the-parties-on-the-eve-of-the-2016-election-two-coalitions-moving-further-apart/.

48 Mauricio Alvarez and Markus Kemmelmeier, "Donald Trump as the Establishment Candidate of the 2016 Presidential Election," Paper presented at the annual

convention of the International Society for Political Psychology, Edinburgh, Scotland, June 2017.

49 Matthew Hayes, Jeff Sinn, and Scott Huffmon, "Insight into Trump's Populism: Social Dominance Orientation and Authoritarianism in the 2016 Presidential Race," Paper presented at the annual convention of the International Society for Political Psychology, Edinburgh, Scotland, June 2017.

50 Andrea Pereira and Jay Van Bavel, "Political Identity Shapes Perceptions of Value-consistency and Believability of Political Facts," Paper presented at the annual convention of the International Society for Political Psychology, Edinburgh, Scotland, June 2017.

51 Joann Sterling, John Jost, Briony Swire, and Joshua A. Tucker, "Political Psycholinguistics: Epistemic Motivation and Language Differences as a Function of Ideology and Extremity," Paper presented at the annual convention of the International Society for Political Psychology, Edinburgh, Scotland, June 2017.

52 Andrew Gelman and Julia Azari, "Nineteen Things We Learned from the 2016 Election," *Statistics and Public Policy*, 4:1 (2017). Accessed at https://amstat.tandfon line.com/doi/abs/10.1080/2330443X.2017.1356775#.W4QkH7hOlPY. Other research indicates that those attracted to social media posts (and posting) have become especially angry in recent years. See Dan Hiaeshutter-Rice and Brian E. Weeks, "Emotionality and Engagement with News Content in Social Media," Paper presented at the annual convention of the International Communication Association, Prague, Czech Republic, May 2018.

53 As quoted in Peter Hessler, "How Trump Is Transforming Rural America," *New Yorker*, July 27, 2017. Accessed at www.newyorker.com/magazine/2017/07/24/how-trump-is-transforming-rural-america.

54 As quoted ibid., 26.

55 Ibid., 11.

56 John R. Hibbing, "How People's Sensitivity to Threats Illuminates the Rise of Donald Trump," *Washington Post*, December 23, 2016. Accessed at www .washingtonpost.com/news/monkey-cage/wp/2016/12/23/how-peoples-sensitivity-to-threats-illuminates-the-rise-of-donald-trump/?utm_term=.8b1172b96971.

57 Michael Kruse, "Johnstown Never Believed Trump Would Help: They Still Love Him Anyway," *Politico*, November 8, 2017. Accessed at www.politico.com/maga zine/story/2017/11/08/donald-trump-johnstown-pennsylvania-supporters-215800.

58 Ibid.

59 The foregoing quotes are ibid.

60 Ibid.

61 Judy Reams, "Apology Letter to My Grandchildren," *Wichita Falls Times-Record-News*, October 26, 2016. Accessed at www.timesrecordnews.com/story/opinion/readers/2016/10/26/letter-to-the-editor-apology-letter-to-my-grandchildren/92761284/.

62 Statistical patterns for Anger terms in news coverage: 1948–1960 stories = 0.2123; 1964–1976 stories = 0.2138; 1980–1992 stories = 0.2782; 1996–2012 stories = 0.3080; 2016 stories = 0.3905; $F[4, 22189] = 21.167$, $p < 0.000$.

63 As quoted in Willa Frej, "Trump Accuses Google of Rigging Search Results to Feature 'Bad' News about Him," *Huffington Post*, August 29, 2018. Accessed at www.huffingtonpost.com/entry/trump-google-search-bad-news_us_5b851627e4boc f7boo2ec5b1.

64 As quoted in Julie Pace, "Female Voters Condemn 'Negative Bully' Trump: Women React to GOP Candidate's Comments on Women," *Times of Israel*, September 28, 2016. Accessed at www.timesofisrael.com/female-voters-condemn-negative-bully-trump/.

65 Julie Pace, "Clinton Scrambles to Head Off Fallout from Brutal Weekend," *Samoa Observer*, September 13, 2016. Accessed at www.samoaobserver.ws/en/13_09_2016/us/11252/Clinton-scrambles-to-head-off-fallout-from-brutal-weekend.htm.

66 Philip Rucker and Sean Sullivan, "Trump: Women's Claims Are Part of 'Global' Conspiracy," *Washington Post*, October 13, 2016. Accessed at www.washingtonpost.com/politics/trump-says-groping-allegations-are-part-of-a-global-conspiracy-to-help-clinton/2016/10/13/e377d7e4-915a-11e6-a6a3-d50061aa9fae_story.html?utm_term=.67c908e06d67.

67 Jennifer Rubin, "Why We Should Worry About What 2016 Is Showing Us So Far," *Washington Post*, January 21, 2016. Accessed at www.washingtonpost.com/blogs/right-turn/wp/2016/01/21/why-we-should-worry-about-what-2016-is-showing-us-so-far/?utm_term=.7349160ab4fa.

68 As quoted in Peter Wehner, "The Man the Founders Feared," *New York Times*, March 20, 2016. Accessed at www.nytimes.com/2016/03/20/opinion/campaign-stops/the-man-the-founders-feared.html.

69 Karin Wahl-Jorgensen, "Public Display of Disaffection: the Emotional Politics of Donald Trump," in Pablo J. Boczowski and Zizi Papacharissi (eds.), *Trump and the Media* (Cambridge, MA: MIT Press, 2018), p. 79.

70 The foregoing commentary was extracted from www.lexisnexis.com. See Jim Chattin, *Bismarck Tribune*, August 31, 2015; David Weigel, *Washington Post*, October 9, 2016; Rick Drennan, *Mississauga News*, March 1, 2016; Judi Ketteler, *Los Angeles Times*, May 2, 2017; Julia Lichtblau, *New York Times*, April 25, 2018; Una Mullally, *Irish Times*, March 18, 2017.

71 While this chapter has focused exclusively on the language of emotion, Donald Trump also presents a dramatic *visual object* for study, with his histrionic gestures, his dramatic grimaces, and his stalking about the public stage. For more on this line of work, see Kira Hall, Donna M. Goldstein, and Matthew B. Ingram, "The Hands of Donald Trump: Entertainment, Gesture, Spectacle," *Journal of Ethnographic Theory*, 6:2 (2016), 71–100; and Patrick A. Stewart, Austin D. Eubanks, Reagan G. Dye, Scott Eidelman, and Robert H. Wicks, "Visual Presentation Style 2: Influences on Perceptions of Donald Trump and Hillary Clinton Based on Visual Presentation Style During the Third 2016 Presidential Debate," *American Behavioral Scientist*, 61:5 (2017), 545–57.

72 As quoted in Jim Yardley, "After More Than a Decade away, a Foreign Correspondent Comes Back to Take Stock of His Divided Homeland," *New York Times*, November 4, 2016. Accessed at www.nytimes.com/2016/11/06/magazine/an-american-in-a-strange-land.html?.

73 As quoted ibid.

74 As quoted in Elizabeth Kiefer, "'Til Trump Do Us Part: the Relationship Deal Breaker We Never Saw Coming," *Yahoo News*, August 1, 2017. Accessed at www.yahoo.com/news/apos-til-trump-us-part-143000899.html.

75 As quoted ibid.

76 As quoted in Chris Quintana, "Fresno State President Vows to Cooperate in Investigation of Lecturer Who Tweeted, 'Trump Must Hang,'" *Chronicle of Higher Education*, April 11, 2017. Accessed at www.chronicle.com/blogs/ticker/fresno-state-president-vows-to-cooperate-in-investigation-of-lecturer-who-tweeted-trump-must-hang/117717.

77 As quoted in Alexander Burns, "Shooting Is Latest Eruption in a Grim Ritual of Rage and Blame," *New York Times*, June 14, 2017. Accessed at www.nytimes.com/2017/06/14/us/baseball-shooting-is-latest-eruption-in-a-grim-ritual-of-rage-and-blame.html.

78 As quoted in Cheyenne Roundtree, "'I Wouldn't Rent to You If You Were the Last Person on Earth," *Daily Mail*, April 10, 2017. Accessed at www.dailymail.co.uk/news/article-4392494/Woman-denied-Airbnb-snowstorm-Asian.html.

79 As quoted in Jessica Chia, "'Trump Might Deport You': Woman Launches Racist Tirade at Iranian-Born U.S. Citizen on the Train," *Daily Mail*, April 10, 2017. Accessed at www.dailymail.co.uk/news/article-3930596/Trump-deport-Woman-launches-racist-abuse-Iranian-born-citizen-train-calling-Middle-Eastern-terrorist-evil-little-pig-shocking-viral-video.html.

80 Holly Yan, Kristina Sgueglia, and Kylie Walker, "'Make America White Again: Hate Speech and Crimes Post-Election," *CNN*, December 22, 2016. Accessed at https://kutv.com/news/nation-world/make-america-white-again-hate-speech-and-crimes-post-election.

81 As quoted in Burns, "Shooting Is Latest Eruption in a Grim Ritual of Rage and Blame," *New York Times*.

82 Clinton, *What Happened*, p. 430.

83 As quoted in Evan Goldstein, "What Follows the End of History? Identity Politics," *Chronicle of Higher Education*, August 27, 2018. Accessed at www.chronicle.com/article/What-Follows-the-End-of/244369.

5 TRUMP'S STORIES

How did Donald John Trump become president of the United States? That question has bedeviled reporters since November of 2016. The obvious answer – that Trump received the most Electoral College votes – is inadequate for many. "Why Are Conservatives More Susceptible to Believing Lies?" queried *Slate*, drawing on social science research suggesting that while "finding facts and pursuing evidence and trusting science is part of liberal ideology," conservatives place their faith in faith (and intuition) and thus are more likely to have difficulty "judging accurately what is true and what is false." With conservatives coming "disproportionately from rural areas and small towns," *Slate* reports, their "social networks remain smaller" and hence they are prone to accepting "misinformation and outright lies."[1] "Nearly 80 percent of white evangelicals plan to vote for Mr. Trump," observed opinion writer Daniel K. Williams in August of 2016. "Are they dupes or hypocrites?"[2] In providing evangelicals with at least two options, Mr. Williams was more generous than many of the nation's scribes.

While some commentators stressed Trumpers' cognitive impairments, others were medical, identifying syndromes like Social Dominance Orientation or Relative Deprivation to explain Trump's popularity.[3] Others were more sociological, noting how attractive Trump was to those who have "relied on public aid for multiple generations" and who live in counties "with the highest mortality rates from alcohol, drugs, and suicide."[4] Academics joined in, arguing that "low-information voters seem to exhibit significantly stronger support for Trump over Clinton," kindly suggesting that Trump supporters "were not deplorable as much as the strategies used to exploit their vulnerabilities."[5] Because "Trump embodies revolutionary hedonism," said another set of scholars, some people are attracted to "his influential branding of architecture, wine, golf courses, and endless luxury items with his name" and, for that reason, they voted Republican.[6]

Some commentators quoted research showing that "the typical Trump voter is not a raging, screaming, white nationalist" but then added that a subset of them is "extraordinarily vocal in their intolerance and white nationalism."[7] This sort of "yes-but" reporting especially offends Trump's defenders, implying that they and their kind can never be wholly free from sin. If you query enough Trump supporters, said another commentator, you will find that "civility is still alive and well, if you know where to look for it."[8] Ah, rectitude.

To balance things, the *New York Times* asked Trump supporters in January of 2018 to explain their support of a President whose "policy and personal conduct" were so desperately lacking. Said Philip Maymin of Greenwich, Connecticut: "Virtually all of my friends or colleagues actively hate Mr. Trump. I'm a minority in every circle I move in. I have a Ph.D. from the University of Chicago and a bachelor's and master's from Harvard. I'm a former hedge fund trader and now an academic. I'm a journalist and author. Imagine being a Trump supporter in even one of these circles! We learn to stay quiet." Said Sonia Schwartz of Valley Stream, New York: "Much of the media, as the hotbed of hatred against Mr. Trump, has pushed me more toward him than his social behavior has done the opposite." Said Alexander Goldstein of Brooklyn: "Before I respond to your questions, I have a question of my own: Did you run similar surveys for Obama voters? Or, for that matter, Eisenhower voters? Trump voters are not circus freaks to be displayed or singled out."[9]

Donald Trump understood these emotions. The tale he told – that the United States had become a disorderly and slovenly place – transcended class and region. His stories of disintegration appealed to older Americans and to strong Republican prizing "brand loyalty," says political psychologist Emily Carty.[10] But it also appealed to economic conservatives like Bill Davis, "a funny, genial sales rep in the packaging industry" who felt that "illegal immigration is killing Southern California" because of people like his neighbor who had "two hundred chickens running around his yard, goats everywhere." "Do you want to live like India?" asked Kathryn Kobor of Phoenix.

"I'm speaking for my descendants. I have a granddaughter. I have a son. I want them to live a decent, clean life. Trump just wants the laws enforced. He's not a mean-spirited person." When seventeen-year-old protester, Esperanza Matamoros, bumped into a supporter at a Trump rally, the supporter yelled, "*Excuse me*. Around here, we say *excuse me*."[11] For many Trump believers, "tumult and confusion actually strengthen his agenda," says Harvard's Michael Sandel, because order is foremost in their minds.[12]

The stories Donald Trump told in 2016 (and later in his presidency) were largely projects of reclamation, returning the nation to its lost sense of self. People who felt trapped in a world that no longer afforded the old gratuities – of space and time, of individuality and independence, of entrepreneurship without taxation – were especially drawn to them. Trump's critics claimed that his stories pointed to a bigoted and misogynistic United States, to an era when things were "orderly" because only some rights were respected and only some lifestyles sanctioned. Dig beneath Trump's stories, they argue, and you will find intolerance, racism, and gendered essentialism. While not denying these claims, I suggest that you will also find narratives designed to heal the wounds – both real and imagined – of Trump's supporters. Although it is easy to dismiss all narratives as mere fiction, Donald Trump knew better and he became president because of what he knew.

The Why of Narrative

As researchers began poring over the results of the 2016 election, they found both questions and answers: How could evangelicals support a wayward person like Donald Trump? Because they treated politics as politics and not morality, said columnist Gary Abernathy.[13] Did the poor and uneducated put Trump over the threshold? No, since many of his supporters did have a college degree and were relatively affluent.[14] Was race or class the more powerful determinant? It was class, some argued.[15] Were Trump supporters monolithic, policy-wise? They were not, ranging from staunch conservatives and free marketeers to American preservationists, anti-elites, and the disengaged.[16] Was white identity or patriotism more predictive? Patriotism.[17] In what ways were Trump voters and Bernie Sanders' supporters similar? They were equally distrustful of government.[18] How could educated women vote for Donald Trump? Because they disliked Hillary Clinton even more.[19] Was Donald Trump's coalition in 2016 dramatically different from Mitt Romney's four years earlier? No.[20] Was terrorism as active a fear in 2016 as it was in 2004 or 2008? Yes.[21]

While all of these factors were part of the picture in 2016, storytelling was one of Trump's go-to weapons. His stories were not Reaganesque, filled with warmth and filigree. They were harsh, soulful, a punch in the face, not a gentle hand on the nation's shoulder. Trump was the protagonist in his stories, almost always their hero. Beat reporters found his stories tedious, false as well. But cheering throngs welcomed them, tall tales included.

Stories are primitive vehicles; they define human community. Stories range from fairy tales to Steven King novels, from Balzac to *Game of Thrones*. In the world of politics, stories often hold sway – Winston Churchill vowing to never surrender, John Kennedy's lunar imagination, Martin Luther King Jr. dreaming his dreams. Political stories take us from a known to an unknown place. They make demands on us but also give us succor. They help us see today what can only be known tomorrow.

And then there is Donald Trump. Balzac would cringe. But Trump and Balzac and the DICTION program know that no matter how grand or plebeian they are, stories have five key elements: They involve people (Human Interest terms) doing something (Motion terms) in some location (Spatial terms) for some duration (Temporal terms) and doing so memorably (Embellishment terms). Prior studies have shown that DICTION's operationalization of Narrative Force cleanly separates novels and short stories from corporate reports, biographies from scientific documents, theatrical productions from scholarly prose. More subtly, Narrative Force also distinguishes broadcast news from print news, showing that the former concentrates on the *action* of an event (higher on Narrative Force) while the latter spends more time *interpreting* it (lower on Narrative Force).[22]

DICTION's ability to calculate Narrative Force – automatically, mechanically – is perhaps an insult to great literature but it is good enough for Donald Trump. As we see in Table 5.1, Trump is a disciplined storyteller. His high Insistence scores (a measure of thematic repetition) show that he continually reinforces the same stories – that the nation is in decline, that the gerontocracy must be disemboweled, that unfettered capitalism will pave the nation's roads with gold. When combined with

Table 5.1 Trump's Storytelling Elements vs. Other Presidential Candidates, 1948–2016

Type	Token	Trump Rank (out of 26)	Highest	Lowest
Storytelling elements	Narrative Style	5	Dukakis	Truman
	Exaggeration terms	1	Trump	Stevenson
	Insistence scores	9	Kerry	HClinton

Source: Data from Campaign Mapping Project.

an unprecedented use of Exaggeration (words like *colossal, extraordinary, fabulous, huge,* etc.), Trump's statements become overstatements and his little stories become grand narratives.

As E. J. Dionne and his colleagues report, many were moved by Trump's stories "out of a yearning for forms of community and solidarity that they sense have been lost." This was especially true of what Andrew Greeley called neighborhood people, "people who do not aspire to being 'citizens of the world' and who love the particular patch where they were raised."[23] Feelings like these gave rise to a kind of "rhetorical realignment," says Penn State's Mary Stuckey, thereby creating an opening for a "purifying" and "nostalgic" vision that was "as at once resentful (mourning that which was taken away) and optimistic (hopeful that it can be restored)."[24]

But Donald Trump's stories were hardly pretty. Most of them were spur-of-the-moment reflections bereft of purpose and direction. It was *the telling* of the stories that entertained his audiences, so he told them again and again. On one occasion, for example, he sounded like a teenage boy, teasing his audience with events of dubious provenance:

> You know, I read a story, it's a terrible story, but I'll tell you. Early in the century, last century, General Pershing – did you ever hear of such a rough guy? – and they had a terrorism problem. And there's a whole thing with swine and animals and pigs and, you know the story. OK. They didn't like that and they were having a tremendous problem with terrorism and, by the way, this is something you can read in the history

books – not a lot of history books, because they don't like teaching this – and General Pershing was a rough guy and he sits on his horse and – very astute, like a ramrod, straight in the air – and this was the early nineteen hundreds and this was a terrible problem . . .

And he caught some terrorists who did tremendous damage and killed many people. And he took the terrorists and he took his men and they dipped bullets in pig's blood – you heard that right – he took bullets and he dipped them in pig's blood and he had his men load their rifles and he lined up the people and they shot those people and then [he took] one person and he said "you go back to your people and you tell them what happened" and for years there wasn't a problem.[25]

Storytelling like this is a kind of interpersonal flattery. Trump knows he shouldn't tell the Pershing story but he does so anyway because he cares so much about his audience. Stories like this give people a sense of purchase in a confusing world. Even when a story has an unclear ending (did the "Pershing medicine" really eliminate Islamic terrorism?), it implies that an endpoint will eventually be reached. In the meantime, one can rest content, bathed in narrative's potential.

"A friend of mine," Trump once said, "buys excavating equipment," but because China has so devalued its currency, "for the first time in his life he's buying excavating equipment from Komatsu." "I said 'what's the difference?'" and Trump's friend replies, "Caterpillars are better but this is good enough." Given the price differentials, the friend continues, "I owe it to my family. I owe it to my wife. I owe it to the employees of my company." "I understand what he's saying," Trump concludes, "Caterpillar is happening to all of us."[26] Stories like this tell Trump's audiences, "I know where you live, I understand the choices you're forced to make, I am with you." Even though Caterpillar is happening to all of us, Trump implies, "*they* can't keep us down."

Trump thinks-by-narrative. For him, the gap between personal experience and public policy is no gap at all: "I said to my friend, jokingly, jokingly, when you started excavating for your building in the middle of the South China Sea, did you get an environmental impact statement? And he said, actually, his daughters came up with the idea on Friday at four o'clock and they started excavating on Saturday morning."[27] The conclusion is obvious: Any law obtruding on the lived life must be dispatched.

Trump's ability to tell stories in a brisk, punchy style lent energy to his campaign and gave him something to do as he wandered around looking for a point. Most of his stories lead to the same tantalizing conclusion – that Donald Trump is special:

> So we started on June sixteenth and I came down the escalator and I said to my wife "Melania, come on, let's go, let's do it. And it takes guts running for president. I never did this stuff before. It takes guts. I didn't know this was going to happen. I thought we were going to do well. I thought it was going to be like a horse race; I'd be in the middle of the pack and maybe by the very end inch it out.
>
> I didn't know we were going to be in this position. I didn't know we were going to be in this place and the people of New Hampshire were unbelievable. I have to tell you. Last week, we won every single category. We won rich, poor, fat, thin, tall, short. We won women; we won men; we won highly educated. We won smart, smart, smart people ... We won every single category and it was such an honor. They were incredible people.[28]

Trump's stories often seize on an aside buried within an earlier aside, making his narratives ragtag things. But his stories also exhibit the kind of self-risk friends exhibit when gossiping over a glass of wine. Based as they are on his personal experiences, Trump's stories defy traditional forms of fact-checking. Instead, they say this: You live in the world, I live in the world, and we share experiences: "I just found out from a friend of mine, a doctor, who called me and said 'we don't get our drugs and we're the biggest country in the world ... and we pay almost the same as you pay if you walk into a drugstore.'"[29]

Trump's stories show where he has been and what he has learned. This is stock political stuff – the politician comes, the politician smiles, the politician goes. But when a billionaire-cum-TV-star, someone who has been in your living room, shares his travels with you, a special intimacy develops:

> In the course of this campaign, I have travelled all across this country and I've met the most amazing people. Every day, I've

seen the goodness and character of our country, and brave citizens proudly fighting through hard times and difficult circumstances. In many parts of our country, the hard times never seem to end. I've visited cities and towns in upstate New York where half the jobs have left and moved to other countries. Politicians have abandoned these places all over our country and the people who live there.

Worse still, politicians have heaped scorn and disdain on these wonderful Americans. My opponent described tens of millions of American citizens as deplorable and irredeemable – how can Hillary Clinton seek to lead this country when she considers its citizens beyond redemption? The hardworking people she calls deplorable are the most admirable people I know: they are cops and soldiers, teachers and firefighters, young and old, moms and dads, blacks, whites and Latinos – but above everything else, they are all American. They love their families, they love their country, and they want a better future. These are the forgotten men and women of America.[30]

Trump's stories are pedestrian but that, of course, is the point. Sophisticates may not like his stories – self-promoting stories, aimless stories – but sophisticates, like everyone else, only get one vote. Donald Trump is smart but hardly brilliant. Fortunately for him, stories require only a plot, some characters, and something that feels like a conclusion. Mr. Trump came to the 2016 campaign with a ready supply of all three. He used them artfully.

The How of Narrative

For Donald Trump, an understated story is no story at all. He used more *Exaggeration* than anyone running for the presidency between 1948 and 2012; he also used more than any Republican or Democrat running in 2016. His style was neoplastic – heavily dependent on adjectival constructions. He regarded nouns as the weakest part of speech because they showed neither imagination nor commitment. Adjectives, in contrast, make ordinary things (golf courses, pieces of legislation) impressive and impressive things (*great* golf courses, *the best* legislation) extraordinary. Trump treats adjectives as a New Yorker's inheritance: He always uses "the best words," his "IQ is one of the highest," he knows more about ISIS than anyone in the entire "history of the world."

Trump's exaggerations give structure to a world of possibilities ("we've passed more bills than anyone ..."). While most politicians are somewhat careful about overpromising (perhaps because they were trained as lawyers), Trump has no such reticence. Remarkably, his admirers have learned to listen for the prayers-within-Trump and not to his literal promises. Says laborer Todd Hiester: "I think his intentions are good. His heart is very good." Says his co-worker Bill MacCaulley: "Whether you like Trump or not, the fact remains: everybody's doing better than they were a year ago." Says steelworker John Gathercole: "I don't know how Trump is on unions. I like him because he was change."[31]

"The Wall had to be imagined," says sociologist Julia Sonnevend. "Whether it could actually be built was secondary."[32] All politicians try to stretch people's imaginations in these ways, but voters do not always comply. Al Cross, director of the Institute for Rural Journalism and Community Issues at the University of Kentucky, notes that rural Americans have learned to listen carefully to politicians because they have suffered so much "moral injury"; 62 percent of them supported Donald Trump in 2016 by taking his stories to heart. "Our ears are tuned to intonation," Cross declares, "we think people are talking down to us. What ends up happening is that we don't focus on policy – we focus on the tones, the references, the culture."[33] For those living in hardscrabble America, Trump's stories had what rhetoric scholar Walter Fisher has called "narrative fidelity."[34]

But all narratives are, in a sense, lies since they superimpose one reality atop another. Because each of us is trapped in our own experiences, we inevitably leave out "extraneous" details when telling a story, concentrating on "this" aspect of our reality and not "that." Although it is said that people are entitled to their own meanings but not to their own facts, that is untrue. We all have facts at our command at all times – "I may look grayer but I'm also thinner, so I'm getting better." We also make decisions based not on facts alone but on facts-plus-values – "I bought the dress because it was cheaper; you bought it because it was blue." Although some worry that the dissimulations of modern media have thrown us into a world of "post-fact," that, too, is untrue. We have always lived with facts; we have always lived with narratives.

Vox published a story a few years ago entitled "Trump Supporters Know Trump Lies. They Just Don't Care." The author reports a series of behavioral science experiments showing that people hew to their own understandings of events rather than change their ideological presuppositions. Contrary facts can momentarily unsettle them but, generally speaking, they go back to the most comfortable place.[35] Trump supporters are no different and so they frequently feel insulted by Hollywood liberals and legacy journalists. "Their views about abortion, gay marriage, gender roles, race, guns, and the Confederate flag," says sociologist Arlie Hochschild, "were held up to ridicule in the national media as backward," leaving Donald Trump with an opening, an opening he filled with narrative.[36]

Linguist Jennifer Sclafani argues that, technically speaking, Trump is not an especially good storyteller. He starts his stories *in medias res*, rarely provides enough details to make events clear, and his characterizations of people are often too sketchy to be memorable. More positively, by using "constructed dialogue," Trump immerses himself in his audience's culture, making his ideas accessible.[37]

While all of this may be true, the most important thing about Trump's narratives was Trump himself. "I am your voice. The world may be crashing in on you but I am here." Such themes, says cultural anthropologist Albion Butters, launched a thousand memes – Trump as the Incredible Hulk, Trump as the new Superman, Trump as Captain America.[38] While meant to disparage Trump, such memes reinforced the story he wanted told – that he was no ordinary politician. Trump was the "alpha male," says the University of Helsinki's Pekka Kolehmainen, giving him a "transgressiveness" that many welcomed.[39]

Donald Trump was not the only one telling stories during the 2016 race but he was the most persistent. As we see in Figure 5.1, Trump larded his stories with more exaggeration than Hillary Clinton, and he stuck to his themes more faithfully.[40] Indeed, Hillary Clinton had the lowest Insistence scores of any major-party candidate running for the presidency since 1948, indicating that she flitted from topic to topic. Her gold-plated resumé may have been her undoing. She became the fox who knew too many things while Trump, the hedgehog, knew only the stories he told.

Clinton saw all of this in retrospect. "I am an unapologetic policy wonk. It's true that I sweat the details, whether it's the precise level of lead in the drinking water in Flint, the number of mental health facilities in Iowa, the cost of prescription drugs, or how exactly the nuclear triad works." "Those aren't just details if it's your kid or your

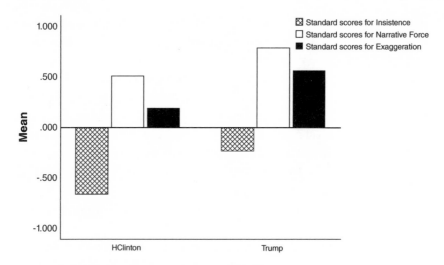

Figure 5.1 Storytelling Elements for Donald Trump vs. Hillary Clinton
Source: Data from Campaign Mapping Project.

aging parent whose life depends on it," she continued; "those details ought to be important to anyone seeking to lead the country." Admirable though her experiences were, says one scholar, they turned Clinton into a rhetorical incrementalist.[41]

"Clinton's story was difficult to pin down," says Michigan State University's Kenneth Levine. Trump, in contrast, did what all successful leaders do – he was innovative, touching on "themes that have been important to the group in the past, but temporarily lost or overshadowed by other stories."[42] On the face of it, "Make America Great Again" does not sound inherently superior to "Stronger together" but the former had Ronald Reagan's stamp on it while Clinton's slogan was vaguer and less lyrical, placing more demands on the voter. But Clinton did have a story and it meant a great deal to her. "I wish so badly," she says, that "we were a country where a candidate who said 'My story is the story of a life shaped by and devoted to the movement for women's liberation'" could win an election, but "I've never felt like the American electorate was receptive to this one."[43]

The story Clinton settled on in 2016 was this: "I am not Donald Trump." But there is no vision here, just the avoidance of disaster. Clinton's story "wound up being muddled, attack-oriented, and vague," say Stephanie Martin and Andrea Terry, helping to ensure that Trump would remain center stage throughout the campaign.[44]

Clinton's communication director, Jennifer Palmieri, said that her proudest moment of the campaign occurred when Clinton delivered her alt-right speech against Trump but, as the *Washington Times*' Kelly Riddell observes, that was exactly Mrs. Clinton's problem. "She needed something more than – 'It's my turn, I'm a woman, I deserve the crown, and he's terrible.'"[45]

Well before the 2016 campaign, Katie Gibson and Amy Heyse laid out the components of the "feminine style" in rhetoric, a style "characterized by its personal tone, references to personal experiences, inductive reasoning, the use of anecdotes and examples as evidence, audience participation, and identification between the speaker and audience."[46] Improbably, Gibson and Heyse seem to be talking here about Donald Trump and not Hillary Clinton. Interestingly, researchers have found that people are quicker to judge warmth when looking at the picture of an unknown person than they are to find competence or efficacy.[47] Voters had twelve months in 2016 to discover the warmth in Clinton but, for whatever reason, they could not find it.[48]

In a thoughtful autopsy of the 2016 campaign, *Salon* surveyed more than a dozen possible explanations for Clinton's defeat, ranging from racism and white supremacy to blatant misogyny and media bias, changing demography, disestablishmentarianism, and, of course, James Comey. But *Salon*'s most compelling explanation was that many Americans felt trapped, bereft of "culture, jobs, community, religion, economics, identity and hope for the future." That sense of displacement, says *Salon*'s reporters, "can be seen as an overarching umbrella that encompasses the polarization, anger, and pessimism prevalent in many parts of the country."[49]

Displacement was Donald Trump's key narrative. He used it to convey "a visceral disdain for the way business is done in Washington that Clinton simply did not," says the *Washington Post*'s Greg Sargent.[50] But he did more than that – he told a story of reactive possibility. His story was hyperbolic in the extreme, based on a vague vision and obscure policy objectives. What he did have, however, was an emotional objective – getting people to feel free again. Although he was rarely eloquent when telling his story, occasionally he was. For people who felt bypassed, Trump offered a roadmap:

> We are going to put our miners and our steelworkers back to work. We will rebuild our roads, bridges, tunnels, highways,

airports, schools and hospitals. American cars will travel the roads, American planes will soar in the skies, and American ships will patrol the seas. American steel will send new skyscrapers into the clouds. American hands will rebuild this nation – and American energy, harvested from American sources, will power this nation. American workers will be hired to do the job.

We will put new American metal into the spine of this country. Jobs will return, incomes will rise, and new factories will come rushing back to our shores. We will make America wealthy again. We will make America strong again. And we will make America great again.[51]

Conclusion

Most of those who supported Donald Trump in 2016 led perfectly normal lives. They were not the angriest people on the planet, nor the most ideologically excessive, nor did they inject a liter of Fox News into their veins each day. They had normal jobs and were raising normal kids but nonetheless felt trapped. Living through eight years of the Obama administration had taxed them. They liked the hope-and-change he preached in 2008 but not the economic collapse they were experiencing. Eventually things improved financially, but the new healthcare plan, in their opinion, infringed on their rights as did Obama's catering to special-interest groups, groups to which they were not aligned. More regulations, more immigrants, more political correctness. By 2016 they were ready for something else.[52]

Donald Trump lifted up his supporters although he had none of Barack Obama's rhetorical brilliance. He had no sense for the electricity of language or for its ability to touch the soul. What Trump did have was a clear, crude way of telling stories about his life and about how things could be made better for others. His stories were usually self-serving, often obscuring the point he was trying to make. Nonetheless, many liked how he told his stories, and the more they liked them, the more Trump told them.

Amanda Carpenter has written a book entitled *Gaslighting America: Why We Love It When Trump Lies to Us*. Trump's brazen lies, says Carpenter, cause people to question reality and Trump uses a consistent formula to do so – advance a controversial claim, deny responsibility for having done so, create suspense, discredit your opponent, declare victory.[53] Echoing Carpenter, Daniel Effron of the London Business School calculates that during Trump's first 400 days in office he made more than 2,400 false or misleading statements but still retained 82 percent support from Republicans. "A little imagination," says Effron, "can apparently make a lie feel 'truthy' enough to give the liar a bit of a pass."[54] Although Trump "is neither terribly articulate nor a seasoned politician," said the editorial board of the *Los Angeles Times*, "he has a remarkable instinct for discerning which conspiracy theories in which quasi-news source, or which of his own inner musings, will turn into ratings gold. He targets the darkness, anger and insecurity that hide in each of us and harnesses them for his own purposes. If one of his lies doesn't work – well, then he lies about that."[55]

I find all of these claims to be overstated. They underestimate Trump as well as the people who support him. True, Trump often lies, which is to say, he puts miscellaneous facts into his blender and then pours out something outlandish but tasty. But all narratives are outlandish, in part because they superimpose structure on a world of blooming, buzzing confusion. Politicians exploit that confusion but so do all of us, telling ourselves stories simply to get through the day: "That new medication worked for Joan so surely it will work for me." Journalists do the work of the Lord when spotting the outrageous stories politicians tell, but journalists themselves traffic in stories, sometimes overworking the supply of available facts, thereby rendering their stories speculative as a result: Does Putin have something on Trump? Is Ivanka a secret Democrat? Will Roe vs. Wade be overturned?

Trump's supporters do not believe every jot and tittle of the stories he tells. They know he stretches the truth but, in their minds, he does so for fine purposes. True, as Mark Thompson says, "Exaggeration is a drug. It delivers an instant high but can have deleterious long-term effects."[56] But Krista Tippett also offers wisdom: "I can disagree with your opinion ... but I can't disagree with your experience."[57] In 2016, Donald Trump understood people's experiences and he barnstormed the country tying into them. The elite media hated his doing so, as did his political opponents. As a result, they too entered the public square, thereby constituting what is known as a political campaign. Then November 8, 2016, happened. Somewhat later, the new President said this: "The overall audience was, I think, the biggest ever to watch an inauguration address, which was a great thing."[58] Mr. Trump's supporters wondered: Was it really the biggest audience ever? Then they pondered Trump's second claim: Was it a great thing? They concluded that it was.

Notes

1 John Ehrenreich, "Why are Conservatives More Susceptible to Believing Lies?" *Slate*, November 9, 2017. Accessed at www.slate.com/articles/health_and_science/science/2017/11/why_conservatives_are_more_susceptible_to_believing_in_lies.html.

2 Daniel K. Williams, "Why Values Voters Value Donald Trump," *New York Times*, August 20, 2016. Accessed at www.nytimes.com/2016/08/21/opinion/sunday/why-values-voters-value-donald-trump.html.

3 Bobby Azarian, "A Psychological Analysis of Trump Supporters Has Uncovered Five Key Traits about Them," *Psychology Today*, December 31, 2017. Accessed at www.psychologytoday.com/us/blog/mind-in-the-machine/201712/analysis-trump-supporters-has-identified-5-key-traits.

4 Sarah Brown, "In a Region with Few College Degrees, People Pin Their Hopes on Trump," *Chronicle of Higher Education*, January 12, 2018. Accessed at www.chronicle.com/article/In-a-Region-With-Few-College/242226.

5 Richard C. Fording and Sanford F. Schram, "The Cognitive and Emotional Sources of Trump Support: the Case of Low-information Voters," *New Political Science*, 19:4 (2017), 670–86.

6 Donna M. Goldstein and Kira Hall, "Postelection Surrealism and Nostalgic Racism in the Hands of Donald Trump," *HAU: Journal of Ethnographic Theory*, 7:1 (2017), 402.

7 Thomas B. Edsall, "The Trump Voter Paradox," *New York Times*, September 28, 2017. Accessed at www.nytimes.com/2017/09/28/opinion/trump-republicans-authoritarian.html.

8 George Saunders, "Who Are All These Trump Supporters? At the Candidate's Rallies, a New Understanding of America Emerges," *New Yorker: American Chronicles*, July 11–18, 2016. Accessed at www.newyorker.com/magazine/2016/07/11/george-saunders-goes-to-trump-rallies.

9 The foregoing comments can be found in "Vision, Chutzpah and Some Testosterone," *New York Times*, January 17, 2018. Accessed at www.nytimes.com/2018/01/17/opinion/trump-voters-supporters.html.

10 See Emily Carty, "Do It for the Brand: Political Leaders, Brand Attachment, and Political Participation," Paper presented at the annual convention of the International Society of Political Psychology, Edinburgh, Scotland, July 2017.

11 The foregoing comments can be found in Saunders, "Who Are All These Trump Supporters?" *New Yorker: American Chronicles*.

12 As quoted in Brett Milano, "To Understand Trump, Learn from His Voters," *Harvard Gazette*, February 22, 2017. Accessed at https://news.harvard.edu/gazette/story/2017/02/to-understand-trump-learn-from-his-voters/.

13 Gary Abernathy, "Why Most Evangelicals Don't Condemn Trump," *Washington Post*, September 1, 2017. Accessed at www.washingtonpost.com/opinions/why-most-evangelicals-dont-condemn-trump/2017/09/01/64baab1c-8e79-11e7-91d5-ab4e4bb76a3a_story.html?utm_term=.8c931cca4bc8.

14 Nicholas Carnes and Noam Lupu, "It's Time to Bust the Myth: Most Trump Voters Were Not Working Class," *Washington Post*, June 5, 2017. Accessed at www .washingtonpost.com/news/monkey-cage/wp/2017/06/05/its-time-to-bust-the-myth-most-trump-voters-were-not-working-class/?utm_term=.d3bb5e84efca.

15 Ross Douthat, "Race and Class and What Happened in 2016," *New York Times*, November 29, 2017. Accessed at www.nytimes.com/2017/11/29/opinion/donald-trump-2016-election.html.

16 Emily Elkins, "The Five Types of Trump Voters: Who They Are and What They Believe," *Democracy Fund Voter Study Group*, June 2017. Accessed at www .voterstudygroup.org/publications/2016-elections/the-five-types-trump-voters.

17 Wayne P. Steger, "Populism and Parties in the 2016 Presidential Nominations," Paper presented at the annual meeting of the Midwest Political Science Association, Chicago, April 2018.

18 Joshua J. Dyck, Shanna Pearson-Merkowitz, and Michael Coates, "Primary Distrust: Political Distrust and Support for the Insurgent Candidacies of Donald Trump and Bernie Sanders in the 2017 Primary," *PS Now*, April 2018. Accessed at www .politicalsciencenow.com/primary-distrust/.

19 Keli Goff, "Roseanne Could be a Turning Point for Conservative Women: Women Had a Lot of Reasons to Vote for Trump, Starting with Hillary Clinton," *Daily Beast*, May 31, 2018. Accessed at www.thedailybeast.com/roseanne-could-be-a-turning-point-for-conservative-women.

20 Nate Cohn and Alicia Parlapiano, "How Broad, and How Happy, Is the Trump Coalition?" *New York Times*, August 9, 2018. Accessed at www.nytimes.com/interactive/2018/08/09/upshot/trump-voters-how-theyve-changed.html.

21 Mirya Holman, Jennifer Merolla, Elizabeth J. Zechmeister, and Ding Wang, "Terrorism, Gender, and the 2016 Presidential Election," Paper presented at the annual meeting of the American Political Science Association, San Francisco, CA, September 2017.

22 See Roderick P. Hart, Jay P. Childers, and Colene J. Lind, *Political Tone: How Leaders Talk and Why* (Chicago: University of Chicago Press, 2013).

23 E. J. Dionne, Jr., Norman J. Ornstein, and Thomas E. Mann, *One Nation After Trump: A Guide for the Perplexed, the Disillusioned, the Desperate, and the Not-Yet Deported* (New York: St. Martins Press, 2017), pp. 14, 216.

24 Mary E. Stuckey, "American Elections and the Rhetoric of Political Change: Hyperbole, Anger, and Hope in U.S. Politics," *Rhetoric and Public Affairs*, 20:4 (2017), 675.

25 Donald J. Trump, "Campaign Rally in Charleston, South Carolina," February 19, 2016. Original transcription. Accessed at https://moody.utexas.edu/centers/strauss/campaign-mapping-project.

26 Ibid.

27 Ibid.

28 Ibid.

29 Donald J. Trump, "Town Hall in Pawley's Island, South Carolina," February 19, 2016. Original transcription. Accessed at https://moody.utexas.edu/centers/strauss/campaign-mapping-project.

30 Donald J. Trump, "Campaign Remarks in New York City," *Time Magazine*, September 15, 2016. Accessed at http://time.com/4495507/donald-trump-economy-speech-transcript/.

31 As quoted in Molly Ball, "Donald Trump's Forgotten Man," *Time Magazine*, February 26, 2018, pp. 28–29. Accessed at https://time.com/5159859/why-trumps-forgotten-man-still-supports-him.

32 Julia Sonnevend, "Facts (Almost) Never Win Over Myths," in Jody C. Baumgartner and Terri L. Towner (eds.), *The Internet and the 2016 Presidential Campaign* (Lanham, MD: Lexington Books, 2017), p. 89.

33 Al Cross, "'Stop Overlooking Us': Missed Intersections of Trump, Media, and Rural America," in Robert E. Gutsche, Jr. (ed.), *The Trump Presidency, Journalism and Democracy* (New York: Routledge, 2018), p. 247.

34 Walter R. Fisher, *Human Communication as Narration: Toward a Philosophy of Reason, Value, and Action* (Columbia: University of South Carolina Press, 1989).

35 See Brian Resnick, "Trump Supporters Know Trump Lies. They Just Don't Care," *Vox*, July 10, 2017. Accessed at www.vox.com/2017/7/10/15928438/fact-checks-political-psychology.

36 Arlie R. Hochschild, *Strangers in Their Own Land: Anger and Mourning on the American Right* (New York: New Press, 2016), p. 221.

37 See Jennifer Sclafani, *Talking Donald Trump: A Sociolinguistic Study of Style, Metadiscourse, and the Politics of Identity* (London: Routledge, 2018).

38 Albion M. Butters, "Changing Faces of Change: Metanarratives in the 2016 U.S. Presidential Election, *European Journal of American Studies*, 12:2 (2017). Accessed at https://journals.openedition.org/ejas/12147.

39 Pekka Kolehmainen, "Social Media Narratives as Political Fan Fiction in the 2016 U.S. Presidential Election," *European Journal of American Studies*, 12:2 (2017). Accessed at https://journals.openedition.org/ejas/12147.

40 Statistical patterns for Narrative Force: Hillary Clinton = 0.5072; Donald Trump = 0.7937; $F [1, 2423] = 68.212$, $p < 0.000$; for Insistence: Hillary Clinton = -0.6651; Donald Trump = -0.2267; $F [1, 2423] = 401.773$, $p < 0.000$; for Exaggeration: Hillary Clinton = 0.1910; Donald Trump = 0.5574; $F [1, 2423] = 89.573$, $p < 0.000$.

41 Stuckey, "American Elections and the Rhetoric of Political Change," 684.

42 Kenneth J. Levine, "Understanding the Stories of Presidential Candidates: a Comparison Between the Stories of 2012 and 2016," *American Behavioral Scientist*, 61:9 (2017), 1026.

43 Hillary R. Clinton, *What Happened* (New York: Simon & Schuster, 2017), p. 114.

44 Stephanie A. Martin and Andrea J. Terry, "Social Media, Candidate Attacks, and Hillary Clinton's Failed Narrative in the 2016 Presidential Campaign," in Jim A. Kuypers (ed.), *The 2016 American Presidential Campaign and the News: Implications for American Democracy and the Republic* (Lanham, MD: Lexington Books, 2018), p. 135.

45 Kelly Riddell, "The Five Real Reasons Hillary Clinton Lost the White House," *Washington Times*, December 14, 2106. Accessed at www.washingtontimes.com/news/2016/dec/14/hillary-clinton-lost-white-house-because-these-fiv/.

46 Katie L. Gibson and Amy L. Heyse, "The Difference between a Hockey Mom and a Pit Bull': Sarah Palin's Faux Maternal Persona and Performance of Hegemonic Masculinity at the 2008 Republican National Convention," *Communication Quarterly*, 58:3 (2010), 238. For more on the feminine/masculine style vis-à-vis Hillary Clinton, see Jennifer J. Jones, "Talk 'Like a Man': the Linguistic Styles of Hillary Clinton, 1992–2013," *Perspectives on Politics*, 14:3 (2016), 625–42.

47 Susan T. Fiske, Amy J. C. Cuddy, and Peter Glick, "Universal Dimensions of Social Cognition: Warmth and Competence," *Trends in Cognitive Science*, 11:2 (2006), 77–83.

48 Interestingly, when analyzing two of Hillary Clinton's memoirs, David Kaufer and Shawn Parry-Giles found that Clinton was more than able to combine a "first-person literary style laced with personal experience, interactivity, and positive emotion, the language of choice for describing networks of family, friends, and intimates."

Why she could not add this rhetorical texture to the 2016 presidential campaign remains a mystery. See David S. Kaufer and Shawn J. Parry-Giles, "Hillary Clinton's Presidential Campaign Memoirs: a Study in Contrasting Identities," *Quarterly Journal of Speech*, 103:1–2 (2017), 7–32.

49 Don Hazen, Kalli Holloway, Jenny Pierson, Jan Frel, Les Leopold, Steven Rosenfeld, Michael Arria, Ilana Novick, and Janet Allon, "Why Donald Trump Won – and How Hillary Clinton Lost: Thirteen Theories Explaining the Stunning Election," *Salon*, December 26, 2016. Accessed at www.salon.com/2016/12/26/13-theories-on-why-trump-won-and-how-clinton-lost_partner/.

50 Greg Sargent, "'Feel the Bern': Hillary's Agonizing Loss and the Future of the Democratic Party," in Larry J. Sabato, Kyle Kondik, and Geoffrey Skelley (eds.), *Trumped: the 2016 Election that Broke All the Rules* (Lanham, MD: Rowman & Littlefield, 2017), pp. 120–21.

51 Trump, "Campaign Remarks in New York City," *Time Magazine*.

52 Dramatizing the popularity of such views, a Pew Research Center survey found that nearly half of white Republicans became upset when hearing a fellow American speak a foreign language in their presence. See Christopher Ingraham, "Nearly Half of White Republicans Say It Bothers Them to Hear People Speaking Foreign Languages," *Washington Post*, May 8, 2019. Accessed at www.washingtonpost.com/business/2019/05/08/nearly-half-white-republicans-say-it-bothers-them-hear-people-speaking-foreign-languages/?utm_term=.f52ebaeeca5e.

53 Amanda Carpenter, *Gaslighting America: Why We Love It When Trump Lies to Us* (New York: Harper Collins, 2018), pp. 14, 65.

54 Daniel A. Effron, "Why Trump Supporters Don't Mind His Lies," *New York Times*, April 28, 2018. Accessed at www.nytimes.com/2018/04/28/opinion/sunday/why-trump-supporters-dont-mind-his-lies.html. According to the *Washington Post*, by the beginning of June 2019, Trump had issued well over 10,000 lies since assuming office, with no end of them in sight. See Glenn Kessler, Salvador Rizo, and Meg Kelly, "President Trump has Made 10,796 False or Misleading Claims over 869 Days," *Washington Post*, June 10, 2019. Accessed at www.washingtonpost.com/politics/2019/06/10/president-trump-has-made-false-or-misleading-claims-over-days/?utm_term=.ba50e0278770.

55 Editorial Board, "Why Trump Lies," *Los Angeles Times*, April 3, 2017. Accessed at www.latimes.com/projects/la-ed-why-trump-lies/.

56 Mark Thompson, *Enough Said: What's Gone Wrong with the Language of Politics?* (New York: St. Martins, 2016), p. 277.

57 Krista Tippett, *Becoming Wise Deluxe: an Inquiry into the Mystery and Art of Living* (New York: Penguin Books, 2017), p. 22.

58 As quoted in Justin Fishel, "Analysis: Seven of Some of the Most Glaring Inaccuracies of Trump's First Year," ABC News Online, January 20, 2018. Accessed at https://abcnews.go.com/Politics/analysis-glaring-inaccuracies-trumps-year/story?id=52481595.

Part IV
FEELING BESIEGED

6 TRUMP'S MEDICINE

Some people think that Donald Trump is crazy. Many of them live in Washington, DC. When consulting the Lexis-Nexis database of news coverage, for example, one finds 329 uses of the collocate <*Trump* + *25th Amendment*> during the first three months of the Trump presidency. Between July 1st and September 30th, 2018, however, that same pairing jumped to 3,833 hits. "Members of Congress 'Holding Secret Conversations about Removing Donald Trump from Office,'" blared the *Independent*, quoting such quotables as Bill Kristol, who declared that the chance of removing the President was "somewhere in the big middle ground between a 1 per cent and 50. It's some per cent. It's not nothing," thus providing a valuable lesson in both politics and basic mathematics. The *Independent* also relied on Harvard's Laurence Tribe ("invoking Section 4 of the 25th Amendment is no fantasy but an entirely plausible tool"), gladdening the hearts of many Americans in the process.[1]

Unquestionably, the nation has not experienced a leader like Donald Trump in years past. Richard Nixon's occasional madness (he is said to have conversed with White House paintings on one occasion) and Lyndon Johnson's manly histrionics (e.g., requiring uptight Kennedy holdovers to swim naked with him in the White House pool) seem staid when compared to Trump-the-Latenight-Tweeter. Those who really know him know that Trump is an emotional fellow. Divisiveness is "built into ... his DNA," said Senator John Thune of South Dakota. "Trump's shtick is that he's the grievance candidate," said veteran Republican consultant Mike Murphy; "he is speaking to that rage."[2]

Once he was elected, Trump's emotionality took center stage. The President is best perceived as "Trumplethinskin," said psychologist Leonard Cruz, because every time he "stomps his foot in an angry, indignant rant, he appears to become more stuck than before."[3]

This chapter takes up the mind-of-Trump but turns it outward rather than inward. It does little good, says psychologist Steven Reisner, to speculate about Donald Trump's demons since "to call it madness is to try and bring it into the realm of the familiar and to miss the real threat that Trump embodies." Trump "thrives in turmoil," Reisner notes, and "has an uncanny ability to bend the world to his reality; he is charismatic and ruthless, hypnotic and terrifying ... and we must abandon the comforting delusion that Trump is delusional."[4] Trump is a "reality artist," Reisner argues, one with "special gifts to mold his fantasies into truths of a new kind," so we must never forget that Donald Trump is, at root, a politician.[5]

Trump is massively unpopular in certain quarters and yet "he dominates the landscape like no other."[6] How is that possible? A reasonable answer is that Donald Trump is the child of television. As television's child, (1) Trump lives in the moment, leaving history to the pedants; (2) he trusts only that which can be visualized – people's actions, their emotional displays; (3) he shares with others that which can be shown easily – tangible things, evocative things; (4) he concentrates on life's changefulness rather than its essences; and (5) he treats television as an expressive medium, a way of making national politics feel intimate. Making emotional contact with others is Trump's game.

This chapter treats the President as an ersatz physician good at diagnosing why people feel besieged. I explore his use of what historian Richard Hofstadter described in the early 1960s as the Paranoid Style of argument, a style that identifies clandestine figures haunting the body politic.[7] Most of us from time to time entertain such thoughts, using imagined others to explain why life has gone wrong for us. Donald Trump is not crazy, I shall argue, but he does understand the normal craziness we feel from time to time. During the 2016 campaign and thereafter, Trump exploited these feelings. He told the electorate, with scant evidence, how a dangerous cadre – immigrants, bureaucrats, the intelligentsia, and China, specifically – had deprived them of their birthright. When stated baldly like this, such a rhetoric may seem daft but, when interpolated by Trump, it rang true for many Americans. Trump presented himself as a curative.

A Troubled President?

When *Psychology Today* published its first issue in 1967, it was a sign of the times. The nation was then beginning to reject the hide-bound 1950s; Erhard Sensitivity Training and bell-bottoms would soon launch their own emancipations. Dr. Nicholas Charney founded the magazine, hoping that clear, lively prose would shake up the social sciences. At the height of its circulation in 1981, *Psychology Today* reached a circulation of 1,171,362, a figure that dropped dramatically when all magazines hit turbulent times.[8] More important, though, the magazine gave the nation new things to talk about. People's internal states – their *libidos*, their *latent needs*, their *neural signatures* – became as popular as hors d'oeuvres at suburban cocktail parties. People learned they were *hard-wired* to do certain things, causing them to seek *closure* lest they develop one *fetish* or another. To avoid *acting out* in socially unacceptable ways, people found their *God spots* via *mind–body therapies*.

When Donald Trump decided to run for office, psychobabble finally found its cause célèbre. In a pretentious tome edited by Yale psychiatrist Bandy X. Lee, the new chief executive was treated to a raft, nay a flotilla, of at-a-distance diagnoses.[9] Mr. Trump was said to be suffering from *extreme present hedonism, blocked empathy, antisocial personality disorder*, and *severe character pathology*, as well as the run-of-the-mill *cognitive impairments* and *anxiety disorders* plaguing everyone in Sioux Falls. Despite these weighty charges, none of the volume's authors had collected scientifically verifiable data, instead using anecdotes to buttress their claims.

In another venue, San Francisco psychiatrist Thomas Singer traced Mr. Trump's failed psyche to the American people themselves. "Trump mirrors, even amplifies our collective attention deficit disorder, our socio-pathy, and our narcissism," declared Singer, so we must all pay the price for the President living inside each of us.[10] Trump, said Singer, "is a perfect compensatory mirror for the narcissistic injuries of those who support him," a charge that would have surprised blue-collar workers in Michigan who hoped Trump would get them a better job.[11] The "woundedness at the core of the American group Self," Singer concludes, produced the monster with which 330 million Selves must now reckon.[12]

Health metaphors are always dangerous when attached to non-medical matters but they seem especially cruel when applied to everyday voters. Donald Trump is "a dangerous president who has dangerous followers," said Bandy Lee.[13] He is an "opportunistic infection, a skin rash rising from a systemic, deeper pathology" that "can become vulnerable to a bacteria or virus it would normally be able to fight off," observed Thomas Lavin.[14] Another psychiatrist, Allen Frances, also targeted voters, arguing that "we can't expect to change Trump, but we must work to undo the societal delusions that created him."[15]

Given the illness Trump contracted from voters, perhaps he should be put under protective custody. That is what attorney James A. Herb had in mind when suing the President on psychiatric grounds. According to Mr. Herb's petitions, the President is unable to "separate fact from fiction," cannot differentiate "acceptable decisions from horrendous decisions," does not know how to "deal reasonably and effectively with other people," requires "excessive admiration," and has "a sense of entitlement."[16] Even worse, Mr. Herb accuses the President of being a ... politician, one who is "excessively impressionistic and lacking in detail," habitually displaying "self-dramatization" and "theatricality," and unduly "influenced by others."[17]

All of this would be risible if it were not so profoundly insulting to Trump's supporters. Reflecting on the rash of psychiatric mumbo jumbo, Allen Frances, who authored the definitive *Diagnostic and Statistical Manual of Mental Disorders*, called it as he saw it: "What's going on is bullshit." Call Mr. Trump "a liar, call him evil, call him a threat to democracy, call him impulsive, call him ignorant," says Frances, "but saying he has a mental disorder doesn't really add force to the argument."[18]

And yet such claims remained popular as the Trump administration wore on. Even elite journalists were not averse to them. "It's Time to Talk about Trump's Mental Health," declared an opinion piece in the *Washington Post*. The author proceeded to do so, using a mixture of anonymous sources, hyperbolic claims, and moral grandiosity: "It is uncomfortable to talk about the President's mental health. But at this point it is irresponsible not to ... To this layman's eyes and ears, there seems to have been deterioration" in the President's mental health.[19] "Trump Is Cracking Up," said a rival column in the *New York Times*. Again quoting unnamed sources, the author points to "an increasingly unhinged and chaotic president," an "untethered maniac" sitting atop a "powder keg," casually "flicking a lighter that Republicans in Congress could take away but won't."[20] Not to be outdone, CNN called Mr. Trump "psychotically demented" after the President was raucously received by followers at a rally in Arizona.[21]

"Mental work" like this has distinct rhetorical advantages. Reducing the chief executive to his primitive needs rearranges the social hierarchy, making the President one-of-us. By democratizing expertise in this manner, everyone becomes a star student in sophomore psychology class. Elsewhere on campus, the rhetoric surrounding such claims became lyrical. In a commentary on "The Loneliness of Donald Trump," Rebecca Solnit imagined Trump as "fortune's fool," "king of the air," and "a hungry ghost" and then rose to a crescendo in her conclusion: "The man in the white house sits, naked and obscene, a pustule of ego, in the harsh light."[22]

Such commentaries take the Trump out of Trump. He ceases to be a historical human being. He becomes gossamer instead, a fantasy of floating instincts, a move that gives an author complete authority over the psyche being autopsied. The id lies there naked on the gurney and then, suddenly, the ominous sound of a bone saw:

> To the Times, Queens is Cleveland. Bush league. You are Queens. The casinos were totally Queens, the gold faucets in your triplex, the bragging, the insults, but you wanted to be liked by Those People. You wanted Mike Bloomberg to invite you to dinner at his townhouse. You wanted the Times to run a three-part story about you, that you meditate and are a passionate kayaker and collect 14th-century Islamic mosaics. You wish you were that person but you didn't have the time.[23]

"By all accounts," says *New York Magazine*'s Eric Levitz, "most GOP Congress members recognize that Donald Trump is a pathological narcissist with early-stage dementia and only peripheral contact with reality." "They have, nonetheless, decided to let him retain unilateral command of the largest nuclear arsenal on planet Earth," Levitz continues, and "you don't need a degree in psychiatry to call that crazy."[24] As it turns out, members of Congress were not really responsible for making Donald Trump the nation's 45th president. The American people did that.

For some, that is precisely the problem. "The hell of his election," says the *New York Times*' Frank Bruni, "wasn't that [Trump] tricked American voters. It was that they'd fully seen the florid whole of him and supported him nonetheless."[25] In other words, crazy people picked a crazy president. In a 2,100-word article describing the Phoenix rally where the President hinted he would pardon infamous Sheriff Joe Arpaio, nine Arizona citizens were mentioned, only one of whom was an avid Trump supporter – Brian Ratchford. In the article, Ratchford declared himself "an American for Americans" and came to the rally equipped with a .357-caliber gun in case any of his fellow Trumpers needed defending.[26] The implication is clear: Like breeds like.

One of Trump's old pals, Tony Schwartz, says that Trump is "100 percent self-absorbed, incapable of interest in other human beings and completely self-referential."[27] Hardly a recipe for popularity. And yet there it is – the recipe for a president. How is that possible? In the following section, I describe the formula Donald Trump used to address people's emotional needs. "We've watched a lot of our friends lose their jobs," said Caterpillar worker Brad Dorff in April of 2016, "they have homes that now they can't afford. They have families they have to support. They lost their insurance. Their kids have diabetes and they're trying to get medication. It literally breaks your heart."[28] Jungian half-creature though he was, Donald Trump understood such people and the conditions they faced. He addressed them during his campaign and when serving as chief executive. That, too, is a story that must be told.

A Troubled People?

When writing his much-touted essay on the Paranoid Style, Richard Hofstadter reflected on an aggressive, protectionist discourse popular in the United States from its beginning. Those using the Paranoid Style included the anti-Masonic movement of the late 1820s, anti-Catholics in the late nineteenth century, opponents of FDR's New Dealism in the 1930s, the devotees of the John Birch Society and McCarthyism in the 1950s, and members of both the White Citizens' Councils and Black Muslims in the 1960s. "I call it the paranoid style," said Hofstadter, "simply because no other word adequately evokes the sense of heated exaggeration, suspiciousness, and conspiratorial fantasy that I have in mind." In the United States in particular, says Hofstadter, "ethnic and religious conflict have plainly been a major focus for militant and suspicious minds of this sort, but class conflicts also can mobilize such energies."[29]

Suspicions about the military-industrial complex gave rise to the anti-war movement in the late 1960s and then to activists concerned with Chicano laborers, feminism, gay rights, environmentalism, and, more recently, to Occupy Wall Street and Black Lives Matter. The object of paranoia varied from one group to another but suspicions about clandestine power animated them all. On the Right, groups concerned with prayer-in-schools, Second Amendment freedoms, abortion restriction, and charter schools – as well as anti-vaxxers and Tea Party enthusiasts – also produced a rhetoric of mistrust.

According to sociolinguist Adam Hodges, the Paranoid Style has a number of stylistic elements. Among them are a focus on hidden schemes, an us-versus-them dialectic, respect for national purity, and an imperative to act quickly.[30] While such elements seem obvious enough when described broadly, operationalizing them is another matter entirely. Aware of the dangers of reductionism, I used the DICTION program to tap the Paranoid Style, keying on three key elements:

(1) *Isolation.* In a large nation like the United States, it is easy to feel alone. The more strangers one encounters in daily life, the sharper that feeling becomes. As any second-grader looking for a lunch-mate will attest, life can be cruel in these ways. Things become crueler still when money and power are at stake. Scholar Laila Lalami notes that modern tribes, like ancient ones, develop distinct languages to protect themselves: "One faction might speak of 'illegal aliens,' 'traditional families,' and 'the life of the unborn,' while the other talks of 'undocumented workers,' 'marriage equality,' and 'my body, my choice.'"[31] Such tribes, says Lalami, rule over separate territories and listen to different oracles, thereby sealing themselves off from those with contrary views.

The presidential election of 2016 brought such feelings to a head. *The Wall* became a dominant trope, a signal that the most open nation in the world was profoundly questioning itself. A confit of Muslim incursions, free trade protectionism, difficulties with NAFTA, and concerns about the porousness of the southern border opened the door to Trumpism. Not surprisingly, says one team of researchers, Trump voters were "less socially connected to their neighbors and friends" (often for geographical reasons) and less connected to government-sponsored benefits (food stamps, Earned Income Tax Credit, etc.) as well.[32] Trump spoke directly to such people, said rhetoric scholar Robert Terrill; instead of opening them up to dialogue, Trump policed "the borders of their imagined community."[33]

(2) *Affliction.* A feeling of isolation is central to the Paranoid Style but restricted communities can also be life-giving. The nuclear family, the local parish, and civic groups are attractive precisely because they are small and set apart. When micro-communities accrete power, however, power from which we feel excluded, things change. Suddenly, the small group becomes our tormentor – they live in gated communities while I live in a ten-story apartment building in a neighborhood of ten-story apartment buildings. When that happens, people's imaginations go into overdrive and cosmopolitanism becomes a curse.

Of the 241 nation-states in the world, the United States ranks 3rd in population. How can a nation so large be made to feel small? Through rhetoric. "We must stop the massive inflow of refugees," Donald Trump declared endlessly: "I met a family in Ohio whose crops had all been eaten by illegal immigrants."[34] "America is dying, folks, just like Hillary is dying. Jobs are gone. Jobs have been replaced by regulations, believe me. Clowns everywhere. Hillary wants open borders."[35] No real facts are introduced here and yet the world suddenly feels claustrophobic. Trump's rhetoric of victimhood is often incoherent, says communication scholar Paul Elliott Johnson, but that bug became a feature when Trump used it to shrink people's horizons.[36]

(3) *Indignation.* Less room, greater privation. It's enough to make one indignant. And it does. The Paranoid Style is an animated style fueled by a list of endless grievances. This was a natural style for Donald Trump, a notoriously thin-skinned fellow. "Every day there are lies about me in the very dishonest media," said Trump; "the *New York Times*, which is failing, broke into Trump Tower and stole forged documents from my office. I have the surveillance tape, but you can't see it because I'm under IRS audit."[37] Few Americans knew what Trump was talking about here nor did they care about the specifics of his arcane plight. But they knew what it felt to be picked on and so they became indignant by association.

"Trump simply could not abide the knowledge that somebody was getting a leg up at his expense," says Michael Wolff. "His was a zero-sum ecosystem. In the world of Trump, anything that he deemed of value either accrued to him or had been robbed from him."[38] Indignation – the sense that one has been wronged unfairly – is by its nature a subjective discourse, connected to one's personhood: "I have been wronged. I say again, *I* have been wronged." Trump's informality and spontaneity, says Mark Thompson, often produced confusion but they also made him sound authentic to those who, like Trump, could not lay out their grievances in strictly linear fashion.[39] Billionaire and stevedore linked emotionally.

This three-part formulation of the Paranoid Style comes down to this: *I have been cast adrift, beset by dark and malign forces, and I am outraged that this has happened to me.* To operationalize this construct, some of DICTION's native search lists were used and new ones were created to fill out the Paranoid Style. Table 6.1 presents the dictionaries used. Because the word lists varied in size, their counts were standardized before being combined to create the individual components and, then, the overall score. For most speakers, the three subsidiary components are not well correlated; that is, those who feel indignant may not feel particularly isolated.[40] But when people like Donald Trump use them together (thereby manifesting the Paranoid Style), a distinct discourse emerges.

As we see in Table 6.2, Trump scored highly on the three individual components and, as we see in Figure 6.1, he also used the Paranoid Style more aggressively than any of the major presidential candidates between 1948 and 2016. Scores for the Paranoid Style have drifted upward over the years for both Democrats and Republicans, although the latter have used it more fulsomely. The McCain/Trump usage is particularly noteworthy, perhaps reflecting an increasing concern that (1) the nation is becoming a majority minority nation too rapidly and that (2) the world outside is pressing in too forcefully. It may also be true that the boldness of the postwar years (scientific exploration, the United Nations, the growth of higher education, new global markets) has given way to concern about the financial, military, and cultural challenges the nation now confronts.

That was certainly Donald Trump's take on things. Trump doubled Hillary Clinton's use of the Paranoid Style, outdid all of his Republican rivals during the primaries, and scored equally highly in his speeches, ads, and campaign debates.[41] Paranoia came naturally to Trump: When his off-the-cuff speeches were compared to his prepared remarks, no differences – none – could be discerned. He found evil forces skulking about during the primaries as well as during the general

Table 6.1 Components of the Paranoid Style

Domain	Components (*search terms*)	# Search terms	Contributes	Detracts
Isolation	Subversion (*sabotage, radical, illegals, lobbyists*, etc.)	50	x	
	Exclusion (*disconnected, exit, ignore, boycott*, etc.)	375	x	
	Collectives (*associations, council, organization, public*, etc.)	114		x
	Social terms (*farmers, school, homeowners, neighborhood*, etc.)	165		x
	Family terms (*children, women, household, families*, etc.)	23		x
	International places (*Vienna, Turkey, Pacific, overseas*, etc.)	652	x	
	Domestic places (*Austin, DC, Midwest, Sacramento*, etc.)	178		x
Affliction	Blame (*dangerous, deceptive, crazy, monstrous*, etc.)	346	x	
	Aggression (*conflict, demolish, cross-fire, bully*, etc.)	581	x	
	Hardship (*agonizing, deficit, embarrassed, failure*, etc.)	470	x	
	Denial (*can't, won't, nothing, without*, etc.)	39	x	
Indignation	Self-references (*I, me, my, mine*, etc.)	7	x	
	Moral terms (*just, cruel, rights, fairness*, etc.)	173	x	

election, when addressing partisan crowds or the general public, and when barnstorming in the South or the Northeast. In which direction does the causal arrow point? Did the electorate "call forth" Donald Trump because of their grievances or did Trump arrive on the scene

Table 6.2 Trump's Paranoia vs. Other Presidential Candidates, 1948–2016

Type	Token	Trump Rank (out of 26)	Highest	Lowest
Paranoid Style	*Affliction* scores	4	Goldwater	Truman
	Indignation scores	8	GHW Bush	Reagan
	Isolation scores	1	Trump	Kennedy
	Overall	1	Trump	Truman

Source: Data from Campaign Mapping Project.

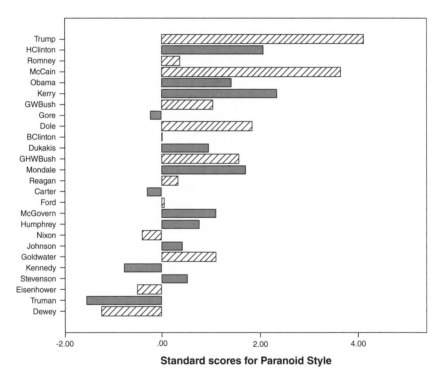

Figure 6.1 Paranoid Style by Candidate and Party, 1948–2016
Source: Data from Campaign Mapping Project.

unbidden, angry at certain economic and social trends and determined to reverse them? In either case, his speech found ears to listen.

Hillary Clinton was not so lucky, although she, too, made more athletic use of the Paranoid Style than most Democrats had in times past. She too addressed people's sense of having been ignored or dismissed. She too felt their pain. But the pain she felt most acutely was Donald Trump. When I examined the Clinton speeches scoring highest on the Paranoid Style, all of them were Trump-oriented. As we will see in Chapter 8, Clinton's focus on Trump caused her to run an overly narrow race. "Feel alone and ignored?" she asked her audiences. It's because Donald Trump thinks you're irrelevant. "Are you having a hard time?" she queried. Donald Trump doesn't care. "Are you angry about racism and sexism?" Donald Trump is their author. Wherever Clinton turned she found Trump:

- Let's not get distracted from the real choice in this election. Donald Trump has proven himself to be temperamentally unfit and totally unqualified to be president and commander-in-chief.
- I wonder if he even knows that a single – a single – nuclear warhead can kill millions of people? That is why dozens of retired nuclear launch officers took the unprecedented step of saying that Donald should, and I quote, "not have his finger on the button."
- Donald says guns should be allowed in nightclubs that serve alcohol. He's even said, on his very first day in office, he would require every school in America to let people carry guns into our classrooms. How can anyone think our schools would be safer with more guns?
- The Donald Trump campaign strategy is pretty simple. They've announced it. Their strategy is: Get women to stay home, get young people to stay home, and get people of color to stay home. It's all part of his scorched-earth campaign.[42]

Trump attacked Clinton too but his was more a *cultural* campaign than a personal one. Trump sensed people's feelings of marginalization and he took those feelings on the road. He was prescient when doing so. Near the end of his second year in office, the *New York Times* announced a poll of 3,555 likely voters in California, Illinois, Kentucky, Minnesota, and West Virginia, finding that – regardless of region – 47 percent of Trump supporters felt like strangers in their own land while 44 percent of those who disapproved of Trump felt the same way. Despite a flourishing economy, despite the absence of war, a great many American people felt distanced from the center of action. Such feelings of estrangement, said the *Times*, touch "something more fundamental than policy preferences, more personal than how people view individual leaders."[43]

The hearings surrounding the nomination of Judge Brett Kavanaugh to the highest court in the land brought those feelings to a head. "With Trump in power," says reporter Emily Badger, "partisans have simply traded views on who feels estranged."[44] "It's a very scary time for young men in America," declared the President during the hearings, "when you can be guilty of something you may not be guilty of."[45] In a passionate and unscripted monologue, *The Daily Show*'s Trevor Noah called out Trump for "trying to convince men that they are the victims of the #MeToo movement."[46] "He knows how to offer victimhood to people who have the least claim to it," said Noah, "which is a really, really powerful tool."[47]

According to researchers Eric Oliver and Thomas Wood, *magical thinking* has long been popular in the United States. Roughly half the citizenry embraces some sort of conspiracy theory they report, in part because such notions "provide compelling explanations for otherwise confusing or ambiguous events" and in part because certain socioeconomic forces (less education, membership in a minority group, or belief in "end time" thinking) steer them in that direction. A belief in "unseen, intentional forces" bends history toward "a Manichean struggle between good and evil," the authors contend; while such a belief does not make people feel better, it does make them feel correct.[48] Importantly, said Daniel Patrick Moynihan, there is always some factual basis to conspiracy theories (for example, an increase in the number of Mexican migrants in the United States), even though the extrapolations from those data (e.g., immigrants commit more violent crimes) are often baseless.[49]

The Paranoid Style is also fed by *motival thinking*. Things do not "just happen" for the conspiracy-minded. "Decisive events are not taken as part of the stream of history," says Richard Hofstadter, "but as the consequence of someone's evil." "Having no access to political bargaining or the making of decisions," Hofstadter continues, people "find their original conception that the world of power is sinister and malicious fully confirmed."[50] Why did so many women accuse Donald Trump of sexual molestation? "I believe it was [Clinton's] campaign that did it," said Trump. Why were his poll numbers slipping in Florida? Because GOP leaders were not "putting their weight behind the people; there's a whole sinister deal going on" inside the party. Is voter fraud really possible in the United States? The media "is so dishonest and corrupt," Trump observed, that "they've poisoned the mind of the voters" and so anything is possible.[51] Fact–motive–fact–motive–fact–motive.

Structural thinking is also central to the Paranoid Style. Everything connects to everything else, and all effects can be traced to some definitive cause. Barack Obama's odd name made him a foreigner. Global warming is a myth created by the Chinese. Antonin Scalia was murdered because of his conservatism. Muslim-Americans planned the 9/11 disaster. Mexico sends "bad ones" to infiltrate the United States. With Trump, says *Salon*'s Conor Lynch, "every conceivable plot and every conceivable problem – whether it be social, economic, political – can be traced back to a cunning and calculated group of conspirators."[52] Research shows that such "complicated" narratives are attractive to rural, less-educated whites because they show how elites have suppressed them.[53]

A fourth aspect of the Paranoid Style is *pathway thinking*. Tightly knit structures push things in a preordained direction. One thing leads to another and then something important – something dangerous – happens. "Big business, elite media and major donors are lining up behind the campaign of my opponent," Trump complained in September of 2016, "because they know she will keep our rigged system in place." "I'm leading in Florida, the polls all show it. If I lose Florida we will know there's voter fraud [and] if there's voter fraud, this election will be illegitimate."[54] Even when the imagined outcomes are unhappy ones, pathway thinking proves that old lessons still hold, that the game is rigged, that you can't fight City Hall. This solace-of-predictability leaves a bitter taste but it keeps one's worldview intact.

The Paranoid Style requires but modest effort for speaker and listener. When hard data are unavailable, one's imagination fills in the blanks. When outcomes are hard to explain, hidden motives come to the rescue. Politics has long depended on such easy thinking, in part because things change quickly in that domain and in part because public policy is so complicated. Being able to depend on old prejudices, old stories, becomes a fine gratuity, especially for neophytes like Donald Trump. Because he knew so little about the nonbusiness world when running for office in 2015, Trump needed a rhetorical formula emanating from his life experience and his hard-bitten view of the world. As a result, the Paranoid Style found him.

A Troubled Era?

Although the Paranoid Style has been widely appropriated by politicians, its roots lie deep within the citizenry. Because the nation has been hounded by its size and diversity since its beginning, Americans

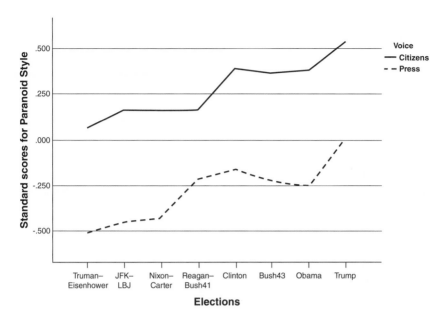

Figure 6.2 Paranoid Style in Citizens' Letters vs. Press Coverage over Time
Source: Data from Campaign Mapping Project.

have habitually looked over their shoulders when assessing their comparative advantage. This has been especially true for those interested in politics. When comparing citizens' letters to the editor to politicians' speeches and campaign coverage, I found massive differences in use of the Paranoid Style, with politicians using it three times more reliably than members of the press and with voters using it 50 percent more than campaigners.[55] Moreover, as we see in Figure 6.2, there has been a modest increase in letter writers' use of the Paranoid Style over the years, with the 2016 campaign topping all prior elections.[56]

These findings partially reflect those who write letters to the editor: They care deeply about the nation's direction. They are imaginative, constantly on the outlook for structures, motives, and obstacles inhibiting enlightened governance. They also love rhetorical excess. Whether Left or Right, whether massively disconsolate or just disconsolate, they are quick to spot a plot:

- *In behalf of Clinton*: I can't help but chuckle when I hear a rich, white, male, major-party candidate complain about a political system "rigged" against him. The political system in this country has been rigged since our nation was formed – rigged against women who were prohibited from voting by our infallible Founding Fathers for the first 130 years of our nation's existence, rigged for 175 years against poor people who could not afford a poll tax, rigged against African-Americans who were "discouraged" in a variety of ways from voting in the South for 100 years after slavery was nominally abolished, rigged by a two-party system of Republicans and Democrats that makes it virtually impossible for a third-party candidate to win.[57]

- *In behalf of Trump*: I urge those who might still be on the fence about their preference for a presidential candidate to check out the outrageous protests at some of the rallies and events for Republican candidate Donald Trump. These protesters are an embarrassment to society; their protests are a pathetic example of political discourse. I question the true motives for their disgusting and, in some cases, criminal behaviors. Perhaps they fear that if Trump is elected they might actually have to get a job and earn a paycheck. That's got to be utterly frightening to some of them, especially since many employers require drug testing these days. Ask yourself: Do you want to be on the same side as these protesters?[58]

- *In behalf of Nobody*: We have two distinguished people running for president. Candidates like never before. One seems to be about "big I and little you" since he is constantly mentioning his name and wealth. The other seems to have dark values overseas since she is gaining wealth in faraway places by talking and making seemingly false promises. She also has the men killed at Benghazi and coverups with DC politics, which are now on the burner once again. It has become hard to pick one over the other as their past does not show them to be untainted nor do they seem to have led honest lives. We do have the privilege of picking old lies or new ones. Whatever you do, don't sit home and not vote. By the way, they both wear pants.[59]

The gradual rise in the Paranoid Style among the writers may signal something cultural afoot: A growing aversion to politics? A sense that foreign interests are unduly affecting ordinary Americans? A belief that people can no longer be trusted? Donald Trump connects to these feelings, says Michael D'Antonio, by favoring "a stubbornly anti-intellectual type of common sense that played to the grievances of the kind of white men represented by the TV character Archie Bunker, who, like Trump, came from Queens."[60] Essayist Charles Kesler notes that, like Ronald Reagan, Trump "spoke as a citizen to fellow citizens, without a trace of the policy expert's condescension, cosmopolitanism, or crocodile tears."[61]

Instead of treating Trump as a psychological object, then, it seems better to think of him in sociological terms, as someone from the tacky underside of American culture. Trump is "a distinctly local product," says Pulitzer Prize winner David Remnick, "like the smell of a Times Square subway platform in mid-August."[62] Unlike Barack Obama, who reasoned from the head, Trump reasons from the gut, connecting him to a world of post-truth fashioned out of people's disappointments. When confronted by a reporter about his own lies and evasions, Trump justified his claims simply: "You know what's important, millions of people agree with me; [people keep saying] 'we agree with Mr. Trump. We agree.' They're very smart people."[63] Although 59 percent of Americans think that Trump makes false claims, 52 percent contend that the news media do as well.[64] So who can you trust? And why trust at all given the conspiracies floating about?

One of the advantages of the Paranoid Style is that it appeals to those with an "aversion to social change." Matt Grossman and Daniel Thaler of Michigan State University have shown that such attitudes are strongly predictive of support for Trump. That was especially true for nonelites, those who are strongly hierarchical and those who uphold traditional standards of morality.[65] Such people are also likely to be Intuitionists, say Oliver and Wood, to believe in nonsensory things like God, ghosts, ESP, reincarnation, "positive thinking," and, of course, conspiracies. Intuitionists are typically less educated, poorer, under financial distress, frequent church attenders, and believe in strict childhood discipline. Many of them, but not all, supported Trump in 2016 because of these "transgressive beliefs."[66] Trump also trusted his intuitions: "I'm a very instinctive person, but my instincts turn out to be right."[67]

With the Paranoid Style increasing in popularity among politicians and citizens, one wonders where all of this is heading. While the press itself normally rejects Intuitionism, there may be a ceiling to that effect. As we see in Figure 6.2, while mainstream reportage starts at a much lower baseline, it has increasingly deployed the Paranoid Style more often in recent years.[68] In part this may be because press reports frequently quote political actors (an indirect effect), but "magical thinking" may also be affecting journalism since it, too, is often captured by storylines of conspiracy, and that may explain why the press has come under increasing attack in recent years. Perhaps news consumers are having a harder time distinguishing news reports from political propaganda, dispassionate analysis from implicit editorializing. If so, perhaps Donald Trump – the press's great tormentor – may not be so crazy after all.

Conclusion

My argument in this chapter has been that Doctor Donald Trump seeks to cure the American people or, at least, half of them – the half that feels beleaguered. As a therapist, Trump ranted about unwanted Mexicans and raved about stealthy Democrats to explain why workers were stuck in dead-end jobs. The more he told such stories and the more he was reinforced for doing so, the more his therapy turned into auto-therapy. Suddenly, he could not stop talking about dark forces and, once elected, he continued to do so. Is Donald Trump himself truly paranoid? Michael Wolff, one of Trump's most delicious tormentors, thinks not. "Narcissism, really, is the opposite of paranoia," says Wolff. "Trump thought people were and should be protecting him," not that they were haunting him.[69] No matter what Mr. Trump's own mental state might be, the more relevant point is that he performs paranoia brilliantly, selling its depredations to others.

Once he was in office, the Paranoid Style became Trump's master more than he its. Typically, he would maintain his reserve as long as possible and then – boom – another explosion. The Senate hearings investigating Dr. Christine Blasey Ford's charges of sexual impropriety against Supreme Court justice nominee Brett Kavanaugh exemplify this. Trump held back as long as he could, describing Dr. Ford's testimony as "very compelling" and describing her as a "very credible witness." Then came Mississippi. Four days before the Senate voted, Trump mocked Dr. Ford at a rally in Southaven, mimicking her description of the sexual attack in vaudeville style: "I don't remember!" "I don't remember!" "Upstairs? Downstairs? Where was it?"[70] After the vote was taken, Trump went on the road again (this time in Orlando), describing the entire Ford–Kavanaugh contretemps as a "hoax," a "disgraceful situation brought about by people who are evil."[71]

A nation that becomes addicted to the Paranoid Style is surely in trouble. In a curious book, George Saunders describes the predations of

"Megaphone Man," an individual who spoils every cocktail party with his loud, shrill, agenda-driven tirades that "antagonize us, make us feel anxious, ineffective and alone."[72] Such a person's unavoidability, says Saunders, makes it hard to change the conversation, so people slink away, abandoning the discussion altogether. On cue, one reliable Megaphone Man, Newt Gingrich, identified the perfect Republican campaign strategy a full two years before the 2020 elections unfolded: "Sanctuary cities could be the future. You too could have an international drug gang like MS-13 gang in your neighborhood."[73]

The Paranoid Style ultimately erodes trust in individuals and institutions, with the paranoiac living in a small space whose boundaries are its main attraction. Masterful though he is when describing unseen dangers, Donald Trump cramps his audiences when doing so, restricting them to what they already know, making them afraid of that which is new. He also renders them incurious about strangers, an odd beneficence for a nation that has in the past eagerly sent missionaries – religious and secular, corporate and philanthropic – to every corner of the globe. There is something unbrave about the Paranoid Style, something sad about those who find respite in it. It is more than a bit ironic that a fellow like Donald Trump, who made millions, lost millions, and made them again – who has spent his life as a wildcatter – would now specialize in making people afraid. Perhaps that is why he sleeps poorly at night.

How long will the Paranoid Style draw a crowd for Trump? Its putative claim, after all, is that (1) a small number of people is (2) secretly plotting to (3) do significant harm. Having to update that formula again and again is burdensome. Each day, fresh plotters and new perfidy must be found lest the tale unravel itself. How long can a nation hear such stuff without tiring of it? How long can hope take a back seat in the United States, the most foolishly optimistic of all nations? Someday, even a bitter performer like Donald Trump must find a new act. Someday, his followers must find something else to motivate them. One hopes that both days arrive soon.

Notes

1 Benjamin Kentish, "Members of Congress 'Holding Secret Conversations about Removing Donald Trump from Office,'" *Independent*, May 4, 2017. Accessed at www.independent.co.uk/news/world/americas/us-politics/donald-trump-impeachment-remove-office-secret-meetings-congress-members-a7716326.html.

2 The foregoing comments can be found in Ashley Porter, Seung Min Kim, and Robert Costa, "'I'm Not Going There': as Trump Hurls Racial Invective, Most Republicans Stay Silent," *Washington Post*, August 18, 2018. Accessed at www.washingtonpost .com/politics/im-not-going-there-as-trump-hurls-racial-invective-most-republicans-stay-silent/2018/08/18/aab7fd8a-a189-11e8-83d2-70203b8d7b44_story.html?utm_term=.5331bdda12f2.

3 Leonard Cruz, "Trumplethinskin: Narcissism and the Will to Power," in Leonard Cruz and Steven Buser (eds.), *A Clear and Present Danger: Narcissism in the Era of President Trump* (Asheville, NC: Chiron Publications, 2017), p. 80.

4 Steven Reisner, "Stop Saying Donald Trump Is Mentally Ill," *Slate*, March 15, 2017. Accessed at www.slate.com/articles/health_and_science/medical_examiner/2017/03/donald_trump_isn_t_mentally_ill_he_s_evil.html.

5 Ibid.

6 Maggie Haberman, Glenn Thrush, and Peter Baker, "Inside Trump's Hour-by-Hour Battle for Self-Preservation," *New York Times*, December 9, 2017. Accessed at www.nytimes.com/2017/12/09/us/politics/donald-trump-president.html.

7 Richard Hofstadter, "The Paranoid Style in American Politics," *Harpers*, November 1964. Accessed at https://harpers.org/archive/1964/11/the-paranoid-style-in-ameri can-politics/.

8 Bruce V. Lewenstein, "Was There Really a Popular Science 'Boom'?" *Science, Technology, and Human Values*, 12:2 (1987), 29–41.

9 Bandy Lee (ed.), *The Dangerous Case of Donald Trump: Twenty-Seven Psychiatrists and Mental Health Experts Assess a President* (New York: St. Martins, 2017).

10 Thomas Singer, "Trump and the American Collective Psyche," in Lee (ed.), *The Dangerous Case of Donald Trump*, pp. 281, 294.

11 Thomas Singer, "President Trump and the American Selfie: Archetypal Defenses of the Group Spirit," in Cruz and Buser (eds.), *A Clear and Present Danger*, p. 32.

12 Ibid., p. 31.

13 As quoted in Paul Basken, "A Yale Psychiatrist Evaluates the Mental Health of Trump – and the Nation," *Chronicle of Higher Education*, January 4, 2018. Accessed at www.chronicle.com/article/A-Yale-Psychiatrist-Evaluates/242157.

14 Thomas P. Lavin, "The Trump Phenomenon," in Cruz and Buser (eds.), *A Clear and Present Danger*, p. 121.

15 As quoted in Carlos Lozada, "Is Trump Mentally Ill? Or Is America? Psychiatrists Weigh In," *Washington Post*, September 22, 2017. Accessed at www .washingtonpost.com/news/book-party/wp/2017/09/22/is-trump-mentally-ill-or-is-america-psychiatrists-weigh-in/?utm_term=.770e1e0c5519.

16 James A. Herb, "Donald J. Trump, Alleged Incapacitated Person: Mental Incapacity, the Electoral College, and the Twenty-fifth Amendment," in Lee (ed.), *The Danger-ous Case of Donald Trump*, pp. 142, 143.

17 Ibid., p. 144.

18 As quoted in Brian Resnick, "The Psychiatrist Who Wrote the Guide to Personality Disorders Says Diagnosing Trump Is 'Bullshit,'" *Vox*, February 10, 2017. Accessed at www.vox.com/policy-and-politics/2017/2/10/14551890/trump-mental-health-nar cissistic-personality.

19 Eugene Robinson, "It's Time to Talk about Trump's Mental Health," *Washington Post*, August 21, 2017. Accessed at www.washingtonpost.com/opinions/its-time-to-talk-about-trumps-mental-health/2017/08/21/40d86eac-86ac-11e7-961d-2f373b39 77ee_story.html.

20 Michelle Goldberg, "Trump Is Cracking Up," *New York Times*, December 1, 2017. Accessed at www.nytimes.com/2017/12/01/opinion/trump-is-cracking-up.html.

21 Sam Levine, "CNN Panel Openly Questions Whether Trump Is Fit for Office after Wild Arizona Rally," *CNN*, August 23, 2017. Accessed at www.huffingtonpost .com/entry/trump-fitness-for-office_us_599d92d6e4b0a296083b76a7.

22 Rebecca Solnit, "The Loneliness of Donald Trump: on the Corrosive Privilege of the Most Mocked Man in the World," *Literary Hub*, May 30, 2017. Accessed at https:// lithub.com/rebecca-solnit-the-loneliness-of-donald-trump/.

23 Garrison Keillor, "When This Is Over, You Will Have Nothing That You Want," *Chicago Tribune*, August 31, 2016. Accessed at www.chicagotribune.com/news/ opinion/commentary/ct-donald-trump-losing-garrison-keillor-20160831-story.html.

24 Eric Levitz, "The President Is Mentally Unwell – and Everyone around Him Knows It," *New York Magazine*, January 4, 2018. Accessed at http://nymag.com/daily/ intelligencer/2018/01/trump-is-mentally-unwell-and-everyone-around-him-knows-it .html.

25 Frank Bruni, "Donald Trump's Radical Honesty," *New York Times*, January 19, 2018. Accessed at www.nytimes.com/2018/01/19/opinion/sunday/donald-trump-lies-honesty.html.

26 John Wagner, Jenna Johnson, and Danielle Paquette, "Trump Threatens Shutdown, Suggests Controversial Pardon at Arizona Rally," *Washington Post*, August 23, 2017. Accessed at www.washingtonpost.com/politics/trump-holds-campaign-style-rally-amid-large-protests-in-arizona/2017/08/22/dd7c83c0-8796-11e7-961d-2f373b 3977ee_story.html?utm_term=.7f3409b83779.

27 As quoted in Jon Wiener, "Trump's Ghostwriter Says the President Is Now in Survival Mode," *The Nation*, November 3, 2017. Accessed at www.thenation .com/article/donald-trumps-ghostwriter-says-the-president-is-now-in-survival-mode/.

28 As quoted in David Goldstein, "Blue-Collar Voters: Trade Is Killing Us," *Charlotte Observer*, April 2, 2016. Accessed at www.charlotteobserver.com/news/politics-gov ernment/article69551672.html.

29 Hofstadter, "The Paranoid Style in American Politics," *Harpers*.

30 Adam Hodges, "The Paranoid Style in Politics: Ideological Underpinnings of the Discourse of Second Amendment Absolutism," *Journal of Language Aggression and Conflict*, 3:1 (2015), 87–106.

31 Laila Lalami, "Does American 'Tribalism' End in a Compromise or a Fight?" *New York Times Magazine*, June 26, 2018. Accessed at www.nytimes.com/2018/06/26/ magazine/does-american-tribalism-end-in-a-compromise-or-a-fight.html.

32 Christopher F. Karpowitz, Jeremy Clayne Pope, and Kelly D. Patterson, "The Disconnected Trump Voter," Paper presented at the annual convention of the American Political Science Association, Boston, MA, September 2018.

33 Robert Terrill, "The Post-Racial and Post-Ethical Discourse of Donald J. Trump," *Rhetoric and Public Affairs*, 20:3 (2017), 501. See also Linda Bos and Jonas Lefe-vere, "Echoes of Populism: The Stickiness of Populist Messages," Paper presented at the annual convention of the International Communication Association, San Diego, CA, June 2017.

34 Donald J. Trump, "Remarks to the RNC in Cleveland, Ohio," July 23, 2017. Accessed at www.politico.com/story/2016/07/full-transcript-donald-trump-nomin ation-acceptance-speech-at-rnc-225974.

35 Donald J. Trump, "Campaign Remarks in Boynton Beach, Florida," October 24, 2016. Accessed at www.youtube.com/watch?v=Wuy1Mo5DM38.

36 Paul Elliott Johnson, "The Art of Masculine Victimhood: Donald Trump's Dema-goguery," *Women's Studies in Communication*, 40:3 (2017), 19.

37 Donald J. Trump, "Campaign Remarks in Manheim, Pennsylvania," October 1, 2016. Accessed at https://moody.utexas.edu/centers/strauss/campaign-mapping-project.

38 Michael Wolff, *Fire and Fury: Inside the Trump White House* (New York: Henry Holt and Co., 2018), p. 248.

39 Mark Thompson, "Trump, Brexit, and the Broken Language of Politics," John Donne Lecture, Oxford University, March 17, 2017, 20.

40 For 56,711 passages processed by DICTION, Isolation and Indignation produced a bivariate correlation of 0.165, Isolation and Affliction of 0.172, and Affliction and Indignation of 0.091.

41 Statistical patterns for the Paranoid Style during general election speeches and debates: Hillary Clinton = 0.4015; Donald Trump = 0.8889; F [1, 2423] = 231.490, p < 0.000. During the Republican primary debates: Trump 1.4245; Rubio = 0.3701; Cruz = 0.86543; JBush = 0.4566; Kasich = 0.3100; Carson = 0.6788; F [5, 342] = 39.173, p < 0.000.

42 Hillary R. Clinton, "Remarks on Gun Control and National Security," Cincinnati, Ohio, October 31, 2016. Accessed at www.youtube.com/watch?v=_uqmcnwjHrY. For kindred (albeit more qualitative) observations about Hillary Clinton's tendency to become excessively negative when discussing her opponent, see Fielding Montgomery, "The Monstrous Election: Horror Framing in Televised Campaign Advertisements during the 2016 Presidential Election," *Rhetoric and Public Affairs*, 22:2 (2019), 281–322.

43 Emily Badger, "Estranged in America: Both Sides Feel Lost and Left Out," *New York Times*, October 4, 2018. Accessed at www.nytimes.com/2018/10/04/upshot/ estranged-america-trump-polarization.html.

44 Ibid.

45 As quoted in Allyson Chiu, "Noah: Trump Convincing Men They Are the 'True Victims,'" *Washington Post*, October 5, 2018. Accessed at www.washingtonpost .com/news/morning-mix/wp/2018/10/05/trevor-noah-calls-out-trump-for-trying-to-convince-men-they-are-the-true-victims-of-the-metoo-movement/?utm_term=.obda 392b7257.

46 Ibid.

47 Ibid.

48 J. Eric Oliver and Thomas J. Wood, "Conspiracy Theories and the Paranoid Style(s) of Mass Opinion," *American Journal of Political Science*, 58:4 (2014), 964.

49 Daniel Patrick Moynihan, "The Paranoid Style in American Politics Revisited," *The Public Interest*, 81 (1985), 119. Craig Allen Smith adds an important addition to this notion, finding that paranoid thinkers feel the need to "document" their claims more often than nonparanoids. See Craig Allen Smith, "The Hofstadter Hypothesis Revisited: the Nature of Evidence in Politically 'Paranoid' Discourse," *Southern Communication Journal*, 42 (1977), 274–89.

50 Hofstadter, "The Paranoid Style in American Politics," *Harpers*, 85, 86.

51 Foregoing Trump quotations extracted from William Saletan, "Trump Is a Madman. The Third Debate Settled it: He's Not Just Cynical. He's Paranoid," *Slate*, October 20, 2016. Accessed at https://upload.democraticunderground.com/12512528990.

52 Conor Lynch, "Paranoid Politics: Donald Trump's Style Perfectly Embodies the Theories of Renowned Historian," *Salon*, July 7, 2016. Accessed at www.salon .com/2016/07/07/paranoid_politics_donald_trumps_style_perfectly_embodies_the_ theories_of_renowned_historian/. For more on the structuralism built into paranoid rhetoric, see G. Thomas Goodnight and John Poulakos, "Conspiracy Rhetoric: from Pragmatism to Fantasy in Public Discourse," *Western Journal of Communication*, 45 (1981), 299–316.

53 See Rafael DiTella and Julio J. Rotemberg, "Populism and the Return of the 'Paranoid Style': Some Evidence and a Simple Model of Demand for Incompetence as Insurance against Elite Betrayal," working paper, National Bureau of Economic Research, Cambridge, MA, December 2016. Accessed at www.nber.org/papers/w22975.

54 As quoted in Thomas B. Edsall, "The Paranoid Style in American Politics Is Back," *New York Times*, September 8, 2016. Accessed at www.nytimes.com/2016/09/08/opinion/campaign-stops/the-paranoid-style-in-american-politics-is-back.html.

55 Statistical patterns for the Paranoid Style for voters = 0.2121; for politicians = 0.1470; for the press = -0.2721; $F_{[2, 43295]}$ = 1178.133, $p < 0.000$.

56 Statistical patterns for letter writers' use of the Paranoid Style during Truman–Ike elections = 0.0698; JFK–LBJ elections = 0.1661; Nixon–Carter elections = 0.1601; Reagan–Bush41 elections = 0.1664; Clinton elections = 0.3907; Bush43 elections = 0.3655; Obama elections = 0.3819; Trump election = 0.5390; $F_{[7, 11264]}$ = 40.734, $p < 0.000$.

57 Robert Beymer, "'Rigged Election' Complaint Comes from the Candidate with All the Advantages," *Duluth News Tribune*, October 24, 2016. Accessed at https://moody.utexas.edu/centers/strauss/campaign-mapping-project.

58 Jeff Bushnell, "Protestors Make Trump Look Good by Comparison," *Duluth News Tribune*, June 3, 2016. Accessed at https://moody.utexas.edu/centers/strauss/campaign-mapping-project.

59 Dick Waltrip, "Both Candidates Dishonest," *Lake Charles American Press*, July 3, 2016. Accessed at https://moody.utexas.edu/centers/strauss/campaign-mapping-project.

60 Michael D'Antonio, *Never Enough: Donald Trump and the Pursuit of Success* (New York: Thomas Dunne Books, 2013), p. 193.

61 Charles R. Kesler, "Thinking about Trump," *Claremont Review of Books*, 18:2 (2018), 12, 16.

62 As quoted in Singer, "President Trump and the American Selfie," p. 10.

63 As quoted in Thomas B. Edsall, "Is President Trump a Stealth Postmodernist or Just a Liar?" *New York Times*, January 25, 2018. Accessed at www.nytimes.com/2018/01/25/opinion/trump-postmodernism-lies.html.

64 Ibid.

65 Matt Grossman and Daniel Thaler, "Mass–Elite Divides in Aversion to Social Change and Support for Donald Trump," *American Politics Research*, 46:5 (2018), 753–84.

66 J. Eric Oliver and Thomas J. Wood, *Enchanted America: How Intuition and Reason Divide Our Politics* (Chicago: University of Chicago Press, 2018), p. 70.

67 As quoted ibid., p. 106.

68 Statistical patterns for use of the Paranoid Style in news coverage during Truman–Ike elections = -0.5061; JFK–LBJ elections = -0.4441; Nixon–Carter elections = -0.4228; Reagan–Bush41 elections = -0.2040; Clinton elections = -0.1622; Bush43 elections = -0.2219; Obama elections = -0.2502; Trump election = 0.0070; $F_{[7, 26707]}$ = 105.501, $p < 0.000$.

69 Michael Wolff, *Siege: Trump under Fire* (New York: Henry Holt & Co., 2019), p. 55.

70 As quoted in Josh Dawsey and Felicia Sonmez, "Trump Mocks Kavanaugh Accuser Christine Blasey Ford," October 2, 2018. Accessed at www.washingtonpost.com/politics/trump-mocks-kavanaugh-accuser-christine-blasey-ford/2018/10/02/25f6f8aa-c662-11e8-9b1c-a90f1daae309_story.html?noredirect=on&utm_term=.b9e42fc5fde2.

71 As quoted in Peter Baker, "Trump Bets Kavanaugh 'Hoax' Can Turn into Midterm Gains," *New York Times*, October 8, 2018. Accessed at www.nytimes.com/2018/10/08/us/politics/trump-kavanaugh-accusations-hoax.html.

72 George Saunders, *The Braindead Megaphone* (New York: Riverhead Books, 2007), p. 11.

73 As quoted in Katie Rogers and Maggie Haberman, "Trump Sees a 'Red Wave' Where His Party Sees a Red Alert," *New York Times*, September 20, 2018. Accessed at www.nytimes.com/2018/09/20/us/politics/trump-republicans-midterms.html.

7 TRUMP'S JOURNALISM

Politics is a deadly serious business until 11:30 p.m. Eastern Standard Time. Then the klieg lights shine. Donald Trump's name is embossed in gold on his penis, declares Stormy Daniels on *Jimmy Kimmel Live*.[1] Ivanka Trump is a "feckless cunt," observes Samantha Bee on *Full Frontal*.[2] Donald Trump is a "presidunce" and a "pricktator," announces Steven Colbert on *The Late Show*.[3] Clearly, nothing is now off-limits when it comes to presidential humor. Researchers have found that Trump was the butt of late-night jokes three times more often than Hillary Clinton during the 2016 presidential campaign, a ratio that seemed foreordained given Trump's media history.[4] Before running for office, after all, Trump had mugged with *Duck Dynasty* characters, overseen the Miss America pageant, and fired people on *The Apprentice* – all on national TV. What could possibly be verboten in a Trump presidency?

Savaging politicians is fine, says the University of Delaware's Danna Young, but it comes with a cost. If comedians "are looking to capitalize on the special sauce of humor," she observes, they should "take that anger and use it to inform their craft, but not have it *become* their craft."[5] As the Trump presidency wore on, that distinction was lost. Never one to laugh at himself, Trump boycotted the White House Correspondents Association Dinner, a venue for inverting the pyramid of power, from 2017 onward. Trump himself appreciated inversions but always on his own terms. He liked putting people in their place, especially women: actress Alicia Machad, a.k.a. "Miss Piggy"; reporter

Megyn Kelly, a.k.a. "Bimbo"; and columnist Gail Collins, a.k.a. "Face of a Dog."

Given his penchant for hitting back twice as hard as he is hit, Mr. Trump perhaps deserves little sympathy when comics belittle him. Except for two things: (1) He is now the President of the United States and (2) half the nation supports him. As a result, anti-Trump comedy now has cultural implications. Journalist Alexander Zaitchik notes that comedian Bill Maher "basically makes eugenics-level arguments about anyone who votes for Donald Trump." "You would never get away talking that way about any other group of people," Zaitchik notes, "and still have a TV show."[6] Trump supporters see jokes about Trump as jokes about them – about their stunted intelligence, about their social awkwardness, about their love of fried chicken. "There is plenty of money to be made," says conservative columnist Mollie Hemingway, "in making cultural elites feel morally superior."[7]

This chapter examines the ongoing war between Donald Trump and the media, a contest that some say has classist undertones. "American journalism has been willfully obtuse about the grievances on Main Street for decades," says commentator Sarah Smarsh, having dug a "hole of resentment that Trump's venom now fills."[8] Not surprisingly, says the University of Leeds' Ric Bailey, market segmentation predominates in the United States, with conservatives tuning in to Fox News and with liberals cavorting with late-night humorists.[9] Laughing at Donald Trump has become cultural laughing, ideological laughing. Humor has gone nuclear.

The news has gone nuclear as well and Donald Trump is part of that story, combining the force of personality with a keen understanding of TV perquisites. *In effect, Trump has set up a rival system of reportage; he has become the nation's publisher-in-chief.* When the various Democratic candidates began introducing themselves to the American people in 2019, for example, Mr. Trump became both play-by-play announcer and color commentator. *On Beto O'Rourke*: "Made to fall like a rock." *On Elizabeth Warren*: "Pocahontas, I think, is probably out." *On Pete Buttigieg*: "I don't think he stands a chance." *On the front-runners*: "Looks to me like it's going to be SleepyCreepy Joe over Crazy Bernie. Everyone else is fading fast!"[10]

To be sure, all presidents use the White House's press office to make their best case, but Trump has gone further, issuing the press releases himself via Twitter and using his natural contentiousness to put reporters on the defensive. As a result, 43 percent of Republicans now declare a willingness to let the President shutter "bad" media outlets; an even higher proportion, 85 percent, say it should be easier to sue journalists who knowingly publish false information.[11] A civil war of news consumption has developed, with 35 percent of the American people feeling that the press is too hard on Trump and 34 percent saying it has not been tough enough.[12]

Partisanship is one thing but issue coverage is something else. Combining different datasets, *Ricochet*'s Jon Gabriel estimates that while the mainstream media devoted 75 percent of its coverage to the Russia scandal during one period of time, only 6 percent of its viewership felt the topic was important. In contrast, 35 percent said that healthcare was a vital matter, a topic the media treated at the 4 percent level. Twenty-one percent of news consumers wanted to hear more about immigration and terrorism, but the media gave it only 6 percent of its attention.[13] Other studies show that, while voters want to hear more about policy issues and moral character during political campaigns, the press largely delivers personality-based stories and horserace coverage.[14] Some observers feel that media imperialism is now undermining American pluralism.

There is, of course, a mutuality between the press and the President. As the *New Yorker*'s John Cassidy observes, "the news media needs content, which the administration provides. The administration needs distribution, which the media provides."[15] Consider Trump's side of the equation: No candidate received as much uncompensated airtime as he did during the 2016 presidential campaign, and no sitting president has ever dominated the airwaves like Trump did once he assumed office. Following his old pal Steve Bannon's advice, Mr. Trump has made his long-term mission short-term – winning the ratings war each hour of each day of each week. According to Fox News' Tucker Carlson, Trump believes in television more than opinion polls because it gives him a richer understanding of the public mood.[16]

Trump often crows that he has improved the media's bottom line and he is not wrong about that. Four months after the 2016 campaign, the *New York Times* boasted 132,000 new subscribers while the *Washington Post* said it would expand its newsroom by 8 percent.[17] "Fake news" is good news for cable channels as well. Trump helped CNN double its audience and he tripled viewers for MSNBC. Not to be outdone, Fox News added 700,000 viewers during the 2016 campaign.[18] "An odd fellowship" has been created, say Silvio Waisbord and his colleagues, "between a candidate who tapped into old conservative sentiments against 'the media' and the profit objectives of mainstream news."[19]

Like any symbiotic relationship, mutual costs must be borne. Try as he might, Trump cannot control the press's agenda – the topics it deems most important (e.g., the Mueller investigation vs. the stock market). But there are costs to the media as well. While "intense dislike of Mr. Trump turns out to be good for the suffering news industry," columnist Michael Kinsley notes, it also forces the press to become his waiting attendant.[20] "At cocktail parties, on cable television, at the dinner table, at the water cooler," says the *New York Times*' Nicholas Kristof, "all we [reporters] talk about these days is Trump. So we complain about Trump being insular and parochial – but we've become insular and parochial as well. We've caught the contagion that we mock."[21]

This chapter focuses on the specifics of the Trump–media relationship, examining how the press covered the President and how he, in turn, covered them back. In some ways, the media have framed Trump as a landed baron and his supporters as mere vassals, thereby increasing the chasm between the public and the Fourth Estate. But Donald Trump also demonizes the media, so there is plenty of contentiousness to go around.

Covering the Monster

It will take many books, and perhaps a psychiatrist or two, to fully understand Donald Trump's relationship with the mainstream press. Each is fascinated with the other and each reviles the other. Why? There are overt and covert reasons. Overtly, Trump believes that the press is blatantly unfair to him; covertly, he is jealous of their influence. Overtly, reporters denounce Trump's disregard for the truth; covertly, they are jealous of his influence. Neither will admit to their neediness but it is there: (1) During the 2016 primaries, for example, Trump received 63 percent of the coverage in a bloated Republican field; (2) Trump also received 15 percent more coverage than Hillary Clinton during the general election; (3) despite her much-polished resumé, Clinton received less foreign policy coverage than Trump and her honorific ("Secretary of State") was mentioned less often than was her marital status; (4) not surprisingly, Trump maintained a crucial 5 percent edge in what people "have heard lately about the candidates" as a result of the extra coverage he received.[22]

Quantity of news coverage is one thing, quality another. Trump's coverage during the 2016 election was overwhelmingly sour, with CBS emphasizing the negative at a 9:1 ratio and even the *Wall Street Journal* providing four times as much bad news as good.[23] The press's drubbing of Trump continued when he assumed office. His ratio of positive-to-negative coverage was much lower than that of his three predecessors and, notably, issues of leadership and character were emphasized more often than they were for prior chief executives.[24] In many ways, says communication scholar Mike Ananny, the press has become an "anticipation industry," displaying an "inability to imagine politics without" Trump.[25]

Headlines are not preordained. Someone writes them. Consider, for example, a headline that appeared in the *Washington Post*: "President Trump Has Made 4,229 False or Misleading Claims in 558 Days." This headline contains no "breaking news" but it does make a factual charge in a professionally careful way. Consider another headline also appearing in the *Post*: "In a New Tweetstorm, Trump Gives His Voters the Middle Finger."[26] Here we see the difference between Old Journalism – evidence-based, restrained – and New Journalism, where everything hangs out. Donald Trump grew up on the edginess of the New York tabloids and so, on the very day he was elected president, he was already "a sore winner."[27]

As his young administration wore on, Trump went from attacking the press for spreading "fake news" to describing them – in the argot of Joseph Stalin and Mao Zedong – as "the enemy of the people." Doing so added thrust to Trump's emotional engine and it galvanized his followers. Anne Schulz and her colleagues report that Trumpers' anti-media attitudes sprang from two bedrock beliefs: (1) that all institutions ignore people like them and (2) that the "public opinion" reported in the press bears no resemblance to their own beliefs.[28] The press has kept the anti-media narrative alive, sometimes turning non-news into news, as when it reported that 89 percent of Republicans trusted Donald Trump more than CNN while 91 percent of Democrats felt the opposite.[29] Print reporters told such stories with barely concealed outrage, broadcasters with barely concealed lust.

Donald Trump's antipathies have caused the press to spin out of control. One especially popular trope has treated Trump as a demon from the underworld: "The Creature That Ate the GOP" (*Philadelphia Inquirer*); "Godzilla Wants the White House – and We Brought It on Ourselves" (*Sunday Times* [London]); "The Unstoppable Trump Monster" (*Atlantic*); "How the Republican Elite Created Frankentrump" (*Mother Jones*). Even a casual search of the Lexis-Nexis news database finds 646 pairings for *Trump* and *monster* between January 1, 2016, and election day vs. only 111 instances of *Clinton* and *monster*. What can that mean? Why did it happen?

Cultural studies scholars have investigated this matter of monstrosity. Their root premise is that monsters are frightening not because they are foreign to us but because they are similar – grotesquely similar. Trump-the-monster is commonly described in the press as a man whose ordinary traits – his rudeness, his shapeshifting, his volubility – are uncontrollable and hence dangerous. "Monsters teach us who or what we need to fear," says Edward Ingbretsen.[30] Monsters police our imaginations, doing exactly what they desire when they desire it, unchained from normal human constraints. Monsters tell us "who we are and how we are to live," says Ingbretsen; the monster "is a pedagogue; he or she teaches fear."[31]

Trump is the perfect monster: When will he spring forth? How obscene will he become? Monsters, says philosopher Slavoj Žižek, are especially appealing during liminal moments, when things are radically changing.[32] Donald Trump was a liminal candidate. He was a person from Reality Television, a place characterized by its grotesqueness and unpredictability. Trump also hailed from Manhattan, a land of wanton excess. He was therefore a Frankensteinian creature made of equal parts billionaire and populist. What reporter could resist such a story?

Like any good monster, Trump could not be killed. People like Marco Rubio and Karen McDougal, people like Michael Wolff and Robert Mueller, tried to do him in but he escaped, ready to frighten us once again. "We distrust and loathe the monster at the same time," says Jeffrey Cohen, but we also "envy his freedom," his utter unpredictability.[33] As a result, Trump has become an endless source of invention for Washington reporters, "a shocking creature whose very existence defies laws of science, society, and religion."[34] Trump regularly questions the research underlying global warming and he questions the moral necessity of welcoming immigrant families. He abhors institutions. He is a man apart. And yet he persists.

Covering the Monster's Retinue

All politicians want to be liked but many treat their supporters as a mere electoral necessity. Not Donald Trump. He adores his people almost as much as he adores himself. Before becoming president, Trump liked being recognized on the streets of New York, thereby proving that his TV ratings were real, that he was real. All of this amped up considerably during his run for the presidency. Dashing from rally to rally, saying too much and lingering too long, Trump boarded his campaign plane reenergized. People were his thing.

Members of the press also paid attention to Trump's supporters but not because they loved them. When tracking references to *Trump supporters* on the Lexis-Nexis news database, I found 9,352 such references between January 1, 2016, and November 30, 2016, but fewer than half as many allusions to *Clinton supporters* (n = 4,246). Such are the numbers. Here is what the numbers look like in the words of Marc Shapiro, a guest commentator for the *San Gabriel Valley Tribune*:

> Donald Trump is not the monster. He's not Jason, Freddy, Pinhead or Frankenstein. What he is, quite simply, is the manifestation of some very real zombies who follow him like lap dogs, cheer and boo on command and basically see in their psychological political creation the justification of every uneducated stereotype and racist attitude, and the willingness to believe anything that comes out of Donald Trump's mouth without, for a nanosecond, even stopping to consider that he might be full of crap.[35]

Mr. Shapiro's observations were not his alone. To get a broad understanding of how Trump's supporters were characterized, I downloaded print coverage from a great variety of newspapers, including elite sources as well as regional and local dailies. Using AntConc software, and with the assistance of a superb group of trained coders, I randomly selected 3,772 "windows" of news coverage. Each window consisted of the ten words preceding the phrase *Trump supporters* as well as the ten words following that phrase. Table 7.1 shows how Trump's supporters were "constructed" by the press.

Two-thirds of the coverage was devoted to analyzing Trump's supporters (their demography, their psychological state, their relationship to the issues), with considerably less space being given to what they

Table 7.1 Descriptions of *Trump Supporters* in Print News Coverage

Component	Specification	# mentioned	%
Supporters' roles		3,772	
	Object of analysis		65.9
	Source of action or opinion		34.1
Supporters' activities		1,535	
	Denouncing a person or group		36.2
	Praising a person or group		33.0
	Responding to questions		26.1
	Protesting a policy position		4.6
Supporters' moods		406	
	Angry or hostile		52.0
	Frustrated or afraid		24.6
	Hopeful or cheerful		15.5
	Feeling empowered		7.9
Supporters' issues		642	
	Jobs and the economy		22.1
	Illegal immigration		20.2
	Religious identity		15.6
	Racial disparities		13.9
	Unresponsive politicians		13.0
	International pressures		8.7
	Governmental inefficiency		3.1
	Sexual identity		1.7
	Healthcare		1.6
Supporters' qualities		637	
	Violent tendencies		28.1
	Uninformed or misguided		22.0
	Xenophobic or racist		14.3

Table 7.1 cont'd

Component	Specification	# mentioned	%
	Loyal and enthusiastic		12.1
	Surprisingly tolerant		11.3
	Biased or sexist		6.9
	Concerned about issues		5.3

Source: Coverage from January 1 through November 30, 2016, randomly selected from Lexis-Nexis database; n = 3,772 news reports.

did, less still to what they said (direct quotations were especially scarce). Mostly, the press laid Trump's supporters on the dissection table, poking them here and there but not really treating them as fully human. During the post-campaign period (i.e., November 9th through the 30th), the reportage became even more clinical, with 77.3 percent of the coverage speculating about why people would cast a ballot for Donald Trump but rarely asking them for an explanation (the post-campaign coverage contained even fewer direct quotes from Trump voters).

The "activities described" in the campaign reportage largely reflect the pro-and-con story the press tells so well. Emotionally, though, things were different. Trump supporters were described as either angry or hostile, a characterization that followed them into the Trump presidency itself. The energy Trump generated in supporters during his campaign rallies was often overlooked, with less than a quarter of the coverage capturing their enthusiasm. On the other hand, the press performed well when identifying policy matters important to Trump voters. The "issues mentioned" in Table 7.1 nicely parallel public opinion surveys and also point up the diversity of Trump's constituents – Rust Belt voters, evangelicals, and voters decrying open borders, as well as people fed up with traditional politicians and governmental inefficiency.

Seventeen percent of the press coverage contained either overt judgments – statements revealing the author's attitudes toward Trump supporters or, more commonly, statements attributing such viewpoints to third-party sources. Most of the judgments were roundly negative, often unconsciously so, and they fed directly into Trump's narrative of press bias. Examining such coverage shows why so many Americans have turned against the Fourth Estate. It is not just the know-it-all editorials that bother them but the taken-for-granted, "everyone knows" style of news coverage. They are disturbed by three refrains in particular:

- *Trump supporters are hopelessly provincial*: This theme holds that Trump supporters hail from "downscale communities" and are "in thrall to a vicious, selfish culture." Such people are said to "live in Trump's world of vanity, hate, arrogance, untruth, and recklessness." As result, they become "negative assets" incapable of processing new data and who, as a result, must resign themselves to joining in a "dance of the dunces."[36] According to Daniel Kreiss and his colleagues, many Trump supporters saw themselves portrayed in the media as ignorant Bible thumpers and as "white strangers in their own land."[37] Removed from civilization as they are, such people could not possibly see into the real Donald Trump, a man who embodies "all the dirty, embarrassing, mean-spirited little thoughts that pop into our brains."[38]

- *Trump supporters are highly gullible*: Because Trump supporters abhor modernity, they are "willfully hornswoggled, consciously choosing to ignore the truth."[39] Scholar Tony Perucci says the press treated the Trump campaign as performance art, portraying his supporters as mindlessly absorbing the phantasmagoria and with no native ability to distinguish between reality television and their healthcare benefits.[40] One commentator, Charles Blow of the *New York Times*, discovered Trumpers in the movie *Gladiator*. After quoting one of the Roman senators in the film – "Rome is the mob. Conjure magic for them and they'll be distracted. Take away their freedom and still they'll roar" – Mr. Blow adds a postscript: "Sounds like someone's supporters we know?"[41]

- *Trump supporters are morally degenerate*: This, of course, is the most upsetting characterization of the Trump voter but it appeared regularly. Rhetorically, the racist/sexist stereotype is irresistible – it draws on historical precedent (i.e., such people have been around since the Founding); it is narratively evocative (movies and TV shows have archived its themes); and it is wonderfully visual (angry, shouting people can be spliced into any news story). The racist voter often became a synecdoche for all Trump voters. Said a *Boston Globe* editorialist: "Those bent on understanding Trump supporters – as if there is something deep to understand – wonder how his working-class acolytes can vote against their own economic interests. What they refuse to see is that all Trump supporters, from the working class to the upper class, have voted their chief interest: maintaining American identity as white, Christian, and heterosexual."[42] There. Said that. Done.

Even though nothing – nothing – can be comprehensively said when half the U.S. electorate votes the same way, it is nonetheless said: "It was a combination of white racial resentment, old-fashioned racism and sexism as opposed to some vague type of 'economic insecurity' that motivated Trump's voters."[43] According to this logic, there was no overlap between Barack Obama's 69,498,516 votes in 2004 and Donald Trump's 62,984,828 votes in 2016, a logic that defies all forms of electoral mathematics. According to Zach Goldberg, such "broad-brush 'whitelash' interpretations allow the Left to demonize millions of Americans and dismiss their concerns." Should this continue, says Goldberg, "the appeal of the Democratic Party will forever be confined to cosmopolitan bubble-land."[44]

Voters are complex. During the blizzard of a national political campaign, it is easy for reporters to forget that. The election of Donald Trump surprised everyone, so one must look charitably at some of the coverage the campaign generated. Reporters did the best they could but the facts on the ground shifted constantly ("shy Trumpers" did not help in that regard). Nonetheless, the 2016 coverage too frequently drew on stereotypes of Trump voters. As the Trump presidency wore on, those stereotypes hardened, in part because of Mr. Trump himself. But exoticizing Trump supporters insults them and, worse, it keeps them mysterious. Political journalists must do better.

The Monster Strikes Back

Donald Trump took the savaging of his supporters personally but, then again, he took everything personally. As we see in Figure 7.1, he reliably did two things in his press conferences (n = 18): He made himself the centerpiece of every issue discussed, and he denied any stated or implied inadequacy. Often, he critiqued the questions asked of him as well as the reporters who asked them. Although it is said that all ex-presidents revile the press when leaving office, Trump got a head

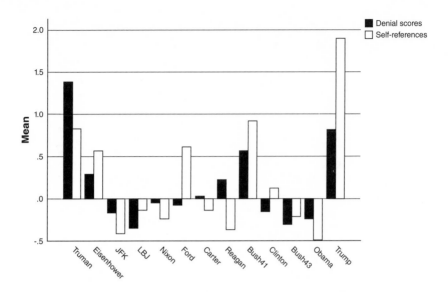

Figure 7.1 Denial Terms and Self-References Used in Presidential Press Interviews
Note: Based on inspection of 1,293 passages (656,600 words) uttered in press conferences from 1949 through 2017.
Source: Data from Campaign Mapping Project.

start. While he enjoyed teasing good coverage from the tabloid folks during his Manhattan days, he found the DC crowd to be a humorless bunch. So he made them the enemy of the people.

As we see in Table 7.2, Donald Trump was obsessed with anything he could not control. He talked about the press constantly, considerably more than Hillary Clinton. He was especially interested in the elite media and, once in office, that preoccupation continued. He once called ABC's Tom Llamas a "sleaze" and CNN's Jim Acosta "a real beauty."[45] He asserted that NBC's Lester Holt should be imprisoned for doctoring his coverage, and he told one female reporter, "I know you're not thinking. You never do."[46] Such insults played well with Republican audiences, only 9 percent of whom saw the *New York Times* as trustworthy (vs. 79 percent for Clinton supporters) and only 10 percent of whom trusted the *Washington Post* (vs. 67 percent for Clinton voters).[47] The media were Trump's "drug of choice," says Sam Nunberg, a former political advisor to Trump. "He doesn't drink," says Nunberg, and "he doesn't do drugs. His drug is himself."[48]

Table 7.2 Use of Media-Related Terms by Donald Trump vs. Hillary Clinton

Domains (*search terms*)	# Search terms	Trump 2015–2016 (531 speech and debate segments)		Clinton 2015–2016 (461 speech and debate segments)		Trump 2017 (247 speech segments)	
		n	%	n	%	n	%
Elite broadcast (*FOX, CNN, MSNBC, PBS*, etc.)	8	47	5.6	1	0.2	47	6.3
Generic broadcast (*media, networks, TV, audience, cameras*, etc.)	33	375	44.4	219	47.7	307	41.2
Elite print (*New York Times, Washington Post*)	2	137	16.3	48	10.5	68	9.1
Generic print (*newspaper, press, reporters, headlines, quotes*, etc.)	25	226	26.8	123	26.8	293	39.3
Generic online (*websites, tweets, podcast, bites*, etc.)	8	58	6.9	67	14.6	30	4.0
Total hits		843		458		745	
Hits/segment		1.58		0.99		3.01	

Source: Data from Campaign Mapping Project. Based on searches of speeches, ads, and debates during presidential campaigns from 1948 to 2016, n = 9,207 passages.

Trump is intimidated by the media – because of their visibility, longevity, and relentlessness – and he is jealous of them as well. As Michael Wolff reports, the New York media formerly treated Trump "as a wannabe and lightweight," a man who was "famous for being infamous" and who, as a result, only had "joke fame."[49] To combat this, Trump became his own publicist during the 2016 campaign, issuing "breaking news" and "editorials" nonstop. He also rhetorically reengineered the race: *journalism* became *fake news*; *Congress* was *The Establishment*; *sexual harassment* was mere *locker room talk*; *undocumented workers* were *aliens*; and the *electorate* was *us*. In addition, he constantly meta-campaigned:

Press is right over there, can you see them? Some of them are wearing little hats? I can't see, maybe. They all work for Hillary and they lie. They lie, folks. Lyin' press, that's what I call them. I do great things, perfect things, and they lie. They say I lost the debate. How can anyone say that? Hillary gets the questions ahead of time. Chris Wallace – who is a real loser, father would be ashamed, bad guy – was shining a laser pointer in my eyes. Camera didn't catch it. I wonder why? Did Hillary the Ripper have the cameraman murdered?[50]

Trump threw everything he had at the press, describing them as incompetent on Mondays, biased on Tuesdays, moneyed on Wednesdays, business failures on Thursdays, and unpatriotic on Fridays. Especially interesting was how the Trump people combined ideological attacks with performative assessments. Said former press secretary Sean Spicer: "We recognize that there's, you know, a few thousand readers or so left that still look at the *New York Times*, and so it's worth probably talking to them."[51] Trump himself once described *Saturday Night Live* as "sad," "unwatchable," and "not funny," charges that probably surprised the Nielsen folks.[52] Channeling her boss but unartfully so, Kellyanne Conway remarked that "if the mainstream media were a thriving private sector business that actually turned a profit," they would have "failed to protect their shareholders and their board members and their colleagues" and would have been driven out of business.[53]

Trump reinscribes the media's power when he is on the attack and that, too, enrages him. While he knows that Twitter is useful, he also knows that *that is only because the press shares his tweets*. In other words, the media hold Trump's mortgage. If they suddenly foreclosed on his social media outpourings, he would be just another fellow typing alone in the dark. Twitter expands Trump's bandwidth but it expands the press's bandwidth as well. The result is an unhappy chief executive who simultaneously courts and insults reporters, behavior that primatologist Jane Goodall sees as almost primate-like:

In many ways the performances of Donald Trump remind me of male chimpanzees and their dominance rituals ... In order to impress rivals, males seeking to rise in the dominance hierarchy perform spectacular displays: stamping, slapping the ground, dragging branches, throwing rocks. The more vigorous and imaginative the display, the faster the individual is likely to rise in the hierarchy, and the longer he is likely to maintain that position.[54]

This sort of thrashing about is vividly seen during press interviews. I selected nineteen such encounters for analysis, half from the campaign and half after election day. After the interviews were divided into four equal segments (see Figure 7.2a and b), a steady progression of the Paranoid Style emerged. While some progressions were more linear than others, *all* of the interviews showed much higher use of the Paranoid Style at the end than at the beginning. Trump either got "on message" as the interviews progressed or the press increasingly grated on him, thereby changing his behavior. In reality, both things probably happened.

Consider, for example, the presidential press conference of February 16, 2017. This was one of Mr. Trump's first formal events at the White House and it showed the Paranoid Style in action:

- *First quarter – Gentle teasing*: This morning, because many of our nation's reporters and folks will not tell you the truth, and will not treat the wonderful people of our country with the respect that they

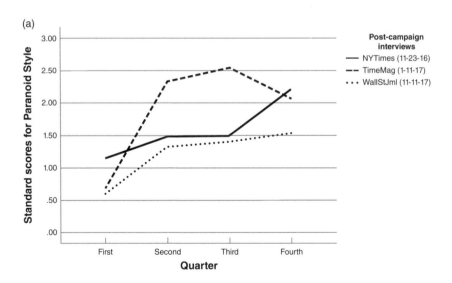

Figure 7.2a Paranoid Style during Selected Trump Press Interviews after the Campaign
Source: Data from Campaign Mapping Project.

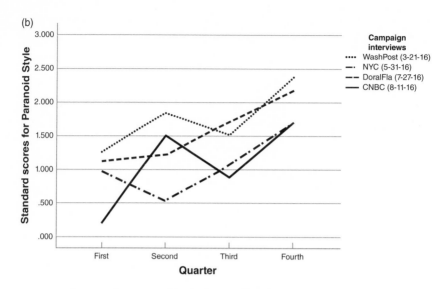

Figure 7.2b Paranoid Style during Selected Trump Press Interviews during the Campaign
Source: Data from Campaign Mapping Project.

deserve. And I hope going forward we can be a little bit – a little bit different, and maybe get along a little bit better, if that's possible. Maybe it's not, and that's OK, too.

- *Second quarter – Adding some bite*: The failing *New York Times* wrote a big, long front-page story yesterday. And it was very much discredited, as you know. It was – it's a joke. And the people mentioned in the story, I notice they were on television today saying they never even spoke to Russia. They weren't even a part, really – I mean, they were such a minor part. They – I hadn't spoken to them.
- *Third quarter – Drawing a line in the sand*: I don't mind bad stories. I can handle a bad story better than anybody as long as it's true and, you know, over a course of time, I'll make mistakes and you'll write badly and I'm OK with that. But I'm not OK when it is fake. I mean, I watch CNN, it's so much anger and hatred and just the hatred … You're not the only one so don't feel badly. But I think it should be straight. I think it should be – I think it would be frankly more interesting. I know how good everybody's ratings are right now but I think that actually – I think [they'd] actually be better. People – I mean, you have a lower approval rate than Congress.

- *Fourth quarter – In your face*: Are you a friendly reporter? Watch how friendly he is. Wait. Wait. Watch how friendly he is. Go ahead ... he said he was gonna ask a very simple, easy question. And it's not, it's not, not – not a simple question, not a fair question. OK sit down, I understand the rest of your question. So here's the story, folks. Number one, I am the least anti-Semitic person that you've ever seen in your entire life. Number two, racism, the least racist person. In fact, we did very well relative to other people running as a Republican – quiet, quiet, quiet – see, he lied about – he was gonna get up and ask a very straight, simple question, so you know, welcome to the world of the media. But let me just tell you something, that I hate the charge, I find it repulsive. I hate even the question because people that know me and you heard the prime minister, you heard Ben Netanyahu yesterday, did you hear him, Bibi? He said, I've known Donald Trump for a long time and then he said, forget it. So you should take that instead of having to get up and ask a very insulting question like that.[55]

We see here an admixture of anger and bravado, both an interpersonal reaction to the press's impertinence but also a playing-to-the-crowd. Trump often attacked other people and groups but none provided as much satisfaction for him as the press. Not surprisingly, his use of the Paranoid Style was (1) higher for his press encounters than for his speeches and debates and (2) higher as well versus his twelve immediate predecessors in office.[56]

The Paranoid Style was a natural one for Trump because he is by nature a "riffer." Often in his press encounters he will use one word (e.g., *Russia*) that triggers another word for him (e.g., *Mueller*) and then another (e.g., *Sessions*). Suddenly he is off to the races, slashing at everything (e.g., *the hearings*) and everyone (e.g., *the press*) in sight. By his very nature, says the University of Bremen's Elizaveta Gaufman, Trump thrives in a "carnival-like atmosphere" prizing overstatements, hyperpersonalization, reversals-of-logic, irreverence, and crudeness.[57] The press brings out the worst in Donald Trump; he is happy that it does so.

Conclusion

As the Trump administration brought its second year to a close, everyone was exhausted. Mr. Trump's supporters were tired of being underanalyzed and overpilloried. Mainstream reporters were tired of the cheap shots directed at them by the President. Voters became weary when cable news personalities applied yesterday's venom to today's news. Surprisingly, the only one who still seemed perky was Donald Trump. He roared into each news conference, never fully prepared to discuss the issues but always ready to dress down a reporter. Donald Trump loved the press. Donald Trump hated the press.

Doing so gave Trump intellectual focus – elites must be purged – as well as sociological appeal – he and the people were one. These were not Donald Trump's refrains alone, says Syracuse University's Kendall Phillips. They were part of an emerging "affective shift" in the nation found in such films as *American Sniper*, *Lone Survivor*, *Captain America*, and *Maze Runner*, where "the state is cast not as the bulwark against cruelty but as the source of cruelty. The imperiled citizens, usually white and threatened by the racialized Other, come to recognize that the state will not be a source of support or protection." Instead, says Phillips, "the state is depicted as uncaring and incompetent, as malevolent and manipulative, and as inherently untrustworthy."[58]

Trump gorged himself on such themes and for that reason, says Karin Wahl-Jorgensen, "Trump supporters seemed to be angry at nothing in particular. Instead, anger seems to be essential to their identity."[59] That, at least, was the story the mainstream press told but that cannot possibly be the whole story. Most Americans – including most Trump supporters – are "clocking in and out of work, sorting their grocery coupons, raising their children to respect others, and avoiding political news coverage," says Sarah Smarsh. "Media makers," Smarsh argues, "cast the white working class as a monolith and imply an old, treacherous story convenient to capitalism: that the poor are dangerous idiots."[60] When the media deploy such stereotypes, says Gary Abernathy, they fail to understand the people who read their coverage, people who simply want a fair shake.[61]

But Donald Trump also does a disservice when savaging reporters. A nation that loses trust in its messengers of truth is a nation at risk; a chief executive who abets that cause is no friend of freedom. "The preening, the boasting, the torrent of careless tweets and the avalanche of lies, the seemingly reckless assaults on pillars of the establishment," says stalwart reporter Ted Koppel, "provokes reactions that confirm precisely what Trump's most avid supporters already believe: The creatures of 'the swamp' belong to a secret society from which they are excluded."[62]

Both Trump and the press derive considerable advantage from their fractious relationship. The more they fight, the more cynicism they generate, and that attracts a certain kind of viewer. But when the sniping is over, who will be left to care about politics? Who will vote?

Two of the finest journalists in the nation – Jill Abramson and Jane Mayer – are particularly worried about the speed of today's news and about Trump's online mentality. While they offer no prescriptions for Mr. Trump (for obvious reasons), they do feel that demands for more information and less knowledge, for more sentiment and less engagement, are overstressing journalism. Having taken three years to write the definitive account of the Clarence Thomas–Anita Hill story (*Strange Justice*), Abramson and Mayer admonish their fellow reporters to slow down and not let Donald Trump set their pace:

> We realize what we are urging runs counter to the rhythms of the Internet and the impatient attention spans of readers who demand to know the news the instant it happens. But at a time when readers feel deluged by the onslaught of news alerts, and bombarded by fragments of Twitter-length items lacking context, characters, and comprehensive analysis, there is more need than ever for the kind of journalism that can connect the dots into meaningful coverage … In his influential 2011 book, *The Filter Bubble*, Eli Pariser asked a question that has only become a more urgent since: 'Is the truth loud enough?' It is up to us to make sure it is – not only by reporting and writing it – but also by differentiating it loudly and clearly from the rest of today's growing partisan brawl.[63]

Notes

1 Sara M. Moniuszko, "Stormy Daniels' 'Toad' Remark about Trump Mushrooms into Late-Night Jokes," *USA TODAY*, September 19, 2018. Accessed at www.usatoday.com/story/life/entertainthis/2018/09/19/stormy-daniels-compared-trump-toad-and-late-night-hosts-loved/1355358002/.

2 As quoted in Brian Steinberg, "Not so Funny? Late-Night's Trump-Fueled Humor Has Limits," *Variety*, June 8, 2018. Accessed at https://variety.com/2018/tv/news/late-night-tv-donald-trump-samantha-bee-crossroads-1202837365/.

3 As quoted in "Three Views: Is Colbert's Off-Color Trump Joke a Firing Offense?" *CNN.com*, May 7, 2017. Accessed at www.cnn.com/2017/05/06/opinions/stephen-colbert-gold-callan-cevallos/index.html.

4 Stephen J. Farnsworth, S. Robert Lichter, and Deanne Canieso, "Donald Trump and the Late Night Political Humor of Campaign 2016: All the Donald, All the Time," Paper delivered at the annual convention of the American Political Science Association, San Francisco, CA, September 2017.

5 As quoted in Steinberg, "Not so Funny? Late-Night's Trump-Fueled Humor Has Limits," *Variety*.

6 As quoted in Sarah Smarsh, "Dangerous Idiots: How the Liberal Media Elite Failed Working-Class Americans," *Guardian*, October 13, 2016. Accessed at www.theguardian.com/media/2016/oct/13/liberal-media-bias-working-class-americans.

7 Mollie Hemingway, "How Jon Stewart and 'The Daily Show' Elected Donald Trump," *The Federalist*, November 11, 2016. Accessed at http://thefederalist.com/2016/11/11/how-jon-stewart-and-the-daily-show-elected-donald-trump/.

8 Smarsh, "Dangerous Idiots," *Guardian*.

9 Ric Bailey, "When Journalism and Satire Merge: the Implications for Impartiality, Engagement, and 'Post-Truth' Politics. A UK Perspective on the Serious Side of U.S. TV Comedy," *European Journal of Communication*, 33:2 (2018), 200–13. One political scientist makes the interesting point that for all of its chest-beating, late-night humor can also disempower liberals by distracting them from more overt, consequential political action. See Patrick T. Giamario, "Beyond Liberal Laughter: Adorno and the Democratic Dangers of Laughing at Trump," Paper presented at the annual convention of the American Political Science Association, Boston, MA, September 2018.

10 Ashley Parker and Robert Costa, "The Narrator in Chief: Trump Opines on the 2020 Democrats – and So Much More," *Washington Post*, May 20, 2019. Accessed at www.washingtonpost.com/politics/the-narrator-in-chief-trump-opines-on-the-2020-democrats–and-so-much-more/2019/05/20/3a8da512-7688-11e9-bd25-c98955e7766_story.html?utm_term=.8f820c815a4a.

11 David Beard, "Is the 'Enemy of the People' Talk Working?" *Poynter.org*, August 8, 2018. Accessed at www.poynter.org/news/enemy-people-talk-working.

12 Art Swift, "Americans Remain Divided on Media's Coverage of Trump," *Gallup.com*, July 12, 2017. Accessed at https://news.gallup.com/poll/213902/americans-remain-divided-media-coverage-trump.aspx.

13 Jon Gabriel, "What Americans Care About vs. What the Media Cares About," *Ricochet*, July 18, 2017. Accessed at https://ricochet.com/archives/americans-care-vs-media-cares/.

14 See Jeffrey Gottfried, "Most Americans Already Feel Election Coverage Fatigue," *Pew Research Center*, July 14, 2016. Accessed at www.pewresearch.org/fact-tank/2016/07/14/most-americans-already-feel-election-coverage-fatigue/.

15 John Cassidy, "Steve Bannon's War on the Press," *New Yorker*, January 27, 2017. Accessed at www.newyorker.com/news/john-cassidy/steve-bannons-war-on-the-press.

16 As quoted in Jeet Heer, "The Post-Literate American Presidency," *New Republic*, September 23, 2017. Accessed at https://newrepublic.com/article/144940/trump-tv-post-literate-american-presidency.

17 Susan J. Douglas, "Trump vs. the Media: Who Will Win?" *In These Times*, March 17, 2017. Accessed at http://inthesetimes.com/article/19980/trump-vs-the-media-who-will-win.

18 See Amy Chozick, "Why Trump Will Win a Second Term," *New York Times*, September 20, 2018. Accessed at www.nytimes.com/2018/09/29/sunday-review/trump-2020-reality-tv.html.

19 Silvio Waisbord, Tina Tucker, and Zoey Lichtenheld, "Trump and the Great Disruption in Public Communication," in Pablo J. Boczowski and Zizi Papacharissi (eds.), *Trump and the Media* (Cambridge, MA: MIT Press, 2018), p. 31.

20 Michael Kinsley, "How Did We Do on the Trump Beat?" *New York Times*, January 20, 2018. Accessed at www.nytimes.com/2018/01/20/opinion/sunday/news-media-trump-beat.html.

21 Nicholas Kristof, "Our Addiction to Trump," *New York Times*, May 5, 2008. Accessed at www.nytimes.com/2018/05/05/opinion/sunday/trump-obsession.html.

22 For details about Trump's news coverage during the election, see Thomas E. Patterson, "News Coverage of the 2016 General Election: How the Press Failed the Voters," working paper, Harvard Kennedy School, December 7, 2016. Accessed at https://shorensteincenter.org/news-coverage-2016-general-election/; Diana Owen, "Twitter Rants, Press Bashing, and Fake News: the Shameful Legacy of Media in the 2016 Election," in Larry J. Sabato, Kyle Kondik, and Geoffrey Skelley (eds.), *Trumped: the 2016 Election That Broke All the Rules* (Lanham, MD: Rowman & Littlefield, 2017), pp. 167–80; Carrie Skulley, "'You Should Smile More!' Gender and Press Coverage of Candidates during the 2016 Presidential Primary," in Jeanine E. Kraybill (ed.), *Unconventional, Partisan, and Polarizing Rhetoric: How the 2016 Election Shaped the Way Candidates Strategize, Engage, and Communicate* (Lanham, MD: Lexington Books, 2018), pp. 59–80; Frank Newport and Andrew Dugan, "Americans Hear, Read and See More about Trump Than Clinton," *Gallup.com*, October 28, 2016. Accessed at https://news.gallup.com/opinion/polling-matters/196730/americans-hear-read-trump-clinton.aspx.

23 Peter VanAelst and Rens Vliegenthart, "The U.S. 2016 Election in the News: the Whole World is Watching," Paper presented at the annual convention of the International Communication Association, San Diego, CA, May 2017.

24 Amy Mitchell, "Covering President Trump in a Polarized Media Environment: A Comparison to Early Coverage of Past Administrations," *Pew Research Center*, October 2, 2017. Accessed at www.journalism.org/2017/10/02/covering-president-trump-in-a-polarized-media-environment/.

25 Mike Ananny, "Anticipating News: What Trump Teaches Us about How the Networked Press Can and Should Imagine," in Boczowski and Papacharissi (eds.), *Trump and the Media*, pp. 105, 107.

26 Glenn Kessler, Salvador Rizzo, and Meg Kelly, "President Trump Has Made 4,229 False or Misleading Claims in 558 Days," *Washington Post*, August 1, 2017. Accessed at www.washingtonpost.com/news/fact-checker/wp/2018/08/01/president-trump-has-made-4229-false-or-misleading-claims-in-558-days/?utm_term=.3d9dbd116e73; Greg Sargent, "In a New Tweetstorm, Trump Gives His Voters the Middle Finger," *Washington Post*, July 31, 2018. Accessed at www.washingtonpost.com/blogs/plum-line/wp/2018/07/31/in-a-new-tweetstorm-trump-gives-his-voters-the-middle-finger/?utm_term=.f9f2cad01ad6.

27 As quoted in Sean Hannity, "CNN's Anti-Trump Bias Embarrassing," *FoxNews.com*, November 30, 2016. Accessed at www.foxnews.com/opinion/sean-hannity-cnns-anti-trump-bias-embarrassing.

28 Anne Schulz, Werner Wirth, and Philipp Müller, "We Are the People and You Are Fake News: a Social Identity Approach to Populist Citizens' False Consensus and Hostile Media Perceptions," *Communication Research*, 45 (2018), 1–26. For additional commentary on popular media stereotypes of Trump, see Will Penman and Doug Cloud, "How People Make Sense of Trump and Why It Matters for Racial Justice," *Journal of Contemporary Rhetoric*, 8:1 (2018), 107–36.

29 Carla Herreria, "CNN Has the 'Trust' Advantage over President Trump in a New Poll," *Huffington Post*, July 4, 2017. Accessed at www.huffingtonpost.com/entry/more-americans-trust-cnn-than-trump-poll_us_595bc9e9e4b0da2c73258bf2.

30 Edward J. Ingebretsen, *At Stake: Monsters and the Rhetoric of Fear in Public Culture* (Chicago: University of Chicago Press, 2001), p. xvi.

31 Ibid., pp. 6, 153. The logical result of all this is the apocalypse, a theme that also pervades much of the journalism devoted to Donald Trump. See Trischa Goodnow, "Signs of the Apocalypse: an Analysis of Trump Magazine Covers during the 2016 Presidential Campaign," *American Behavioral Scientist*, 61 (2017), 1–10.

32 Slavoj Žižek, "Living in the Time of Monsters," *Counterpoints*, 422 (2012), 32–44.

33 Jeffrey Jerome Cohen, "Monster Culture: Seven Theses," in Jeffrey Jerome Cohen (ed.), *Monster Theory: Reading Culture* (Minneapolis: University of Minnesota Press, 1996), p. 17.

34 Debbie Jay Williams and Kalyn L. Prince, *The Monstrous Discourse in the Donald Trump Campaign* (Lanham, MD: Lexington Books, 2018), pp. 38–39.

35 Marc Shapiro, "Is Trump the Monster at Halloween?" *San Gabriel Valley Tribune*, October 30, 2016. Accessed at www.sgvtribune.com/2016/10/27/is-trump-the-monster-this-halloween-guest-commentary/.

36 The foregoing sentiments derive from a variety of news outlets collected in Stephen D. Cooper, "The Othering of Donald Trump and His Supporters," in Jim A. Kuypers (ed.), *The 2016 American Presidential Campaign and the News: Implications for American Democracy and the Republic* (Lanham, MD: Lexington Books, 2018), pp. 37, 39.

37 Daniel Kreiss, Joshua O. Barker, and Shannon Zenner, "Trump Gave Them Hope: Studying the Strangers in Their Own Land," *Political Communication*, 34 (2017), 474.

38 Patrick Fletchall, "This Halloween, the Scariest Monsters Are the Trump and Hillary inside Us All," *The Federalist*, October 11, 2016. Accessed at http://thefederalist.com/2016/10/11/halloween-scariest-monsters-trump-hillary-inside-us/.

39 Kurt Schlichter, "Trump Is Making Performance Art out of His Fans, But His Supporters Are Doing the Same to Him," *Independent Journal Review*, January 25, 2016. Accessed at https://ijr.com/.

40 Tony Perucci, "The Trump Is Present," *Performance Research*, 22:3 (2017), 127–35. Some scholars have become intrigued with the "feminized" aspects of reality television, a zone in which "authentic" emotions are both permitted and encouraged, thereby freeing participants from the masculine/formalistic rules of traditional public expression. See, for example, Diane Negra, Kirsten Pike, and Emma Radley, "Gender, Nation, and Reality TV," *Television and New Media*, 14:3 (2012), 187–93; Camilla A. Sears and Rebecca Godderis, "Roar Like a Tiger on TV? Constructions of Women and Childbirth in Reality TV," *Feminist Media Studies*, 11:2 (2011), 181–95. For a broader set of studies, see Geoff King (ed.), *The Spectacle of the Real: From Hollywood to "Reality" TV and Beyond* (Bristol, UK: Intellect Books, 2005).

41 Charles M. Blow, "Senators Save the Empire," *New York Times*, May 4, 2017. Accessed at www.nytimes.com/2017/05/04/opinion/senator-donald-trump.html. For additional commentary on the gullibility of the Trump voter, see Michael McDevitt and Patrick Ferrucci, "Populism, Journalism, and the Limits of Reflexivity: the Case of Donald Trump," *Journalism Studies*, 19:4 (2018), 512–26.

42 Charles Taylor, "Blunt Talk about Trump and His Supporters," *Boston Globe*, June 14, 2018. Accessed at www.bostonglobe.com/opinion/2018/06/14/blunt-talk-about-trump-and-his-supporters/eOoUZ8UHmmLSHEpHuShcYI/story.html.

43 Chauncey DeVega, "Can We Finally Kill Off the Zombie Lie? Trump Voters Mostly Weren't the 'White Working Class,'" *Salon*, June 7, 2017. Accessed at www.salon .com/2017/06/07/can-we-finally-kill-off-the-zombie-lie-trumps-voters-mostly-werent-the-white-working-class/.

44 Zach Goldberg, "Serwer Error: Misunderstanding Trump Voters," *Quillette*, January 1, 2018. Accessed at https://quillette.com/2018/01/01/serwer-error-misunder standing-trump-voters/.

45 As quoted in James Poniewozik, "Trump, 800-Pound Media Gorilla, Pounds His Chest at Reporters," *New York Times*, May 31, 2016. Accessed at www.nytimes .com/2016/06/01/arts/television/to-understand-trump-and-the-news-media-watch-the-clips-of-harambe-the-gorilla.html.

46 Jason Schwartz, "Trump to Reporter: 'I Know You're Not Thinking. You Never Do,'" *Politico*, October 1, 2018. Accessed at www.politico.com/story/2018/10/01/ trump-reporter-insult-854870.

47 Peter L. Francia, "'Going Public' in the Age of Twitter and Mistrust of the Media," in Jody C. Baumgartner and Terri L. Towner (eds.), *The Internet and the 2016 Presidential Campaign* (Lanham, MD: Lexington Books, 2017), p. 208.

48 As quoted in Evan Osnos, "How Trump Could Get Fired," *New Yorker*, May 8, 2017. Accessed at www.newyorker.com/magazine/2017/05/08/how-trump-could-get-fired.

49 Michael Wolff, *Fire and Fury: Inside the Trump White House* (New York: Henry Holt & Co., 2018), p. 73.

50 Donald J. Trump, "Campaign Remarks in Boynton Beach, Florida," October 24, 2016. Accessed at https://moody.utexas.edu/centers/strauss/campaign-mapping-project.

51 As quoted in Louis Nelson, "Spicer: President Trump Won't Be Beholden to Traditional Media Practices," *Politico*, December 29, 2016. Accessed at www.politico .com/story/2016/12/sean-spicer-donald-trump-media-press-conferences-233029.

52 Daniel Politi, "Donald Trump Has Now Criticized 'Biased' *SNL* Three Times on Twitter," *Slate*, December 4, 2016. Accessed at www.slate.com/blogs/the_slatest/2016/ 12/04/donald_trump_has_now_criticized_biased_snl_three_times_on_twitter.html.

53 As quoted in Jason Easley, "Kellyanne Conway Has an Epic Meltdown and Compares Donald Trump to Jesus," *PoliticusUSA*, January 27, 2017. Accessed at www .politicususa.com/2017/01/29/kellyanne-conway-epic-meltdown-compares-donald-trump-jesus.html.

54 As quoted in James Fallows, "When Donald Meets Hillary: Who Will Win the Debates?" *Atlantic*, April 12, 2017. Accessed at www.theatlantic.com/magazine/ archive/2016/10/who-will-win/497561/.

55 Donald J. Trump, "Full Transcript and Video: Trump News Conference," *New York Times*, February 16, 2017. Accessed at www.nytimes.com/2017/02/16/us/politics/ donald-trump-press-conference-transcript.html.

56 Statistical patterns for the Paranoid Style for Trump's campaign speeches = 3.6521; media interviews = 6.1499; campaign debates = 4.6457; F [2, 779] = 51.020, $p < 0.000$. Statistical patterns for the Paranoid Style for Trump's campaign speeches = 3.4946; for predecessors' campaign speeches = 0.3933; for Trump's Oval Office speeches = 0.3933; for predecessors' Oval Office speeches = -0.6097; F [3, 4373] = 229.183, $p < 0.000$.

57 Elizaveta Gaufman, "The Trump Carnival: Popular Appeal in the Age of Misinformation," *Interpersonal Relations*, 32 (2018), 1–20.

58 Kendall R. Phillips, "'The Safest Hands Are Our Own': Cinematic Affect, State Cruelty, and the Election of Donald J. Trump," *Communication and Critical/ Cultural Studies*, 15:1 (2018), 88.

59 Karin Wahl-Jorgensen, "Media Coverage of Shifting Emotional Regimes: Donald Trump's Angry Populism," *Media, Culture and Society*, 40:5 (2018), 775.

60 Smarsh, "Dangerous Idiots," *Guardian*.

61 Gary Abernathy, "Please, Big Media, Visit Us in Trump Country," *Washington Post*, November 9, 2017. Accessed at www.washingtonpost.com/opinions/please-big-media-come-visit-us-in-trump-country/2017/11/09/eccdaa54-c56a-11e7-84bc-5e285 c7f4512_story.html?noredirect=on&utm_term=.15d97d2db1ad.

62 Ted Koppel, "Trump Has Drawn Much of the Media into a Distortion of Their Traditional Roles," *Washington Post*, September 3, 2018. Accessed at www .washingtonpost.com/opinions/trump-has-drawn-much-of-the-media-into-a-distortion-of-their-traditional-roles/2018/09/03/f8046298-ad66-11e8-8a0c-70b618c98d3c_story .html?utm_term=.51a394101b32.

63 Jill Abramson and Jane Mayer, "The Press Has Never Been More Vital to the Survival of Democracy: 2018 Theodore H. White Lecture," Shorenstein Center on Media, Politics, and Public Policy, October 15, 2018. Accessed at https://shorenstein center.org/abramson-mayer/.

Part V
FEELING TIRED

8 TRUMP'S NOVELTY

Well after it ended, the 2016 presidential campaign remained enigmatic. What parallel universe could explain how Donald John Trump became the nation's forty-fifth chief executive? How could an experienced, supremely capable woman like Hillary Rodham Clinton be defeated? The punditocracy sputtered for a while after the final votes were tabulated but its explanations soon poured forth: The *Daily Wire*'s Aaron Bandler offered "Seven Reasons Trump Won," only to be outdone by *CNN*'s Gregory Krieg's "Twenty-Four Theories" for the election's outcome. The *BBC*'s Anthony Zurcher proved a piker, only able to adduce "Five Reasons Donald Trump Won" and was further embarrassed by Howard Gold's "Five *Huge* Reasons Donald Trump Won."[1] Still, Zurcher won the rhetorical war by declaring that Trump "had built a throne of skulls out of his Republican primary opponents."[2]

Today, the explanations for the 2016 election seem clearer: White men without college degrees felt economically disadvantaged and racially resentful and hence turned against the Democrats. Clinton could not match Barack Obama's appeal to minority voters, and sexism still reigned in the United States, especially within the working class. Trump was a business guy, so perhaps he would eliminate income inequality, some voters reasoned. Clinton was overly confident, not spending enough time campaigning in the Midwest. A series of disorderly nouns offered additional explanations for the contest's result: FBI, Twitter, Facebook, Russia, Opioids, Emails, Benghazi, Media, Rust Belt, Whitelash, Supremacists.

All of these matters were no doubt important but some make more macroscopic claims. Philosopher Slavoj Žižek, for example, has argued that global capitalism's disintegration of the welfare state had preordained a disruptive force like Donald Trump, showing how threadbare the "liberal capitalist consensus" had become in the United States.[3] Pollster Patrick Caddell also saw something more encompassing. "The old rules of politics are collapsing," said Caddell, and the deep-state establishment has run its course.[4] In other words, many Americans had become tired – tired of being attacked for their religious beliefs, tired of being called racist and xenophobic, tired of the elite media looking down on them. They were tired of traditional Democrats – hence the attractiveness of Bernie Sanders – and tired of traditional Republicans, especially after hearing that Trump would self-fund his campaign. "Trump made it clear to the American people," says blogger Jordan Kalinowski, "that he would not be running so he can shake hands with a Wall Street executive under the table while fooling American voters; he was running because he saw an America that needed him."[5]

This sort of "system weariness" hit Hillary Clinton with full force. "You have to understand," said Donald Trump on the campaign trail, "it's a rigged system and she's protected."[6] Trump's comments found a deep echo. Said North Carolina voter Pat Bullock: "Anybody but Hillary – I'd take an asteroid over Hillary." Said Deborah Phillips of Pennsylvania: "People are tired of the same-old same-old." Said Annie Linskey of Boston: "Obama was like a new car coming off the boat. This year you're buying a used car where you know all the problems."[7] One gets a sense of bone-weariness here, voters who cannot stand the thought of another insider. "Remember that in the recession, people were losing their homes," said Thomas Baldino of Pennsylvania's hard-hit Luzerne County, "and [Clinton's] giving speeches and taking money from the banking establishment. Those kinds of memories are long here."[8]

Research has found that economic distress per se had no nationwide influence on the outcome in 2016 (although it did affect certain locales), suggesting that something deeper, something cultural, was feeding Americans' weariness.[9] Even though Barack Obama still had high approval ratings on the eve of the 2016 election, voters were "angry about the political system and dismayed at the country's direction."[10] In an important study, political scientist John Sides and his colleagues have argued that nothing less than *American identity* was at stake in the campaign, reflecting cleavages of race, religion, and citizenship status. The campaign was not just about who should occupy the Oval Office, they argued, but about what the United States should become.[11]

While economic and demographic factors were no doubt important, I believe that the candidates' *personal identities* – and Donald Trump's novelty in particular – were also influential. Like Sides and his colleagues, I base my argument on public opinion polls funded by the National Science Foundation and overseen by scholars at the University of Michigan and Stanford University. While the American National Election Studies (ANES) produce a rich set of quantitative findings, they also make available interviewees' spontaneous reactions to researchers' questions such as "What do you think of candidate X?" Often these responses amount to only a word or two (e.g., "inexperienced," "sexist") but sometimes they ramble on for several hundred words. Many of the responses are blunt (e.g., "unlike her, he's not a felon"), others charming (e.g., "Melania would make a great First Lady"), and still others plaintive (e.g., "I know Donald has Christ in his heart").

Collectively, proffered reactions to Trump in the 2016 ANES surveys produced 490,449 words, while the Clinton corpus was slightly smaller (433,360 words). The ANES survey in 2016 only tapped the feelings of registered Republicans, but even that limitation produced a tremendous range of feelings about candidates Clinton and Trump. Of those offering opinions, 1,847 individuals made positive comments about Donald Trump while 2,907 were more negative; Hillary Clinton's proportions were strikingly similar: 1,938 had positive things to say about her, with 2,597 denouncing her. These proportions reflect what numerous other studies have shown: Trump and Clinton were the most "strongly disliked" candidates running for the presidency between 1980 and the present. Other research indicates that they were also the "least-trusted" candidates in recent years.[12]

To make systematic sense of the open-ended responses, and after carefully perusing the respondents' transcripts, I generated a series of word lists (or dictionaries) to guide computerized inspection of their remarks. So, for example, to quantify how often Trump was described as a "successful businessman," I built search files containing such tokens as *background, experience, skills, prosperous, financial*, etc.

Naturally, there is a certain arbitrariness to any such clustering procedure since (1) words are multi-meaningful and (2) a given statement can make multiple, even competing, claims (e.g., "Trump has built a lot of sky-scrapers but he hates the unions"). Analyzing words independent of context cannot tell us everything we need to know but it can call attention to overall patterns that might escape even the most perceptive observer.

Happily, the overall results conform rather well to what other researchers have found, but they have the added benefit of honoring the subtlety and individuality embedded in respondents' spontaneous remarks. Overall, my findings show this: The 2016 presidential campaign was about many things – guns and butter, nativism and collectivism – but mostly it was about the candidates themselves, the candidates-as-persons.

National Identity in 2016

As the midterm elections of 2018 rolled around, the American people were told that the campaign would fundamentally redefine the nation. The bombast of the current chief executive, they were told, would lead to tyranny unless people acted quickly. Nonsense, said Mr. Trump's supporters. The country was indeed redefining itself but doing so by becoming a true meritocracy freed of the nanny state's whinings. All the nation needed on November 6, 2018, both sides agreed, were enough votes to ensure the nation's rightful destiny.

People in the United States had been told such things before. There has always been something incomplete, something anticipatory, about the United States. The country's romanticism ("a nation of ideas") and its bewildering diversity ("one nation under God") have left it searching for an essential self. Its founding in 1776 failed to provide sufficient clarity, and the war between the states added to the cultural uncertainty. Freeing the slaves, emancipating women, and per-mitting gay marriage were historic achievements, but they also made the nation seem mottled and formless to many. The Louisiana Purchase, the Manhattan Project, and Apollo 11 promised to reinvent the United States but the Great Depression, the Kennedy assassination, and 9/11 destabilized things once again. In light of these momentous events, the 2018 midterms seemed trivial and yet some saw them as a final sorting-out of "real Americans and fake Americans."[13]

All of us live in the moment, few of us in history, so we can be forgiven for overembellishing our moment-in-time. Still, the 2016 presidential race – and the midterms in 2018 – clearly featured questions of identity. "This is not who we are," Barack Obama said during the early Trump years, urging his "fellow Americans to reject the exclusionary policies and America-first posturing" of people on the Right.[14] "A globalist is a person that wants the globe to do well, frankly, not caring about our country so much," Mr. Trump retorted.[15] A great many Americans "see themselves more as settlers than as immigrants," the *New York Times'* Ross Douthat says, "identifying with the Pilgrims and the Founders, with Lewis and Clark and Davy Crockett and Laura Ingalls Wilder."[16] Trump's ascent, Douthat believes, was "an attempt to restore their story to pre-eminence" but it is "a restoration attempt that can't succeed because the country has changed too much."[17]

Recent political campaigns have found clear-cut divisions in the nation: an overwhelmingly white, older, evangelical, and declining heartland vs. a growing, wealthy, better-educated, and more diverse network of large cities. While suburbanites counteracted Trumpism during the midterms, the Republicans held their own in the rural United States but their success could only last so long. More dark-skinned Democrats were being born each day. Republican babies? Not so much. For reasons such as these, the 2016 election made questions of identity especially prominent. There are many reasons why.

Region

Victoria Sanders, a remarkably perceptive undergraduate at Bob Jones University, has argued that hate didn't elect Donald Trump, people did. A fifth of the children living in poverty live in rural areas, Sanders notes. Rural Americans have lower life expectancies, are more likely to suffer from alcoholism and depression, and live in heavily polluted, formerly industrialized areas. To dismiss such people as deplorable, Sanders observes, overlooks the fact that desperation drove many of them into the Republican camp. Other than Trump, Sanders says, "no one has listened to these communities' cries for help."[18]

Given the rural/urban divide, *Vox* columnist Sean Illing sees the United States now split between what he calls "nativist" and "identitarian" communities, each of which "defines itself in opposition to the other." "They live in different worlds," Illing notes, "desire different things, and share almost nothing in common."[19] It is not so much that people do not trust government, says Duke University's Timur Kuran, it is that they no longer trust one another.[20] A great many small, isolated "red" enclaves on the one hand; fewer, but massive, "blue" areas on the other. Such was the United States of America when Donald Trump ran for the presidency.

Race

Race and region are often intertwined but the 2016 campaign had a racial component independent of where one lived. In contrast to prior Republican orthodoxy, Trump went full bore against minority communities. "The script of shared American values of self-reliance, hard work, and moral fortitude," says Fairfield University's Gwendoline Alphonso, "had long relied on negative racial imagery to depict (and pathologize) the negative values of immorality, dependency, and criminality."[21] Trump's contrast of "work" and "entitlement" became an oblique way of attacking African-Americans. Lauding "Angel Moms," whom Trump described as "mothers of American children killed by illegal immigrants," brought Hispanics into the picture, albeit negatively. In the waning days of the 2018 midterms, Mr. Trump reintroduced these tropes to what many observers said was considerable effect.

Trump's exploitation of the racial divide began with "Birtherism" in 2011 when he first called Barack Obama's political paternity into question, but it is also true, according to the *Atlantic*'s Adam Serwer, that "had racism been toxic to the American electorate, Trump's candidacy would not have been viable."[22] In other words, says Serwer, "Trump's great political insight was that Obama's time in office inflicted a profound psychological wound upon many white Americans," an indication that cultural forces, not just Trump's insensitivity, were influential in 2016.[23] White voters high on the "racial resentment scale," says Emory University's Alan Abramowitz, preferred Donald Trump by a margin of 73 percent to 22 percent for Hillary Clinton.[24] In many ways, Mr. Trump was pushing on an open door when making coded racism part of his campaign strategy.

Class

While the effects of class and race are often conjoined, they can diverge as well. Trump's appearance on *The Apprentice*, says Joshua

Green, made him strangely appealing to working-class African-Americans who saw themselves as budding entrepreneurs.[25] In contrast, Trump's anti-immigrant message connected with white blue-collar workers even as it alienated those of Latino descent. In many ways, though, some of Trump's unorthodox political positions – protecting Social Security and Medicare benefits, defending Planned Parenthood, restricting free trade, avoiding foreign entanglements, and building a wall – sprang directly from his interactions with ordinary Americans. "Trump arrived at these heterodox views," says Green, "by doing exactly what politicians were supposed to do: listening to voters."[26]

That Trump was able to attract blue-collar workers in 2016 speaks to the intricacy of the American fabric. "In the Gilded Age," says scholar Mary Stuckey, "good citizens were good workers, and good workers made for good citizens," and that made sense to Trump as well as to many working-class Americans.[27] The University of Pennsylvania's Diana Mutz has found that *status threat* – the fear of losing out to a rising tide of the newly enfranchised – spoke to workers' growing sense of psychological displacement and not just to fears of economic dislocation.[28]

Partisanship

All of the preceding variables factor into Americans' party allegiances. As we see in Table 8.1, the 2016 presidential race was strikingly orthodox. When Trump's and Clinton's remarks were searched for "Democratic" and "Republican" tokens, the results were clear-cut: Donald Trump talked like a Republican and Hillary Clinton like a Democrat.[29] Interestingly, though, these results differed from historical trends. While the "Democratic" words do in fact distinguish Ds from Rs in most elections, they do so only modestly. The "Republican" words, in contrast, were used by members of both parties with equal frequency.[30] All candidates, it seems, want a dynamic economy housed in a safe and secure nation.

In an important book, *Neither Liberal nor Conservative: Ideological Innocence in the American Public*, Donald Kinder and Nathan Kalmoe argue that party allegiances are now more culturally driven than ideologically driven.[31] Americans are no longer divided into clear, competing philosophical camps – Big Government people over here, Liberty & Security people over there. Instead, the reverse is true:

Table 8.1 Use of Party-Stereotypical Terms by Donald Trump vs. Hillary Clinton

Type	Tokens (search terms)	Clinton rank (out of 26)	Trump rank (out of 26)	Highest	Lowest
"Democratic" terms	Caretaking (friendship, fairness, opportunity, support, etc.)	5	12	Kerry	Kennedy
	Family (children, household, father, women, etc.)	3	26	Gore	Trump
	Growth (educate, schools, seniors, nurture, etc.)	6	15	Gore	Goldwater
	Labor (workers, job, salaries, livelihood, etc.)	8	21	Kerry	Stevenson
"Republican" terms					
	Economy (dollars, budget, economy, investing, etc.)	19	12	McCain	Nixon
	Capacity (best, important, strong, win, etc.)	16	1	Trump	Goldwater
	Quantity (amount, lots, hundreds, percent, etc.)	17	2	Dole	Stevenson
	Security (criminal, destroy, foreign, invasion, etc.)	24	1	Trump	Kennedy

Source: Data from Campaign Mapping Project. Based on searches of speeches, ads, and debates during presidential campaigns from 1948 to 2016, n = 9,207 passages.

People decide what they are (culturally) and then slot their beliefs into the two available categories. Educated white women and blue-collar white men are now moving in different directions, with the former trending Democratic and the latter Republican. These dynamics were witnessed during the 2016 presidential race as well as during the midterms two years later.

Other Factors

Cultures are complex things. Religion, for example, often impacts politics but it does so in curious ways. White evangelicals found themselves in the Trump camp but not always comfortably. The more often a Trump Republican went to church, for example, the less likely he or she was to embrace identitarian politics or to take populist stands.[32] Church-going Republicans were also more racially tolerant than infrequent church-goers. Age and education also affected things. Young evangelicals, for example, were particularly torn during the 2016 campaign, with many of them canceling out their parents' votes because of Donald Trump's misogyny and ethnocentrism. Similarly, having a college degree "supercharged" the divide among white voters, say Brian Schaffner and his colleagues, in part because better-educated people find themselves in more diverse and open-minded work environments.[33] In contrast, "Trump won white voters without college degrees by a net 50 points among men and 23 points among women."[34]

"As often as Americans have imagined that they inhabit a country of ideas," says legal scholar Jedediah Purdy, "many have insisted instead that it is a nation of identity, a land of blood and soil, more about who you are than about what you affirm."[35] The 2016 presidential campaign brought all this to a head, with issues of class, race, religion, education, and region swirling about one another. That drove pollsters crazy: Who were these Americans? Where had they come from? Where were they going? Michael Paterniti has written, "we remain many chaotic minds at once, a cacophony that sometimes resolves to symphony and then distortion again."[36] Paterniti was describing but one state here, Maine, but he may as well have been speaking of the nation itself.

Hillary Clinton and Donald Trump did their best to sort through this cultural uncertainty in 2016. They spoke of the nation as if it were an accomplished thing when, in fact, it was shifting beneath their feet. Added to that complexity were the candidates themselves. As in all campaigns, they sought to "construct" themselves for voters and to ward off rival constructions. It is to these issues of management that we now turn.

Personal Identity: Hillary Clinton

Hillary Clinton and Donald Trump were perhaps the best-known pair to have run for the American presidency since the Founding. They were celebrities as well as politicians. Earlier campaigns had also featured celebrities – Dwight Eisenhower in 1952 and Ronald Reagan in 1980 – but they squared off against entirely conventional politicians. Clinton and Trump were different. Both had been in the public eye for so long that it seemed that nothing new could be learned about them. Hillary and The Donald had star power.

Table 8.2 is embarrassingly simple but also telling. It is based on a portion of the documents housed in the Campaign Mapping Project – news coverage and letters to the editor – a corpus now amounting to some 20 million words. The table records the ratio of last-name to first-name references made during the initial campaigns that brought each American president to the White House. Generally speaking, the table shows that last-name references were the press's norm for most of the candidates but not all. *Jack*, *Ike*, and *Dick* broke through and the former two also resonated among ordinary letter writers, where they were joined by *LBJ*, *George*, and *Bill*. In some cases, the vice-presidency increased the candidates' familiarity but the letter writers embraced Dwight Eisenhower and Bill Clinton right from the start.

Donald performed about average but *Hillary* outpaced everyone. Being on a first-name basis with the American people might seem like a godsend but it can also be diminishing. As CNN's Peggy Drexler says, "While Clinton is arguably more widely known than any of her to-date opponents, she's also a former U.S. senator and secretary of state. She's not Beyoncé ... Calling Clinton by her first name serves to, at best, reinforce gender and workplace stereotypes – that women need to be 'approachable,' not abrasive or aloof, in order to get the job done and be liked while doing it."[37]

Ms. Drexler's observations were made on April 14, 2015, two days after Mrs. Clinton declared her presidential candidacy. By the time the campaign got underway, the citizenry (in the form of ANES survey

Table 8.2 Last-Name/First-Name Ratios for Selected Presidential Candidates

Year	Candidate	Ratios for print news stories (n = 22,295)	Ratios for citizens' letters (n = 11,276)
1948	Harry Truman	29.52	16.90
1952	Dwight (Ike) Eisenhower	2.72	1.71
1960	John (Jack) Kennedy	6.86	8.49
1964	Lyndon (LBJ) Johnson	18.02	3.32
1968	Richard (Dick) Nixon	7.25	13.16
1976	Jimmy Carter	63.67	18.44
1980	Ronald (Ron) Reagan	191.15	62.25
1988	George H. W. Bush	42.10	4.80
1992	William (Bill) Clinton	21.10	3.11
2000	George W. Bush	34.07	11.92
2008	Barack Obama	117.12	44.52
2016	Donald Trump	37.65	14.46
2016	Hillary Clinton	2.44	1.32
	Average	44.12	15.72

Source: Data from Campaign Mapping Project.

respondents) was also ready. When examining what voters said about Clinton, one hears an admixture of intimacy and cruelty. Voters pored over *Hillary*'s sex life (or lack thereof) and speculated about the size of her pantsuits.[38] They criticized her daughter's sense of *noblesse oblige*, and many accused Hillary of having abetted Bill's serial infidelities.

The difference in ratios for Trump and Clinton in Table 8.2 is telling: Although Americans were inclined to think of *Donald* as a member of the family (a flamboyant uncle, perhaps), they knew *Hillary* far better because women are presumptively easier to know. Mrs. Clinton understood that double standard:

> In my experience, the balancing act women in politics have to master is challenging at every level, but it gets worse the higher

you rise. If we're too tough, we're unlikeable. If we're too soft, we're not cut out for the big leagues. If we work too hard, we're neglecting our families. If we put family first, we're not serious about the work. If we have a career but no children, there's something wrong with us, and vice versa. If we want to compete for a higher office, we're too ambitious. Can't we just be happy with what we have? Can't we leave the higher rungs on the ladder for men?[39]

Table 8.3 categorizes the various open-ended comments expressing some amount of appreciation for Hillary Clinton. Not unexpectedly, her political experience took center stage but that proved to be both a strength and a weakness. While Clinton knew more about everything than Donald Trump did, her competence left few details for voters to fill in on their own. Also, being *Hillary* and being *not-Trump* are different. As we saw in Chapter 7, Clinton often struggled during the fall debates to feature her own priorities, so unsettling was the marauding presence of Donald Trump.

It is also surprising that the author of the phrase "It takes a village" generated only modest scores on "Cares for all Americans" and "Protects minority rights." Who had done more than Hillary Clinton to call attention to the need for universal healthcare, to increasing violence against women, to problems with adoption and foster care laws, and to the need for increased benefits for wounded veterans? Table 8.3 also indicates that two of Clinton's strongest suits – continuing the Obama legacy and breaking through the glass ceiling – did not resonate strongly even for open-minded Republicans.

When examining the specific remarks of those who had something good to say about Clinton, one senses commitment without passion: "She's for the middle class; she's not for the rich like the other one is." "She is for us and trying to get stuff we never had." "She likes kids and poor people." "She wants to pull us all together and not divide us." Clearly, these are endorsements but they are pale ones. "She tells the truth most of the time," said one respondent. "Level-headed; won't set the country on fire," said another. One also hears a great deal of temporizing: "Tries to be a good person." "Ability not to be a jackass in public." "She does not look like she wants to be a star."

Even worse, Clinton's experience was often conflated with her husband's track record, sometimes joyously: "There's nobody better to

Table 8.3 Survey Respondents' Positive Comments about Hillary Clinton

Approving Comments (n = 1,938; corpus = 186,048 words)			
Argument strings	# coded words	% coded words	Sample search terms
Vast experience	1,997	32.8	*Competent, diplomatic, experienced, government, international, leader, qualified, senator, service*
Not Donald Trump	851	14.0	*Corrupt, crazy, extreme, dishonest, evil, idiot, liar, rich, Trump, unstable*
Attractive policy positions	784	12.9	*Agenda, beliefs, education, healthcare, issues, platform, positions, programs, stance, values*
Admirable personal qualities	705	11.6	*Calm, control, good, honest, integrity, knowledgeable, personality, rational, smart, strong, trust*
Cares for all Americans	645	10.6	*Americans, cares, children, community, feels, help, people, social, support, us*
Continue Obama legacy	491	8.0	*Democrat, economy, husband, jobs, liberal, Obama, progressive, working, wages*
Time for a woman	423	6.9	*Abortion, ceiling, choice, deserving, female, lady, time, woman, women's*
Protect minority rights	198	3.2	*Black, diversity, equality, Hispanics, immigration, LGBTQ, minorities, rights, racial*

Source: From searches of open-ended comments, 2016 American National Election Study.

have on your bench that someone that has had the job. In a crisis, we have a good team." At other times, the respondents were dismissive even while being supportive: "Bill was the closest to a genius that we have ever had in the White House. So if Hillary screws up, Bill will straighten her up."

The *Hillary/Trump* comparisons were also not an unalloyed boon for Clinton: "She's not Trump; her daughter is not a mess."

"I don't care who is running against Trump; I would vote for anyone with a pulse." "Relative to Donald Trump, she is sane." Missing here are qualities people admire in a loved one. Occasionally one finds references to Clinton's biographical self – "she may do things from a mother's perspective; she helps the young and cares about the children" – but she was more often treated representationally: "Being a lady would be a good story for the U.S. that may bring lots of honor and opportunity for the females."

Remarks made by Clinton's detractors were often scabrous. As we see in Table 8.4, more than half the comments dealt with scandal, deception, and her wayward husband. Occasionally a policy issue would peek through ("I don't think she's good for the working man; I think she's for handouts"; "She's a criminal and likes to kill babies") but mostly one finds ad feminams: "She's as corrupt as the devil himself." "The only time you can tell if she's lying is when her mouth is open." 'The most corrupt and evil person ever to run for high office in the U.S." Sometimes, the commentators dipped into popular culture: "She comes across as a 'mean girl.'"

The criticisms were also disestablishmentarian. "She's all bought up," said one respondent. She has a "sense of entitlement," said another. And there were more: "It's troubling that two families, namely the Bushes and the Clintons, would be in charge of America for 28 years." "Family history of making her fortune in political dealings." Interestingly, many of the respondents traced Hillary's flaws to those of her husband: "If she is pro-woman she wouldn't be covering up all the crap her husband has been doing all these years."

Not surprisingly, many of the criticisms were gendered: "I think women are overstepping their boundaries; I can see equal pay and all that but I can't see women taking total command." "She can wear pants but sooner or later she will have to wear a dress." But even more troubling was the fusion of policy issues with aspects of personality: "She praises the minorities just for the vote; she has this fake smile; she will stab you in the back." "Illegal activities in the Clinton Foundation; probably has Parkinson's Disease, having seizures and falling down." "Don't like her outlook on gun control and abortion and her attitude in general; her presence, her body language."

An old pro like Hillary Clinton had heard all of this before. But here is one criticism she should have heeded more often: "I don't like the way she's always making fun of Trump instead of telling us her plans."

Table 8.4 Survey Respondents' Negative Comments about Hillary Clinton

Disapproving Comments (n = 2,597; corpus = 249,312 words)			
Argument strings	# coded words	% coded words	Sample search terms
Serial deceiver	2,075	28.0	*Baggage, cheat, deceit, dishonest, hypocrite, liar, phony, secrets, shady, transparency, untrustworthy*
Scandal and corruption	1,635	22.1	*Accusations, Benghazi, corruption, criminal, crooked, email, fraud, investigation, partnership, scandal, thief*
Ignores average Americans	1,128	15.3	*America, banks, class, country, corporations, everyone, middle, national, people, public, support*
Dangerous policy positions	976	13.2	*Abortion, borders, Christianity, decisions, deficit, guns, issues, military, policies, stand, taxes, wall, war*
No leadership skills	651	8.8	*Commander, conflicts, foreign, incompetent, judgment, knowledge, leader, president, weak, understanding*
Insider politician	566	7.7	*Career, change, connections, establishment, interests, politician, power, system, Washington*
Sordid family history	481	6.5	*Background, Bill, Clintons, family, history, husband, lifelong, past, record, years*
Leftist ideology	391	5.3	*Bernie, Democrats, gender, healthcare, illegals, liberal, media, Muslims, Obama, racial, socialist*

Source: From searches of open-ended comments, 2016 American National Election Study.

Post-campaign research has found that (1) Clinton launched many more negative tweets than Trump, (2) her paid advertising was also more castigatory as were (3) her campaign emails, and (4) she found it hard to replicate her buoyancy during the primary debates when going face-to-face with Trump.[40] Habitually, Clinton's tendency was to bristle: "I've had my disagreements with Republicans. I might have disagreed on policies or principles, but I've never doubted their fitness to serve in this office. Donald Trump is different, and that's why there is so much at stake in this election. He has a dark and divisive vision for America that could tear our country apart."[41]

Unlike the suffragist Elizabeth Cady Stanton, Clinton had a hard time turning a large, faceless mass into "an implied intimate."[42] She "is someone so interested in solving problems," says the Brookings Institution's Elaine Kamarck, "that she skips right past the emotions."[43] When sampling the candidates' followers on Reddit, researchers found that Trump scored well on both "male" and "female" traits but that Clinton scored well only on the "male" characteristics.[44] Earlier research in the 2008 campaign showed something similar: Clinton's toughness made her seem removed from the lives of ordinary Americans.[45] Although studies have shown that women are predisposed to "display empathy toward distressed others in society," that proved difficult for Clinton despite her celebrated commitment to such issues.[46]

Clearly, women are cross-pressured when trying to marry emotion with policy. Performance coach Joel Silberman notes that "the most frightening sound" to many men "is their mother's voice in a certain tone," sensations that Hillary Clinton consistently evoked.[47] She understood all of that. "I love to wave my arms," Clinton once said, "but apparently that's a little scary to people. And I can't yell too much. It comes across as 'too loud' or 'too shrill' or "too this' or 'too that,' which is funny, because I'm always convinced that the people in the front row are loving it."[48] Hillary Clinton could overwhelm anyone with her knowledge of governmental affairs but voters were in the market for something else in 2016 – novelty and personality – a combination foreclosed to Clinton.[49]

Political campaigns cannot possibly reveal the essence of a politician but voters feel otherwise, confident in their ability to gauge candidates from a distance. Still, Hillary Clinton did her best. "I'll be glad to take [a selfie] with you," she once said, "but I think selfies come at a cost. Let's talk instead. Do you have something you want to share? I want to hear it ... I'd love to know your name and where you're from and how things are going with you."[50] This entreaty is found in Clinton's campaign biography and reflects the Hillary who wished-to-be. Sadly for her supporters, it was not the Hillary perceived-to-be.

Personal Identity: Donald Trump

Covering the 2016 presidential campaign was an endless struggle for the nation's reporters. They were not built for a Trump campaign. Journalists are serious people, adept at discerning candidates' worldviews. "Trump did not set out to sell voters on an ideological vision or a coherent menu of policies," say Texas A&M's David Fortunato and his colleagues. Instead, he "diverted attention from conventional political criteria for candidate evaluation."[51] One news report (ostensibly meant to disparage Trump's stance on immigration) inadvertently revealed Trump's strength. Its authors quote California-based pastor Samuel Rodriguez, who noted that Trump's "commitment to building a wall and stopping illegal immigration was very rigid ... but the moment I brought up dreamers, everything shifted. In fact, at one point he brought up the fact that he was a father and a grandfather."[52]

Trump's supporters often keyed on revelations like these, engaging in a kind of "magical realism ... where the marvelous seems to grow organically within the ordinary, blurring the distinction between them."[53] So, for example, how might a Trump supporter explain away Trump's lecherous comments about women's bodies? This is how: "He has a wife and daughter, so I believe that somewhere down the line, he understands the needs of a woman. And though he might have said those remarks, I don't think he really meant them in, like, a harmful way or anything like that."[54]

This sort of "double-listening" was found throughout the election. Trump's platform was Trump, not some airy world of ideas. "Political campaigns are usually sober, dull affairs," says author Allen Frances, "but for those who loved him, Trump's daily antics and baroque lies made politics fun again."[55] Trump bodied forth his campaign. Literally. When perusing voters' commentaries, one was struck by a metaphor tapping that most preposterous of all things – Donald Trump's heart: "He has our best interests at heart." "He speaks from the heart." "His heart is in the right place." And even: "He shoots from the heart." Because his heart was pure, Trump "appeared in public guilt-free."[56]

Table 8.5 presents my coding of those who endorsed Mr. Trump in the ANES survey. His protectionism and "traditional Republican values" attracted some individuals, but three-quarters of the

Table 8.5 Survey Respondents' Positive Comments about Donald Trump

Approving Respondents (n = 1,847; corpus = 193,935 words)			
Argument strings	# coded words	% coded words	Sample search terms
Successful businessman	1,276	24.2	*Background, businessman, career, economy, experience, financial, ideas, jobs, money, skills, successful, thinking*
Protects and preserves United States	1,276	24.2	*Americans, borders, control, enforcement, foreign, illegal, immigration, ISIS, law, military, secure, terrorists, veterans*
Great personal energy	846	16.0	*Able, change, forward, fresh, hope, leadership, new, outlook, policies, promise, reform, solutions, views*
Nonconformist politician	550	10.4	*Against, Congress, corruption, different, government, insiders, lobbyists, outsider, parties, politicians, system, Washington*
Populist platform	452	8.8	*Cares, class, everyone, fair, help, loves, people, sincere, supportive, together, us, we*
Refreshingly candid	460	8.7	*Blunt, correctness, genuine, honest, outspoken, says, speaks, straight-shooter, sugar-coat, tells, truth, up-front*
Not Hillary Clinton	271	5.1	*Clinton, Democrat, Democrats, Hillary, liberal, Obama, Obamacare*
Traditional Republican values	131	2.5	*Anti-abortion, beliefs, conservative, guns, pro-life, Reagan, Republican*

Source: From searches of open-ended comments, 2016 American National Election Study.

comments focused on Trump-the-man: his experiences, his candor, his energy, his concern for the average citizen. Trump is said to be a "good father, leader, and truthful American." "He has a big family; he is family-oriented." "He is a true American and wants to fix America." The respondents also unearthed Trump's deepest motivations: "I feel he really loves America and wants to make it strong." "He is a sincere person. How much more sincere can you be?" "I would want him to be my husband's boss."

Comments about Clinton rarely went this deep. Even Trump's flaws proved invitational. Yes, he owned New York City and, yes, his lusts and his temper were legendary, but he was also the billionaire-on-the-corner. Who could resist a guy like that? Mark Singer reports how Trump used to jump out of his car in Manhattan to shake hands with the parking attendants. "It was a quintessential Trumpian gesture," Singer says, "of the sort that explains his popularity among people who barely dare to dream of living in one of his creations." At all times, in all ways, The Donald sought the spotlight: "Trump. Me. Look."[57]

When endorsing Trump, his supporters often overextended their reach, as we see in Table 8.6. Ambivalences about Trump ran throughout the transcripts. People knew what they were getting when supporting him – a bit of this and a great deal of that. Clinton's supporters also had ambivalences but they usually resolved them on policy grounds: "She's too secretive but she'll fix things." In contrast, it was the *person* of Donald Trump that sustained his supporters. He was everyone's brother-in-law – kind of a jerk but one who means well and who will take your kid to the ballgame.

But he was also another kind of brother-in-law, the fellow who never paid back the money he owes you and who left your sister and her kids in the lurch. As we see in Table 8.7, ANES respondents also found this Donald Trump and they did so gleefully: "Dangerously uninformed, egomaniac, hot-tempered." "He has the temperament of a 5-year-old; he is a racist." "He annoys me and he doesn't know how to talk – too high class, thinks he owns everything, and he's a big liar." "If I was close to him and if I had a dozen eggs, I would egg him."

Criticisms of Trump were largely policy-agnostic, focusing on Trump-the-individual. Some of the comments were juvenile (e.g., "blithering idiot," "complete slappy-headed wanker," "monkey in a suit," "a despicable and unqualified primate") and many featured his insensitivities: "He doesn't treat people nicely," "you should protect the weak, not bully them," "if you're going to be president you need to talk about all Americans in a good way." Admonishments like these ran throughout the transcripts, a sign of how homiletic the campaign became because of Trump.

Table 8.6 Supporters' Ambivalences about Donald Trump

Competence
- May have bankrupted a few companies BUT never bankrupted himself.
- He comes off condescending BUT he is intelligent and will help.
- He has some questionable business practices BUT his knowledge of running a business could be effective in running a country.
- I don't necessarily agree with his business tactics BUT he is knowledgeable.

Candor
- He says what he thinks which is not always a good thing BUT he says what he thinks.
- He blurts out stuff and I think it's funny BUT it's honest.
- He might not be as experienced as Clinton BUT I think he would not go back on his word.
- He is an honest man, sometimes that gets him in trouble BUT you can't get into too much trouble by telling the truth.

Clumsiness
- He may say thing that might have offended people BUT they're only words.
- He isn't concerned about being PC BUT doing what is right.
- I agree with a lot that he says BUT his delivery is [too] strong.
- He's a very thoughtful, kind and well-versed gentleman BUT when he gets up before an audience things change.
- He speaks his mind; it may not always be politically correct BUT then, so what?

Freshness
- I was saying this guy is crazy BUT he might bring something different and that is on my mind.
- I kind of like his stance on not bringing in refugees . . . I know it's kind of barbaric BUT I like that.
- New ideas, business-minded BUT don't like his personality.
- Kinda feel like he's trying to change things around to maybe the way they should be BUT he has a hard way of doing it.

Frailty
- I know he has his faults BUT so does everyone else.
- Now he seems like a good family man BUT he was not before.
- I don't believe everything that is said about him groping people he has joked about BUT that doesn't mean he has done it.
- He tells it like it is BUT he doesn't always tell the truth.

Source: From searches of open-ended comments, 2016 American National Election Study.

Table 8.7 Survey Respondents' Negative Comments about Donald Trump

Disapproving Respondents (n = 2,907; corpus = 296,514 words)			
Argument strings	# coded words	% coded words	Sample search terms
No political experience	1,508	20.4	*Countries, foreign, government, ignorance, incompetent, inexperienced, presidency, qualified, skills, unqualified, world*
Racist and sexist	1,240	16.8	*Bigoted, Blacks, deport, discrimination, hate, Hispanics, immigrants, misogynist, prejudiced, racist, sexual, women*
Ignores average Americans	1,050	14.2	*Americans, cares, common, concerned, country, everyone, groups, heart, himself, human, people, poor, support, we*
Pathologically dangerous	1,023	13.9	*Anger, crazy, dangerous, explode, extreme, frighten, hothead, impulsive, irrational, radical, temper, unstable, violence*
Insensitive speech patterns	873	11.8	*Attitude, comments, disrespectful, filter, insult, loud, mouth, says, speaks, statements, tone, unfiltered*
Overbearing and narcissistic	746	10.1	*Arrogance, bully, dictator, ego, idiot, immature, insane, mean, narcissist, personality, rude, selfish, temperament, uncouth*
Bad moral character	524	7.1	*Bad, character, dishonest, fake, hypocrite, immoral, liar, morals, principles, respect, trust, truth, values*
Cares only about money	414	5.6	*Billionaire, business, corporate, crook, deals, financial, greedy, jobs, money, pandering, power, Republicans, rich, tax, wealthy*

Source: From searches of open-ended comments, 2016 American National Election Study.

One finds a considerable number of rhetorical critiques as well: "He speaks like he has a freshman-in-high-school education," "he opens his mouth before he engages his brain," "he speaks out of his ass." Objections to Trump's borderline racism ("he is a hate monger and the absolute worst human") and sexism ("he has sexually assaulted young ladies") were common but one also finds warnings about his political inexperience, the very quality that delighted his supporters. Some of these critiques were harsh ("he's nuts, doesn't know anything about politics"), some more forgiving ("I kind of feel sorry for him because he has no idea what the political process is like"), still others prayerful ("In his speeches he is telling people he is against them, that he doesn't need them. America is a melting pot; when we stop helping people here that is bad").

Identity-based politics inevitably opens the door to therapeutic analyses. Trump's detractors mixed psychobabble ("racist with bipolar tendencies") and medical interventions ("needs to be placed on a 72-hour psych hold") with the rhetoric of the streets ("batshit crazy"). Other commentators linked his weaknesses of character to underlying psychological causes ("wants to be popular," "very immature," "no self-esteem," and "he wants to be king"). Some commentators traced Trump's personal shortcomings to a deficiency in self–object ties ("he sounds like he is not very well brought-up. He has gold chairs and gold everything ... and he displays this as if it were a good thing") while others identified his personal insecurity as the root problem ("he is not self-made and ... has had to trample on many individuals to get to where he is").

If one cannot perform a quick psychoanalysis of Donald Trump, one is not paying attention. "I get along with everybody," he once told CNN's Anderson Cooper. "People love me and, you know what, I've been very successful; everybody loves me."[58] Not quite: 60 percent of the ANES respondents heaped abuse on the man, including many who voted for him. Trump is "a walking inkblot test," says his biographer, Michael D'Antonio. "In him one could see extreme example of ambition, obsession, aggression, and insecurity. He also exhibited creativity, strength and candor."[59] The ANES respondents saw all of this. Supporters and detractors alike were fascinated by Trump's tortured self.

Although all political campaigns are at least, in part, a referendum on those running for office, policy issues usually play a larger role than they did in 2016. In their place were issues of personal identity. The unique personalities and psychological prominence of the candidates crowded out other matters for many voters. To be sure, Trump's supporters wanted a border wall and tax cuts, but mostly they wanted Trump's freshness. Others wanted Hillary Clinton because they loathed Trump.[60] In 2016, everyone was focused on identity.

Conclusion

Ontologically speaking, U.S. voters did not know more about the 2016 candidates than they did about earlier candidates but their *sense of knowing* was off the charts. During my reading of the ANES surveys, I was struck by the respondents' relative inattention to policy issues and by their willingness to wax prophetic about the candidates' interior selves. A "zone of intimacy" surrounded them, fed by a cadre of journalists with an unslakable thirst and by various social media outlets. One would have had to be hiding under a rock not to have known Hillary Clinton in 2016. One would have had to be irredeemably stuffy not to have been galvanized by TV's Donald Trump.

The Dunning–Kruger Effect holds that people with very low levels of information greatly exaggerate what they know. Researcher Ian Anson found such effects to be particularly strong among intense partisans.[61] People with "fixed" worldviews, say political scientists Mark Hetherington and Jonathan Weiler, tend to draw within themselves when threatened by scarcity, conflict, uncertainty, and broad cultural changes.[62] As people become more tribal, it becomes harder for them to take in new information or to entertain questions having no immediate answers. When voters' own partisan identities are comingled with candidates' imagined personalities, voters' essentialism increases, thereby producing the effects described in this chapter.

Is all of this a democratic good? In one sense, we should rejoice when the American people feel a personal connection to those running for the presidency. Such ties can lead to what political scientists call "regime support," a commitment to the nation and its mission, patriotism standing atop charisma. But these kinds of long-distance perceptions are faulty at best. It is especially dangerous when we treat far-distant political candidates as if they rented our back bedrooms.

Popular culture routinely abets this "know-the-person-then-go-vote" mindset. *Saturday Night Live* is particularly adept in this regard. In one scene, an alleged Bernie Sanders and an alleged Hillary Clinton meet in a pub. The former orders "brand new beer, something refreshing and revolutionary," while Alleged Hillary orders a draft that "no one likes, but gets the job done."[63] Innocent fun, but Donald Trump took that same approach when framing Clinton as a deformed individual. People who use "identity insults," says Karina Korostelina, "have a need to boost their own self-respect and confidence" at the expense of public policy.[64] When addressing African-Americans in an audience, Trump once said that Clinton "doesn't care at all about the hurting people of this country or the suffering she has caused them."[65] He further asserted that "it's easy for Hillary Clinton to turn a blind eye to crime when she has her own private security force."[66] And elsewhere this: "[Lobbyists] are throwing money at her because they have total control over everything she does. She is their puppet."[67]

Trump's Clinton is imperious, a woman without a soul; he directly confronts the stereotype of the nurturing female and inverts it. Trump's Clinton is feckless, wooden, a sightless puppet who cannot act on her own. In part because of Trump and in part because of her own shortcomings, Clinton's "unfavorability" ratings increased as the 2016 campaign wore on (although they never quite caught up to Trump's) but, even worse, her "favorability" ratings declined precipitously toward the end of the contest.[68] On election day, the American people *knew* Hillary Clinton, or so they felt.

They knew Donald Trump as well. Again, *Saturday Night Live*: "Donald Trump can't hate women because he loves looking at them" and "he can't hate immigrants because he married them."[69] Said a real voter: "Trump is an oaf, a buffoon, a demagogue, a boor, probably reckless, a liar, probably guilty of sexual assault," but he's better than Hillary Clinton.[70] Said another voter: "He is who I and I'm sure many others around the world aspire to be. He holds America and its citizens in his prayers privately and publicly. He's not a puppet of special interests. He uses Twitter to get it straight from the horse's mouth with no spin. He reminds me of Maximus from *Gladiator*."[71] Again, one searches here for a policy issue, for guidance about what the United States would become under Trump-the-President. One finds, instead, "a hobo's dream of what a rich person is. Everything is gold, even the toilet."[72]

It is worrisome when voters spend so much time focusing on personality rather than policy, even worse when the press does so. I have found that, over the years, news reports have increasingly featured presidents' thoughts and feelings more than their overt actions. As a result, we have become a nation of speculators, fed by our natural interest in other people. But there is more to politics than personality. Governance is ultimately about who gets what from whom at what cost, about which paths to pursue and which to forsake. Identity, in contrast, is but a chimera, alluring though it can surely be. In 2016, there were chimeras enough for all.

Notes

1 Aaron Bandler, "Seven Reasons Trump Won," *Daily Wire*, November 11, 2016. Accessed at www.dailywire.com/news/10733/7-reasons-trump-won-aaron-bandler; Gregory Krieg, "How Did Trump Win? Here Are Twenty-Four Theories," *CNN*, November 10, 2016. Accessed at www.cnn.com/2016/11/10/politics/why-donald-trump-won/index.html; Anthony Zurcher, "U.S. Election 2016 Results: Five Reasons Donald Trump Won," *BBC*, November 9, 2016. Accessed at www.bbc.com/news/election-us-2016-37918303; Howard Gold, "Opinion: Five Huge Reasons Donald Trump Won," *MarketWatch*, November 9, 2016 (italics mine). Accessed at www.marketwatch.com/story/5-huge-reasons-donald-trump-won-2016-11-09.

2 Zurcher, "US Election 2016 Results: Five Reasons Donald Trump Won," *BBC*.

3 As quoted in Stephen Johnson, "Slavoj Žižek: Trump's Rise is a Symptom of a Dark and Subtle Force," *Attack the System*, October 24, 2018. Accessed at https://attackthesystem.com/2018/10/28/slavoj-zizek-trumps-rise-is-a-symptom-of-a-dark-and-subtle-force/.

4 For more on Caddell's views, see Mike Whitney, "Patrick Caddell: the Pollster Who 'Got it Right,'" *Counterpunch*, November 11, 2016. Accessed at www.counterpunch.org/2016/11/11/patrick-caddell-the-pollster-who-got-it-right/.

5 Jordan Kalinowski, "Why People Voted for Trump," *The Odyssey Online*, November 14, 2016. Accessed at www.theodysseyonline.com/why-people-voted-for-trump.

6 As quoted in David Jackson, "Trump Closes Campaign as He Began It: Running against the Establishment," *USA Today*, November 6, 2016. Accessed at www.usatoday.com/story/news/politics/elections/2016/11/06/donald-trump-closing-argument-clinton/93369524/.

7 The preceding on-the-street comments can be found in James Hohmann, "How Donald Trump Won – and Why the Media Missed It," *Denver Post*, November 9, 2016. Accessed at www.denverpost.com/2016/11/09/how-donald-trump-won-and-why-the-media-missed-it/.

8 As quoted in Josh Saul, "Why Did Donald Trump Win? Just Visit Luzerne County, Pennsylvania," *Newsweek*, December 5, 2016. Accessed at www.newsweek.com/2016/12/16/donald-trump-pennsylvania-win-luzerne-county-527861.html.

9 David Byler, "Demographic Coalitions: How Trump Picked the Democratic Lock and Won the Presidency," in Larry J. Sabato, Kyle Kondik, and Geoffrey Skelley (eds.), *Trumped: the 2016 Election that Broke All the Rules* (Lanham, MD: Rowman & Littlefield, 2017), p. 39.

10 Jamelle Bouie, "Is America Really in an Anti-Establishment Rage?" *Slate*, May 31, 2016. Accessed at https://slate.com/news-and-politics/2016/05/is-american-really-in-an-anti-establishment-rage.html.

11 John Sides, Michael Tesler, and Lynn Vavreck, *Identity Crisis: the 2016 Presidential Campaign and the Battle for the Meaning of America* (Princeton: Princeton University Press, 2018).

12 Harry Enten, "Americans' Distaste for Both Trump and Clinton Is Record-Breaking," *FiveThirtyEight.com*, May 5, 2016. Accessed at https://fivethirtyeight.com/features/americans-distaste-for-both-trump-and-clinton-is-record-breaking/. For trust scores, see Pamela S. Shockley-Zalabak, Sherwyn P. Morreale, and Carmen Stavrositu, "Voters' Perceptions of Trust in 2016 Presidential Candidates Clinton and Trump: Exploring the Election's Outcome," *American Behavioral Scientist*, 61 (2017), 1–32.

13 Matt Viser, "Trump, Self-Described 'Nationalist,' Turns Midterms into a Forum on American Identity," *Washington Post*, October 20, 2018. Accessed at www.washingtonpost.com/politics/trump-self-described-nationalist-turns-midterms-into-a-forum-on-american-identity/2018/10/30/dd3a418a-dc4b-11e8-b732-3c72cbf131f2_story.html?utm_term=.1e3b80edf23a.

14 Ross Douthat, "Who Are We?" *New York Times*, February 4, 2017. Accessed at www.nytimes.com/2017/02/04/opinion/who-are-we.html.

15 As quoted in Aaron Blake, "Trump's Embrace of a Fraught Term – 'Nationalist' – Could Cement a Dangerous Racial Divide," *Washington Post*, October 23, 2018. Accessed at www.washingtonpost.com/politics/2018/10/23/trumps-embrace-fraught-term-nationalist-could-cement-dangerous-racial-divide/?utm_term=.3321b00b9e38.

16 Douthat, "Who Are We?" *New York Times*.

17 Ibid.

18 Victoria L. Sanders, "Hate Didn't Elect Donald Trump. People Did," *Wordpress. com*, November 12, 2016. Accessed at https://victorialsanders.wordpress.com/2016/11/12/hate-didnt-elect-donald-trump-people-did/.

19 Sean Illing, "Twenty of America's Top Political Scientists Gathered to Discuss Our Democracy. They're Scared," *Vox*, October 13, 2017. Accessed at www.vox.com/2017/10/13/16431502/america-democracy-decline-liberalism.

20 As quoted ibid.

21 Gwendoline Alphonso, "'One People, under One God, Saluting One American Flag': Trump and Republican Party Construction of American Identity, Nation, and Peoplehood," Paper presented at the annual convention of the American Political Science Association, San Francisco, CA, September 2017.

22 Adam Serwer, "The Nationalist's Delusion," *Atlantic*, November 20, 2017. Accessed at www.theatlantic.com/politics/archive/2017/11/the-nationalists-delusion/546356/.

23 Ibid.

24 Alan J. Abramowitz, "It Wasn't the Economy, Stupid: Racial Polarization, White Racial Resentment, and the Rise of Trump," in Sabato, Kondik, and Skelley (eds.), *Trumped: The 2016 Election that Broke All the Rules*, p. 208.

25 Joshua Green, *Devil's Bargain: Steve Bannon, Donald Trump, and the Storming of the Presidency* (New York: Penguin, 2017), pp. 97–99.

26 Ibid., p. 190.

27 Mary E. Stuckey, *Defining Americans: the Presidency and National Identity* (Lawrence: University Press of Kansas, 2004), p. 82.

28 Diana C. Mutz, "Status Threat, Not Economic Hardship, Explains the Presidential Vote," *Proceedings of the National Academy of Sciences of the United States of America*, May 8, 2018. Accessed at www.pnas.org/content/115/19/E4330.

29 Statistical patterns for Caretaking terms for Clinton = 8.8312, for Trump = 6.8784; $F_{[1, 2423]} = 96.703$, $p < 0.000$; for Family terms for Clinton = 5.3933, for Trump = 2.1882; $F_{[1, 2423]} = 468.053$, $p < 0.000$; for Growth terms for Clinton = 2.0689, for Trump = 0.7851; $F_{[1, 2423]} = 121.195$, $p < 0.000$; for Labor terms for Clinton = 5.0607, for Trump = 3.3427; $F_{[1, 2423]} = 110.344$, $p < 0.000$. Statistical patterns for Economy terms for Clinton = 3.2022, for Trump = 4.7400; $F_{[1, 2423]} = 53.306$, $p < 0.000$; for Capacity terms for Clinton = 4.0721, for Trump = 46.4371; $F_{[1, 2423]} = 161.491$, $p < 0.000$; for Quantity terms for Clinton = 1.7946, for Trump = 3.6476; $F_{[1, 2423]} = 228.809$, $p < 0.000$; for Security terms for Clinton = 1.4261, for Trump = 4.3801; $F_{[1, 2423]} = 279.370$, $p < 0.000$.

30 Statistical patterns for Caretaking terms for Democrats = 8.0199, for Republicans = 7.1948; $F_{[1, 7454]} = 24.073$, $p < 0.000$; for Family terms for Democrats = 4.4175, for Republicans = 3.6864; $F_{[1, 7454]} = 34.470$, $p < 0.000$; for Growth terms for Democrats = 2.1545, for Republicans = 1.5881; $F_{[1, 7454]} = 33.733$, $p < 0.000$; for Labor terms for Democrats = 4.5034, for Republicans = 3.3142; $F_{[1, 7454]} = 18.209$, $p < 0.000$. Statistical patterns for Economy terms for Democrats = 4.8332, for Republicans = 4.8220; $F_{[1, 7454]} = 0.005$, $p < 0.943$; for Capacity

terms for Democrats = 4.1424, for Republicans = 4.2342; F [1, 7454] = 0.803, p < 0.370; for Quantity terms for Democrats = 2.3948, for Republicans = 2.1408; F [1, 7454] = 9.793, p < 0.002; for Security terms for Democrats = 2.0893, for Republicans = 2.7548; F [1, 7454] = 17.561, p < 0.000.

31 Donald R. Kinder and Nathan P. Kalmoe, *Neither Liberal nor Conservative: Ideological Innocence in the American Public* (Chicago: University of Chicago Press, 2017).

32 Emily Ekins, "Religious Trump Voters: How Faith Moderates Attitudes about Immigration, Race, and Identity," *Democracy Fund: Voters Study Group*, September 2018. Accessed at www.voterstudygroup.org/publications/2018-voter-survey/religious-trump-voters.

33 Brian F. Schaffner, Matthew MacWilliams, and Tatishe Nteta, "Explaining White Polarization in the 2016 Vote for President: the Sobering Role of Racism and Sexism," Paper presented at the Conference on the U.S. Elections of 2016: Domestic and International Aspects, IDC Herzliya, Israel, January 2017.

34 Steven Johnson, "How a College Degree 'Supercharges' a Divide among White Voters," *Chronicle of Higher Education*, November 5, 2018. Accessed at www.chronicle.com/article/How-a-College-Degree/245014.

35 Jedediah Purdy, "Is America Still a 'Nation of Ideas'?" *Politico*, September/October 2017. Accessed at www.politico.com/magazine/story/2017/09/05/america-nation-ideas-donald-trump-215532.

36 Michael Paterniti, "A State That Is of Two Minds," *New York Times Magazine*, November 20, 2016. Accessed at www.nytimes.com/interactive/2016/11/20/magazine/donald-trumps-america-maine.html.

37 Peggy Drexler, "Stop Calling Her Hillary," *CNN*, April 14, 2015. Accessed at www.cnn.com/2015/04/14/opinions/drexler-dont-call-her-hillary/index.html.

38 For more on this matter see Roseann M. Mandziuk, "Dressing Down Hillary," *Communication and Critical/Cultural Studies*, 5:3 (2008), 312–16.

39 Hillary Rodham Clinton, *What Happened* (New York: Simon & Schuster, 2017), p. 119.

40 *For tweets*: See Mandi Bates Bailey and Steven P. Nawara, "Women, Social Media, and the 2016 Presidential Election: A Content Analysis," Paper presented at the annual meeting of the Midwest Political Science Association, Chicago, April 2017; Christian R. Hoffman, "Crooked Hillary and Dumb Trump: the Strategic Uses and Effect of Negative Evaluations in US Election Campaign Tweets," *Internet Pragmatics*, 1:1 (2018), 58–87. *For ads and emails*: John C. Tedesco and Scott W. Dunn, "Political Advertising in the 2016 U.S. Presidential Election: ad Hominem ad Nauseam," *American Behavioral Scientist*, 62 (2018), 1–13; Samuel C. Rhodes, Taewoo Kang, and Orion A. Yoesle, "Desperate Measures: Why Candidates Choose to Go Negative in Campaign Emails," Paper presented at the annual meeting of the Midwest Political Science Association, Chicago, April 2017. *For debates*: Raul Madrid, Jr., "The Tone of the Debates: the Difference Between Democrats and Republicans During the Primaries," in Jeanine E. Kraybill (ed.), *Unconventional, Partisan, and Polarizing Rhetoric: How the 2016 Election Shaped the Way Candidates Strategize, Engage, and Communicate* (Lanham, MD: Lexington Books, 2018), pp. 27–42.

41 Hillary R. Clinton, "Remarks on Gun Control and National Security," Campaign speech in Cincinnati, Ohio, October 21, 2016. Accessed at https://moody.utexas.edu/centers/strauss/campaign-mapping-project.

42 See Susanna Kelly Engbers, "With Great Sympathy: Elizabeth Cady Stanton's Innovative Appeals to Emotion," *Rhetoric Society Quarterly*, 37:3 (2007), 307–32.

43 Elaine Kamarck, "Why Hillary Clinton Lost," *Brookings Institution*, September 20, 2017. Accessed at www.brookings.edu/blog/fixgov/2017/09/20/why-hillary-clinton-lost/.

44 Brent J. Hale and Maria Elizabeth Grabe, "Visual War: a Content Analysis of Clinton and Trump Subreddits during the 2016 Campaign," *Journalism and Mass Communication Quarterly*, 95:2 (2018), 449–70.

45 Diana B. Carlin and Kelly L. Winfrey, "Have You Come a Long Way, Baby? Hillary Clinton, Sarah Palin, and Sexism in 2008 Campaign Coverage," *Communication Studies*, 60:4 (2009), 326–43.

46 Clifford P. McCue and David Gopoian, "Dispositional Empathy and the Political Gender Gap," *Women and Politics*, 21:2 (2000), 1–20.

47 James Fallows, "When Donald Meets Hillary," *Atlantic*, October 2016. Accessed at www.theatlantic.com/magazine/archive/2016/10/who-will-win/497561/.

48 Hillary Rodham Clinton, "Hillary Clinton Opens Up about Sexism in New *Humans of New York* Post," *Guardian*, September 8, 2016. Accessed at www.theguardian .com/us-news/2016/sep/08/hillary-clinton-humans-of-new-york-sexism.

49 For more on this kind of "market analysis," see Sudeep Bhatia, Geoffrey P. Goodwin, and Lukasz Walasek, "Trait Associations for Hillary Clinton and Donald Trump in News Media: a Computational Analysis," *Social Psychology and Personality Science*, 9:2 (2018), 123–30.

50 Clinton, *What Happened*, p. 96.

51 David Fortunato, Matthew V. Hibbing, and Jeffery J. Mondak, "The Trump Draw: Voter Personality and Support for Donald Trump in the 2016 Republican Nomination Campaign," *American Politics Research*, 46:5 (2018), 789.

52 Robert Costa and Michael Schrer, "'Amnesty Don'? Trump Tests the Faith of Supporters with Talk of Immigration Deal," *Washington Post*, September 14, 2017. Accessed at www.washingtonpost.com/politics/amnesty-don-trump-tests-the-faith-of-supporters-with-talk-of-immigration-deal/2017/09/14/8d8cec42-9961-11e7-82e4-f1076f6d6152_story.html?utm_term=.a4c3e173f1a9.

53 Trevor Clohessy, Colin Callinan, Thomas Acton, Eoin Whelan, and Murray Scott, "An Analysis of the 2016 American Presidential Nominees' Tweets: a Magical Realism Perspective," NUI Galway, 2017. Accessed at https://aran.library .nuigalway.ie/handle/10379/6829.

54 As quoted in Karina Korostelina, *Trump Effect* (New York: Routledge, 2017), p. 93.

55 Allen Frances, *Twilight of American Sanity: a Psychiatrist Analyzes the Age of Trump* (New York: William Morrow, 2017), p. 135.

56 Charles R. Kesler, "Thinking about Trump," *Claremont Review of Books*, 18:2 (2018), 17.

57 Mark Singer, "Trust Me," *This Land*, October 25, 2016. Accessed at http://thisland press.com/2016/10/25/trust-me/.

58 As quoted in Leonard Cruz and Steven Buser, "The Goldwater Rule," in Leonard Cruz and Steven Buser (eds.), *A Clear and Present Danger: Narcissism in the Era of President Trump* (Asheville, NC: Chiron Publications, 2017), p. xv.

59 Michael D'Antonio, *Never Enough: Donald Trump and the Pursuit of Success* (New York: Thomas Dunne Books, 2013), p. 13.

60 This latter statement is from an anonymous voter quoted in Hamilton Nolan, "Trump Voters Explain Themselves," *The Concourse*, January 3, 2017. Accessed at https:// theconcourse.deadspin.com/trump-voters-explain-themselves-1790711999.

61 Ian G. Anson, "Partisanship, Political Knowledge, and the Dunning–Kruger Effect," *Political Psychology*, 39:5 (2018), 1173–92.

62 Mark Hetherington and Jonathan Weiler, *Prius or Pickup? How the Answers to Four Simple Questions Explain America's Great Divide* (New York: Houghton Mifflin, 2018).

63 As quoted in Outi J. Hakola, "Political Impersonations on Saturday Night Live during the 2016 U.S. Presidential Election," *European Journal of American Studies*, 12:2 (2017). Accessed at https://journals.openedition.org/ejas/12153.

64 Korostelina, *Trump Effect*, p. 51.

65 Donald J. Trump, "Campaign Speech in West Bend, Wisconsin," August 17, 2016. Accessed at www.politico.com/story/2016/08/full-text-donald-trumps-speech-on-227095.

66 Ibid.

67 Donald J. Trump, "Acceptance Speech at the Republican National Convention," Cleveland, OH, *Politico*, July 21, 2016. Accessed at www.politico.com/story/2016/07/full-transcript-donald-trump-nomination-acceptance-speech-at-rnc-225974.

68 Gregory Holyk and Gary Langer, "Poll: Clinton Unpopularity at New High, on Par with Trump," *ABC News*, August 31, 2016. Accessed at https://abcnews.go.com/Politics/poll-clinton-unpopularity-high-par-trump/story?id=41752050.

69 As quoted in Hakola, "Political Impersonations on Saturday Night Live during the 2016 U.S. Presidential Election."

70 Calum Miller, "Why People Voted for Trump," *CalumsBlog*, November 25, 2016. Accessed at https://calumsblog.com/2016/11/25/why-people-voted-for-trump/.

71 Mike Gonzo, "To Make America Great Again," *Quora*, July 16, 2017. Accessed at www.quora.com/What-are-the-main-reasons-why-people-voted-for-Trump-How-do-those-reasons-continue-to-satisfy-Trump-supporters-today.

72 Anonymous interviewee from Farmington, Maine, as quoted in Paterniti, "A State That Is of Two Minds," *New York Times Magazine*.

9   TRUMP'S SPONTANEITY

Everyone has an opinion about Donald Trump's tweets. Lisa Lampanelli, a professional comedian specializing in racy humor, finds his tweets remarkably disgusting. "I saw Trump be a roastmaster at the Friars Club," Lampanelli reports, "but he doesn't have the skill to do this kind of thing with the right intention underneath it. Is it entertaining to some? I don't find these tweets entertaining in the least. It's off-putting and it gets to a scary, bully level."[1] Folks working in the District of Columbia agree. "Stop it!" said Senator Lisa Murkowski of Alaska; "the Presidential platform should be used for more than bringing people down." "This isn't normal," echoed her senatorial colleague, Ben Sasse of Nebraska, "it's beneath the dignity of [the President's] office." Trump's Twitter usage "represents what is wrong with American politics, not the greatness of America," said South Carolina's Senator Lindsey Graham.[2]

Journalists, often the object of Mr. Trump's ire, agree. "On the one hand," says the *Washington Post*'s Kathleen Parker, Trump should stop tweeting. "On the other hand, how else would we have known how truly demented the man is?"[3] Ms. Parker's colleague, reporter Dan Balz, finds that same attitude among the citizens he met in the heartland, people worried that Trump's use of Twitter "reveals a volatile president unable to control his impulses."[4] Indeed, on the eve of the 2018 midterm elections, polls showed that Trump's tweeting was one of three issues (the other two being healthcare and tax reform) that especially vexed voters.[5] "More Twitter rage means a less popular Trump – but we need more data to confirm it," Nate Silver of *FiveThirtyEight* reports.[6] What nationwide polls tell us, say political psychologists Jeremy Frimer and Linda Skitka, is that "the more President Trump insulted others, the lower his approval ratings were among liberals and moderates," with time-lagged analyses also showing that "Trump's uncivil tweets depressed approval with his conservative base several days later."[7]

All such commentary is lost on Trump. "For those few people knocking me for tweeting at three o'clock in the morning," says he, "at least you know I will be there, awake, to answer the call!"[8] Many of his supporters agree. "He talks to us every single day. He tells us what he's doing, what he's thinking. He doesn't hold back much, I think we can all agree to that. And it's pretty unique," says Tricia Hope of Houston.[9] Twenty-two-year-old Emma Leach of Wilkes-Barre, Pennsylvania, agrees, telling a team of reporters that "Trump's use of Twitter energizes younger people such as herself." A few years ago, Leach says, "she could have asked a friend what Obama did in office that day, and she wouldn't have known. But today she'll know what Trump tweeted or what Trump did or what executive order happened. She's involved now."[10]

"By treating words as potent and weightless – potent, as tools to skewer opponents, and weightless, without lasting consequence," says the *Guardian*'s Lawrence Douglas, Trump "greased his way to a spectacular political rise."[11] Essayist George Saunders sees a link between Trump's rhetorical style and his ability to galvanize the electorate. Trump usually avoids teleprompters, says Saunders, because "he is not trying to persuade, detail, or prove; he is trying to thrill, agitate, be liked, be loved, here and now. He is trying to make energy."[12] The energy flows out of him, says Saunders, and "enters the minds of his followers: their cheers go ragged and hoarse, chanting erupts, a look of religious zeal may flash across the face of some non-chanter, who is finally getting, in response to a question long nursed in private, exactly the answer he's been craving."[13] Trump's spontaneity is among his strongest assets. He lives in the moment. He is the moment.

The President "can really improve in the way he says things," a woman in Fountain Hills, Arizona, tells Saunders, "but who gives a shit? Because if he's going to get the job done? I'm just saying. You can't let your feelings get hurt. It's kind of like, get over it, you know what I mean? What's the big picture here?"[14] Many Americans concur. During the 2016 presidential election, Trump's tweets were retweeted five times more often than Hillary Clinton's.[15] Although only 8 percent of the population actually consumed his tweets directly, 75 percent said that they saw, read, or heard of them when the news picked them up.[16] Those who share Trump's missives in their own Twitter streams (via the "liking" function) display higher approval of the President's overall performance.[17] Even Trump's nasty tweets, those housing "a little bit of wrongness," recommend themselves, says the *Wall Street Journal*'s Scott Adams, because, with Twitter, "strategic wrongness is jet fuel."[18]

This chapter focuses on the sense of interaction – the social energy – Trump creates via Twitter. Twitter is a technology but it is also a sign – it's time to wake up. Conventional politics is about old-line power brokers and backroom deals. Conventional politics is also about ponderous speeches, drawn-out debates, news conferences that go nowhere. Twitter, in contrast, is about authenticity and community. Tweets arrive via a smartphone, making them feel personal. Tweets are authored by people we may not know but with whom we willingly associate. Twitter lets us respond directly – although most of us do not – but the invitation to interact lingers.[19] Tweets sidle up to us, demanding nothing, promising much.

Donald Trump's tweets were short, signaling his impatience; routine, signaling his faithfulness; irreverent, signaling a man with a plan. "Twitter has given Trump the illusion of transparency and accessibility without having to actually provide them," says digital journalist Matthew Ingram, and without "the accountability that usually comes with a two-way conversation with the press."[20] "This is the first time," says *Politico*'s Jack Shafer, that "we've had the type of open access to the subconscious of the president."[21]

Or so it would seem. This chapter examines Donald Trump's use of Twitter during the 2016 campaign and thereafter. It looks at how his tweets were covered by the press, how voters reacted to them, and what Twitter says about the President himself. Mindless though his postings often are, they energize people. What makes them so irresistible? Why does the press cover them so assiduously? Trump's use of Twitter is "not a puff of air," says the *New Yorker*'s Adam Gopnik, nor is Trump "just a blowhard from the outer boroughs who keeps making threats without any real intention or ability to follow through on them."[22] His tweets prove that "cruel impulses are easy to awake in large numbers of people," Gopnik argues, especially when "they're told by those in power that those impulses are now acceptable."[23] Donald

Trump's tweets are small things on their way to becoming big things. This chapter traces that trajectory.

What the Press Says

Donald Trump averages around ten tweets per day, although he quadrupled his output during the 2016 presidential campaign.[24] Oddly enough, Hillary Clinton produced more postings than Trump but he got greater "pickup" for two reasons: (1) his tweets were retweeted 6,000 times on average (vs. only 1,500 per tweet for Clinton) and (2) he got considerably more media coverage than the former First Lady, in part because he used Twitter to attack people, thereby stimulating controversy.[25] "Clinton's approach to Twitter appeared to be one of quantity," argue communication researchers Steven Nawara and Mandi Bates Bailey, while Trump's tweets were "more candid, outlandish, and memorable" and hence caught the press's eye.[26] When Trump tweets, said his former press secretary Sean Spicer, "It gets picked up by everybody, it gets read live on the news, you guys will cover it in the paper. We put out a press release and it gets covered much less than when he sends out a single tweet."[27]

As of this writing, Trump has generated well over 10,000 tweets as president and he shows no sign of slowing down. The press love-hates that fact. Although Trump was dead last in national endorsements during the Republican primary in 2016 and even though he was almost last in money raised, he made up for it by getting far more "free media" than his rivals, a commodity valued by one researcher at $4.96 billion vs. only $3.24 billion for Hillary Clinton.[28] Because of his social media followers, Trump also received $402 million in value from his tweets compared to only $166 million for Clinton. Money and media attention are organically related: The more that people retweeted Trump, the more press coverage he received and that, in turn, produced additional postings.[29]

The press's addiction to Trump's tweets sends a meta-message: Trump is powerful, a master of circulation.[30] Attention plus amplification, say Yini Zhang and her colleagues, show that power is transferable – from candidates to tweets, from tweets to the press, from the press to voters.[31] And there is more here than mere partisanship: Trump's tweets were picked up in the United States as well as abroad and by Democrats as well as Republicans. Indeed, more Democrats paid attention to Trump's tweets (64 percent) than did Republicans (50 percent) during the 2016 race.[32] In many ways, Trump brought to Twitter what he brought to reality television, accumulating social power by displaying his outrageous self.

Members of the press are not happy with all of this but they have a predicament: Pay attention to Trump and thereby do his bidding, or ignore him at the risk of reducing the size of their audience. As we see in Table 9.1, reporters respond with their best rhetorical weapon – characterization. This table was generated by tracking in news coverage the kernel cluster "Trump's ____ tweets," with the blank being filled in by one of twenty-six adjectives. As can be seen, the press registers 5.7 negative characterizations for each bouquet it tosses in Trump's direction. Columnist Patrick Fletchall summarizes things this way: "All the dirty, embarrassing, mean-spirited little thoughts that pop into our brains, he [Trump] actually says out loud," and the press cannot get enough of it.[33]

Trump's tweets are plentiful and colorful but the press does its share of counterpunching. Jasmine Lee and Kevin Quealy, who write for the *New York Times*, have made a habit of cataloging Trump's Twitter insults. Not surprisingly, many of the names on the list are politicians Trump has scorned (Bill Clinton: *hypocrite*; Jeb Bush: *weak and ineffective*; and Ted Cruz: *greatly dishonest*) but Hollywood types are also included (Samuel L. Jackson: *not athletic*; Whoopi Goldberg: *in total freefall*; and John Oliver: *very boring*). One also finds plenty of reporters that Trump has attacked, including longstanding pros (Cokie Roberts: *kooky*; Charles Krauthammer: *highly overrated*; and Maggie Haberman: *third-rate reporter*) as well as some conservatives (Major Garrett: *bad reporter*; Shep Smith: *totally biased*; Bill Kristol: *a sad case*; and Frank Luntz: *a total clown*).[34] The most surprising thing about Lee and Quealy's work is that their cataloging began in January of 2016, well before Mr. Trump fired up his Twitter machine. Since then, mayhem has reigned.

It is hardly surprising that the press dislikes Trump's tweets since they are so often directed at journalists, with "fake news" being his battle cry. In response, the press issues dire warnings based on historical antecedents: "a terrifying form of presidential demagogy that the antifederalists warned of two and a half centuries ago."[35] One hears, too, of a fundamentally corrupted citizenry: "Twitter addicts take on this kind of nervous, paranoid, cranky quality, sort of itching

Table 9.1 Characterizations of Trump's Tweets by Elite News Outlets

Characterization	Number of hits
Angry	945
Ill-informed	560
Stupid	183
Negative	102
Positive	101
Crazy	92
Vicious	61
Ignorant	59
Upbeat	58
Dumb	49
Enthusiastic	39
Important	39
Humorous	35
Silly	30
Clever	29
Optimistic	23
Foolish	15
Deranged	14
Bitter	12
Perceptive	12
Happy	12
Irate	12
Irrational	10
Cheery	8
Thoughtful	5
Well-informed	1

Source: Based on searches in the Lexis-Nexis news database from November 9, 2016, through November 9, 2018.

for a fight."[36] One also hears of Trump singling out women for special opprobrium, of his following media cues instead of establishing his own leadership positions, of a nation made insular by the President's tweets, and of a society now so debased that a "collapse of thoughtful, reasoned, and respectful discourse" is foreordained.[37]

All presidents eventually dislike the press but, as we saw in Chapter 7, Donald Trump has made the media both his sparring partner and his inamorata. "They were once mine," one hears him say, "but I am now cut adrift, unnoticed and unloved." So he stands atop the Battleship Twitter, firing his salvos.

There is such a waste of time in all of this. Tweets are no way to run a country. Or a newspaper. By emphasizing interpersonal drama, the press pays insufficient attention to the policy issues Trump's tweets also contain. The press does so for dramatic reasons but that makes the news tiresome, predictable, causing people to tune out. With rare exception, Twitter underserves both the First and Fourth Estates. It underserves the body politic as well.

What Voters Say

While the press is strangely attracted to Trump's tweets, most voters can do without them. Survey after survey shows this. A Fox News poll in March of 2017, for example, found that "a full 50 percent of the sample said they 'disapprove' of Trump's tweeting, with another 32 percent saying that they 'wished he'd be more cautious.'"[38] One year later, a *Politico* survey found that 72 percent felt Mr. Trump used Twitter too much, while 59 percent said it was hurting his presidency.[39] Yet another survey showed that (1) better-educated voters, (2) those who trusted traditional media, (3) those with a high need for political information, and (4) those who embraced political correctness were particularly upset by Trump's tweets.[40] The least popular postings? Those in which Trump attacked other people.[41]

All of this was lost on Mr. Trump, who continued to propagate the notion that he had a "direct line" to the American people. Nonsense, says *Quartz*'s Ana Campoy. At best, she says, Mr. Trump has about 22 million followers, with machine-learning software finding that 60 percent of Trump's alleged 55 million followers have sprung from fake accounts and bots. While the myth holds that Trump "can broadcast a message to those millions of people at any hour of the night or day and be sure they are seeing it," most Americans hear what he says courtesy of the elite media.[42]

Why do voters dislike Trump's tweets? In the spring of 2018, I explored that question via the Texas Media & Society Survey (TMASS), a national random-sample poll conducted by the GfK Group and overseen by the Annette Strauss Institute for Civic Life at the University of Texas at Austin. This is an annual poll examining voters' attitudes about media and politics, news consumption, community involvement, and information habits. The survey consists of a large battery of questions differentially presented (in twenty-minute increments) to survey respondents who also answered a set of demographic questions. In 2018, 2,066 individuals took the TMASS survey, including an oversample of Texas voters.[43]

The respondents were 53.6 years of age on average, with 67 percent having had at least one year of college. Twenty-three percent of the respondents went to church each week, with 25.2 percent avoiding religious services altogether. Fifty-eight percent worked full-time, 27 percent were retired, with the remainder working part-time or going to school; 88.4 percent of the respondents reported living in a metro area and 83.1 percent were registered to vote. Forty-six percent said they were of middle income (i.e., salaries somewhere between $26,000 and $99,000 per year), with 30.1 percent working in skilled occupations, 20 percent in professional positions, and the remainder having either consumer-facing or service jobs.

Politically, 47.7 percent of the sample consisted of Democrats, 45.2 percent Republicans, with the rest being either Independents or having no party preference; 5.7 percent of the respondents "strongly approved" of the Trump presidency, and 39.6 percent "somewhat approved," while 23.1 percent were unsure how they felt. "Strong disapprovers" comprised 19.2 percent of the sample, with 11.1 percent declaring that they "somewhat disapproved" of Mr. Trump. In the sample, 62.4 percent used Facebook regularly but only 15.6 percent tweeted. Texans (n = 1,058) and non-Texans (n = 1,008) were equally represented in the survey, with 77 percent of all respondents saying Mr. Trump should tweet less often. Of these naysayers, 88 percent were Democrats, 68 percent Republicans, and 64 percent Independents. Only 2.9 percent of the sample wanted to hear more from the Tweeter-in-Chief, with 16.5 percent settling for his current output.

The sample did not speak with one voice about Trump's tweets. Younger people and social media devotees were slightly more tolerant of his Twitter usage. Less-educated individuals were not as upset with the President's tweets as better-educated respondents; men were slightly more tolerant of his tweets than were women. Surprisingly, evangelicals said the President should tweet less often (even though most of them supported Trump on other matters).[44]

Interestingly, when respondents were asked about Trump's tweets, Texas voters and the national sample were statistically indistinguishable, a finding that perhaps presaged the "purple" hue the state took on during the 2018 senatorial race between Ted Cruz and Beto O'Rourke. Demographically, though, Texans were still Texans: They were slightly older than the national sample, somewhat more conservative, more likely to be born-again Christians, more urban than rural, more likely to be long-term residents of the state, and far more likely to be Hispanic. In terms of voter registration, party identification, and annual income, on the other hand, the Texas sample and national sample were strikingly similar.

These findings largely conform to what other surveys have found, but I was especially interested in *why* people felt as they did about Trump's tweeting. Did they find his postings untoward or a distraction from the job, or were they upset by the egotism or partisanship they contained? As can be seen in Table 9.2, I asked fourteen questions along these lines, seven inviting positive responses and seven negative ones.[45]

In many ways, the survey responses reflect basic American axiology: Do what's appropriate, don't call attention to yourself, work hard, avoid silly fights, be practical. It is also interesting that strategic and partisan issues (e.g., outmaneuvering one's enemies, making fun of liberals, garnering media coverage, being inveterately Republican) fall to the bottom of the value hierarchy. Also noteworthy are the small standard deviations reported in Table 9.2, an indication that those who took the survey approached the individual questions in similar ways. The respondents knew what they knew and had no trouble saying why.

Table 9.3 shows two things: (1) Republicans were more tolerant of Donald Trump's tweets than were Democrats – an unsurprising finding – but (2) they moved closer to one another when basic values like propriety, functionality, and industry were invoked. In contrast, the partisan divide opened up when the survey questions focused on

Table 9.2 Respondents' Reactions to Trump's Tweets

Order	Item	Mean[a]	s.d.
1	President Trump's tweets often show bad manners on his part.	4.25	1.003
2	President Trump's tweeting is inappropriate for the nation's chief executive.	4.22	1.063
3	President Trump makes a fool of himself when tweeting.	4.18	1.057
4	President Trump's tweeting distracts him from more important work.	4.06	1.162
5	President Trump's tweets speak directly to the average American.	4.03	1.103
6	President Trump's tweets start needless fights with Democrats.	3.97	1.121
7	President Trump's tweets are refreshingly straightforward.	3.97	1.118
8	President Trump's tweets counteract the media's influence.	3.93	1.126
9	President Trump's tweets cruelly attack decent people.	3.91	1.220
10	President Trump's tweets defend basic American values.	3.90	1.160
11	President Trump cleverly outmaneuvers his enemies with tweets.	3.71	1.130
12	It's great when President Trump's tweets make fun of liberals.	3.44	1.161
13	President Trump's tweets explain the Republican Party's take on issues.	3.40	1.099
14	President Trump's tweets really don't affect media's coverage.	2.18	1.266

Source: Data provided by GfK Group/Strauss Institute's TMASS Survey, May, 2018, n = 2,066.
[a] 5 = Strongly agree, 1 = Strongly disagree.

political strategy. Mr. Trump is likely to miss the nuance here, but his long-term popularity may be at stake. Curtailing his tweets would not "solve all of his political problems," says *CNN*'s Chris Cillizza, "but what it would do is to begin the process of reorienting the way in which

Table 9.3 Respondents' Reactions to Trump's Tweets by Partisanship

Item	Republicans (n = 929) Mean[a]	Agreement	Democrats (n = 976) Mean[a]	Agreement	Mean Differential
President Trump's tweets cruelly attack decent people.	2.80	32.30%	4.57	86.20%	-1.77
President Trump makes a fool of himself when tweeting.	3.36	54.90%	4.68	90.10%	-1.32
President Trump's tweeting distracts him from more important work.	3.28	52.30%	4.55	86.00%	-1.27
President Trump's tweets often show bad manners on his part.	3.51	60.30%	4.72	92.10%	-1.21
President Trump's tweets are inappropriate for the nation's chief executive.	3.50	54.80%	4.67	89.00%	-1.17
President Trump's tweets start needless fights with Democrats.	3.29	51.40%	4.40	81.50%	-1.11
President Trump's tweets really don't affect media's coverage.	2.08	11.00%	2.18	19.40%	-0.10
President Trump's tweets explain the Republican Party's take on issues.	3.53	47.40%	2.84	30.80%	0.69
It's great when President Trump's tweets make fun of liberals.	3.71	52.60%	2.21	16.70%	1.50

President Trump cleverly outmaneuvers his enemies with tweets.	4.03	66.20%	2.39	29.40%	1.64
President Trump's tweets counteract the media's influence.	4.25	79.30%	2.52	25.50%	1.73
President Trump's tweets speak directly to the average American.	4.37	84.90%	2.50	31.10%	1.87
President Trump's tweets are refreshingly straightforward.	4.33	83.10%	2.40	30.80%	1.93
President Trump's tweets defend basic American values.	4.26	79.60%	2.29	25.30%	1.97

Source: Data provided by GfK Group/Strauss Institute's TMASS Survey, May, 2018, n = 2,066.

[a] 5 = Strongly agree, 1 = Strongly disagree.

Table 9.4 Advice from Trump's Supporters Regarding Twitter

Advice	Observation	Respondent
Build community	"I voted for you and believe that you can bring change, but your tweeting has to stop. It is too much. We need togetherness."	Stacy Hurley, Dundalk, MD (January 9, 2017)
Be proportional	"SNL has spoofed POTUS since '75. Sorry, it's hilarious. I voted for you but come on! No more Twitter! Be above it! SAD!"	Steve Cvetlovic, Pittsburgh, PA (January 15, 2017)
Act presidentially	"Please stop tweeting this nonsense. Not presidential at all! I voted for you, now start acting like a president, please."	Cindy Nevling, Levittown, PA (January 15, 2017)
Establish priorities	"Some of his tweets are, like, what the hell does that have to do with running the country?"	Francis Smazal, Marshfield, WI (November 5, 2017)
Stay on task	"I think he rants and raves. He doesn't think about it. I think he can do better things with his time."	Scott McCommons, Altoona, PA (March 29, 2017)
Avoid distractions	"He needs to tone it down and forget about Snoop Dogg, forget about Arnold Schwarzenegger. We don't really care about them, do we?"	Ray Starner, eastern Pennsylvania (March 29, 2017)
Watch your mouth	"Presidentially, I kind of like where he's going. Personally, he needs to put that phone down and learn to shut his mouth when he needs to. His mouth is his own worst enemy."	Duane Gray, Boise, ID (November 5, 2017)
Do your job	"He creates too many distractions, which weakens any momentum in policy and legislation."	Ken Cornacchione, Venice, FL (November 5, 2017)
Get some help	"While I like the fact that he uses Twitter, he might think of putting a trusted advisor between himself and the send button. A second opinion on some of his tweets might not be a bad idea."	Lee Mills, Shelby County, TN (January 5, 2018)

Table 9.4 cont'd

Advice	Observation	Respondent
Grow up	"Kill your Twitter. Turn it off, shut it down, block, whatever ... I mean, it's a good tool to be able to mass-communicate quickly, but I think knowing Trump – and this is just the way he is – he gets all 'grrrr.' He gets all hot under the collar."	Anonymous active duty military, Niceville, FL (May 12, 2017)

Source: These citizens' reactions (and more) can be found in Carlos Garcia, "Many of Trump's Supporters Are Pleading with Him to Stop Tweeting," *The Blaze*, January 9, 2017. Accessed at www.theblaze.com/news/2017/01/09/many-of-trumps-supporters-are-pleading-with-him-to-stop-tweeting; Tim Molloy and Brian Welk, "Trump Voters Beg Him: Stop Tweeting," *The Wrap*, January 18, 2017. Accessed at www.thewrap.com/trump-voters-beg-stop-tweeting-snl-meryl-streep-apprentice/; Susan Page and Josh Hafner, "One Year Later, Trump Voters Blame the President's Tweets for His Troubles," *USA Today*, November 5, 2017. Accessed at www .usatoday.com/story/news/politics/2017/11/05/one-year-later-trump-voters-blame-presidents-tweets-his-troubles/828180001/; Suzanne Presto, Brynn Gingras, and Chris Welch, "Trump Voters to President: Stop Twitter Rants," *CNN Politics*, March 20, 2017. Accessed at www .cnn.com/2017/03/28/politics/trump-tweets-supporters-ccntv/index.html; Jenna Johnson, "'I Wish He'd Quit Tweeting': Many Trump Backers Say It's Time for Him to Put Down His Phone," *Washington Post*, May 12, 2017. Accessed at www.washingtonpost.com/politics/i-wish-hed-quit-tweetingmany-trump-backers-say-its-time-for-him-to-put-down-hisphone/2017/05/10/9e806526-319a-11e7-9534-00e4656c22aa_story.html?noredirect=on&utm_term=.461bad64e86c; Natalie Martin, "Trump's Bans and Tweets Spark Diverse Opinions among Supporters," *Daily Helmsman*, February 8, 2017. Accessed at www.dailyhelmsman .com/news/trump-s-bans-and-tweets-spark-diverse-opinions-among-supporters/article_8d9c4d32-ee43-11e6-8f00-4f3954f0855a.html.

the public perceives him to be acting and thinking day in and day out. At the moment, much of the perception of Trump on a daily, weekly and monthly basis is formed by what he tweets. And that perception is not good."[46]

Mr. Trump's supporters understand such matters. As we see in Table 9.4, they come at the issue from multiple perspectives but with a clear sense of urgency: Do what you're being paid to do, get some help, grow up, act like a president. Political professionals agree, arguing that Trump should "hand over the reins to a coordinated team of media strategists who can force him to stay on message – or in his case, articulate one."[47] This advice was provided by *Salon*'s Nico Lang two weeks after Mr. Trump was elected president. A year later, a Quinnipiac poll found that judgments of Mr. Trump's level-headedness and fitness for office were inversely related to perceptions of his Twitter addiction.[48] Another year passed and the TMASS survey again tapped this disquietude. Many Americans continued to support the President, some even loved him, but they hated his nocturnal habits. And yet he types.

"The tweets bother me," says Melissa Hight of Raleigh, North Carolina. "To me, firing off these tweets is just childish. He should be above that."[49] "I think his language is unprofessional," says Annie Anthony, another North Carolinian. "He uses words like 'sad' and 'bad.' That's first-grade language. We're an intelligent population who elected you. Represent us!"[50] "Trump's got to lay off that Instagram and Twitter crack," says Carlos Neal of Detroit. "Put his phone down and stop all the nonsense."[51] The American people rarely speak with one voice but in this case they do. But their message is going unheard and here is why: Donald Trump has his own opinions about such matters.

What Trump Says

While many Americans wish that Donald Trump would stop tweeting, not all do. "I feel it's a great way to reach out to your constituents and create a give-and-take, because people obviously respond to his tweets, retweets. In general, I'm in favor of it," said Ilene Wood of Erasmus, Pennsylvania. Scottie Gontarek of Niceville, Florida, agreed: "I'd rather hear honest and crude than unhonest and sanitized." Anna Para of Youngstown, Ohio, is even more passionate: "He's, like, tenacious sometimes and says stuff off the cuff like we do, like real Americans do. You know, we're not perfect. I'm tired of suave. I'm tired of polished. I'm tired of the teleprompter."[52]

Donald Trump understands. He knows that spontaneity and impatience are his best qualities. Trump is a "man of action" combined with a "man of words." Normally, says social philosopher Eric Hoffer, the man of words launches a mass movement with his prophecies, after which he yields to the man of action who carries out the vision.[53] Via Twitter, Donald Trump does double-duty: 280 characters are more than enough to get done what must be done.

Twitter is a pedestrian tool and that also appeals to Trump, letting him violate rules of grammar he never really understood. Broken syntax, random exclamation points, misplaced modifiers, and capital letters are his way of thumbing his nose at the kids in school who did better in English Composition. Grammatical niceties slow things down but Twitter is all about speed. Twitter lets you say things that have no meaning (e.g., "stable genius") but that sound meaningful; it lets you conflate constructs (e.g., "rigged witch hunt") and turn them into an argument. Twitter lets you make assertions you do not understand (e.g., "collusion is not a crime") that sound conclusory. Twitter also lets you exaggerate like crazy (e.g., "all will be great") and have people treat it matter-of-factly.

To get a better sense of how Trump operates, I subjected some 7,000 of his tweets (randomly selected from the Trump Twitter Archive) to computer-based inspection, paying special attention to the keywords he used.[54] The notion here is that some words – *Obamacare, terrorism, courage* – are emotionally evocative, even when their context is unknown or unclear. Some keywords have sacred meanings – *charity, justice, progress* – so politicians often use them. Other keywords, those that literary scholar Richard Weaver called "devil terms" – words such as *fascism, drugs,* and *un-American* – are heinous and so politicians often use them.[55] Still other keywords, words such as *immigrant* and *China,* conjure up positive associations at one time, dark forebodings at another, so politicians often use them.

Table 9.5 presents an overview of Trump's tweets and the results are hardly surprising. Donald Trump sold himself to the American people as a scion of industry and his linguistic choices reflect that, with economic terms constituting more than a third of his keywords. As we also see, Trump's campaign tweets sounded similar to those he issued as president, although his concern for healthcare ramped up once he took office. As we see in Table 9.6, the values Trump championed on the stump also carried over to his presidency. Clear, pragmatic accomplishment was his call to action. Table 9.6 also shows how potent Equity was in Trump's universe, a rhetorical choice that made him appealing to industrial workers. People need more and better jobs, said Trump; it was their *right* to have them:

- *January 8, 2016:* I hope all workers demand that their @Teamsters reps endorse Donald J. Trump. Nobody knows jobs like I do! Don't let them sell you out!
- *July 30, 2016:* The "Rust Belt" was created by politicians like the Clintons who allowed our jobs to be stolen from us by other countries like Mexico.

Table 9.5 Policy Keywords Used in Trump's Tweets, 2016 and 2017

Dimension	Keyword	2016		2017	
		n	%	n	%
Finances	*Banking*	15	2.51%	2	0.35%
	Wall Street	20	3.35%	4	0.70%
	Economy	33	5.53%	35	6.11%
	Energy	21	3.52%	13	2.27%
	Jobs	153	25.63%	104	18.15%
Social net	*Health*	14	2.35%	86	15.01%
	Obamacare	49	8.21%	80	13.96%
	Schools	5	0.84%	5	0.87%
Immigration	*Muslims*	3	0.50%	3	0.52%
	Immigrants	41	6.87%	24	4.19%
	Border	47	7.87%	56	9.77%
Diversity	*African-Americans*	11	1.84%	1	0.17%
	Hispanics	7	1.17%	4	0.70%
	Women	55	9.21%	47	8.20%
Global threats	*Foreign policy*	11	1.84%	2	0.35%
	Middle East	5	0.84%	8	1.40%
	Terrorism	51	8.54%	44	7.68%
Domestic threats	*Crime*	37	6.20%	38	6.63%
	Guns	10	1.68%	2	0.35%
	Drugs	9	1.51%	15	2.62%
	Total	597		573	

Source: Trump Twitter Archive (http://www.trumptwitterarchive.com/archive). Number of Tweets in 2016 = 4,291, in 2017 = 2,590.

- *September 4, 2016*: To the African-American community: The Democrats have failed you for fifty years, high crime, poor schools, no jobs. I will fix it, VOTE "T."

Trump's tweets are also barometric. Everything has a cost, everyone a price. That which cannot be quantified – education, religion, charity – falls to the bottom of Trump's hierarchy, as we see in Table 9.6. To be a functioning human being is to be one demonstrably so. To fail is to not measure up. When Marco Rubio sweated too much, said Trump, he lost his chance at leadership, as did Hillary Clinton when her annual physical raised questions about her health. Tabloid newspapers are best because they sell more papers; Trump Tower beats Marriott because it has more elevators. To assess people empirically is to be in charge of them; to announce the results of your evaluation is to make life meaningful:

- *Truth*: "I am attracting the biggest crowds, by far the best poll numbers, also by far. Much of the media is totally dishonest."
- *Duty*: "I settled the Trump University lawsuit for a small fraction of the potential award because as President I have to focus on our country."
- *Love*: "I'm so proud of my wife Melania and the launch of her new jewelry line."
- *Loyalty*: "I'm loyal to people who've done good work for me."
- *Journalism*: "I was so happy when I heard that @Politico, one of the most dishonest political outlets, is losing a fortune. Pure scum!"
- *Weather*: "The evening news broadcasts must stop talking about weather – boring and too many other topics."[56]

Empirically based tweets like these especially appeal to those who like beauty pageants, who play the numbers, who compete in fantasy football, and who watch *The Voice* on TV. Trump's world is Hobbesian, a place where winners and losers are easily distinguished. But we would miss the magic of Donald Trump if we concentrated solely on the dark side. *A more careful inspection shows that Trump's tweets are remarkably buoyant and consistently so*, as we see in Table 9.7. To be sure, Trump's tweets are sometimes negative and we hear about them daily. But in many ways Donald Trump became president because of the promises he made.[57] Perhaps he hoodwinked people when doing so; perhaps they were taken in by the best flim-flam

Table 9.6 Values Keywords Used in Trump's Tweets, 2016 and 2017

Dimension	Keyword	2016		2017	
		n	%	n	%
Accomplishment	*Competition*	14	7.22%	6	2.27%
	Individualism	2	1.03%	7	2.65%
	Hard work	3	1.55%	6	2.27%
	Achievement	2	1.03%	6	2.27%
	Progress	2	1.03%	14	5.30%
	Success	15	7.73%	40	15.15%
Equity	*Fairness*	32	16.49%	26	9.85%
	Justice	18	9.28%	30	11.36%
	Equality	5	2.58%	4	1.52%
Protection	*Courage*	6	3.09%	17	6.44%
	Patriotism	5	2.58%	9	3.41%
	Freedom	26	13.40%	27	10.23%
	Liberty	6	3.09%	3	1.14%
Possibility	*Unity*	18	9.28%	20	7.58%
	Peace	8	4.12%	18	6.82%
	Optimism	3	1.55%	16	6.06%
Growth	*Education*	8	4.12%	4	1.52%
	Science	3	1.55%	1	0.38%
Benevolence	*Volunteerism*	5	2.58%	3	1.14%
	Charity	6	3.09%	0	0.00%
Devotion	*Religion*	3	1.55%	5	1.89%
	Faith	4	2.06%	2	0.76%
	Total	194		264	

Source: Trump Twitter Archive (http://www.trumptwitterarchive.com/archive). Number of Tweets in 2016 = 4,291, in 2017 = 2,590.

man since P. T. Barnum. But facts are facts and tweets are tweets. Donald Trump's postings are considerably more positive than negative.

Preposterous as this claim may seem, even a cursory look at the Trump Twitter Archive confirms it. It takes a strong stomach to read Trump's self-congratulatory tweets but his supporters often found them inspiring:

- *March 22, 2016*: "I have proven to be far more correct about terrorism than anybody – and it's not even close."
- *June 6, 2016*: "I have been able to spend far less money than others on the campaign and finish #1."
- *May 31, 2016*: "I have raised/given a tremendous amount of money to our great veterans."
- *August 21, 2016*: "I have been drawing very big and enthusiastic crowds."

Admittedly, there is nothing newsworthy here (unless one is fascinated by the elasticity of the human ego) so reporters ignore such claptrap. But Trump's upbeat style came in handy on the campaign trail, especially since his opponents spent their time attacking him personally. Although hardly a policy wonk, Trump brought a sense of optimism to that realm as well:

- *April 30, 2016*: "Nobody but Donald Trump will save Israel."
- *March 26, 2016*: "Nobody will protect our nation like Donald J. Trump."
- *January 8, 2016*: "I will create jobs like no one else."
- *March 26, 2016*: "Nobody has more respect for women than Donald Trump!"

As we see in Table 9.8, Trump's upbeat style continued into his presidency, with positive emotions dominating negative ones. Much of this consisted of self-puffery and over-the-top promises to make America great again. But to dismiss such sentiments is to miss the very rationale of politics – to give people hope that their problems can be solved. Trump's tweets steamroll over knotty issues and vastly overestimate what a single leader can do. But voters want to know what is grand about life and Donald Trump tells them:

- *December 1, 2016*: "Getting ready to leave for the Great State of Indiana and meet the hard working and wonderful people of Carrier A.C."

Table 9.7 Personality Keywords Used in Trump's Tweets, 2016 and 2017

Dimension	Keyword	2016		2017	
		n	%	n	%
Ignorance	Stupid	10	0.47%	3	0.23%
	Ridiculous	9	0.42%	6	0.46%
	Dumb	23	1.08%	3	0.23%
	Crazy	23	1.08%	11	0.85%
	Boring	11	0.52%	1	0.08%
Malevolence	Bad	139	6.54%	88	6.77%
	Dangerous	4	0.19%	11	0.85%
	Evil	10	0.47%	7	0.54%
	Vicious	9	0.42%	4	0.31%
	Nasty	18	0.85%	2	0.15%
Ineptness	Crazy	23	1.08%	11	0.85%
	Sad	53	2.49%	35	2.69%
	Ineffective	9	0.42%	1	0.08%
	Incompetent	7	0.33%	0	0.00%
	Worthless	4	0.19%	0	0.00%
Dishonesty	Fake	5	0.24%	198	15.23%
	False	31	1.46%	14	1.08%
	Biased	31	1.46%	6	0.46%
	Crooked	280	13.17%	34	2.62%
	Phony	33	1.55%	23	1.77%
Attractiveness	Beautiful	17	0.80%	28	2.15%
	Classy	3	0.14%	0	0.00%
	Fine	17	0.80%	14	1.08%
	Nice	53	2.49%	17	1.31%

Table 9.7 cont'd

Dimension	Keyword	2016		2017	
		n	%	n	%
Intelligence	*Brilliant*	6	0.28%	3	0.23%
	Smart	30	1.41%	17	1.31%
	Wise	8	0.38%	0	0.00%
Probity	*True*	39	1.83%	22	1.69%
	Honest	75	3.53%	31	2.38%
	Fair	32	1.51%	26	2.00%
Integrity	*Decent*	2	0.09%	0	0.00%
	Kind	10	0.47%	5	0.38%
	Good	81	3.81%	86	6.62%
Capacity	*Great*	850	39.98%	498	38.31%
	Wonderful	48	2.26%	49	3.77%
	Amazing	84	3.95%	22	1.69%
	Awesome	5	0.24%	0	0.00%
	Fantastic	27	1.27%	17	1.31%
	Excellent	4	0.19%	3	0.23%
	Perfect	3	0.14%	4	0.31%
Overall	Total	2,126		1,300	
	Positive	1,394	65.57%	842	64.77%
	Negative	732	34.43%	458	35.23%

Source: Trump Twitter Archive (http://www.trumptwitterarchive.com/archive). Number of Tweets in 2016 = 4,291, in 2017 = 2,590.

- *January 16, 2017*: "Martin Luther King Day and all of the many wonderful things that he stood for. Honor him for being the great man that he was!"

Table 9.8 Emotional Keywords Used in Trump's Tweets, 2016 and 2017

Dimension	Keyword	2016		2017	
		n	%	n	%
Positive Feelings	*Respect*	29	5.65%	53	14.68%
	Liking	153	29.82%	62	17.17%
	Love	94	18.32%	44	12.19%
	Honor	52	10.14%	101	27.98%
	Enjoyment	108	21.05%	33	9.14%
Negative Feelings	*Hate*	24	4.68%	23	6.37%
	Fear	6	1.17%	4	1.11%
	Criticism	9	1.75%	1	0.28%
	Anger	31	6.04%	28	7.76%
	Hurt	7	1.36%	12	3.32%
Overall	Total	513		361	
	Positive feelings	436	84.99%	293	81.16%
	Negative feelings	77	15.01%	68	18.84%

Source: Trump Twitter Archive (http://www.trumptwitterarchive.com/archive). Number of Tweets in 2016 = 4,291, in 2017 = 2,590.

- *May 14, 2017*: "Wishing @FLOTUS Melania and all of the great mothers out there a wonderful day ahead with family and friends! Happy #MothersDay."
- *September 6, 2017*: "Wonderful to be in North Dakota with the incredible hardworking men & women @ the Andeavor Refinery."
- *March 14, 2018*: "It was wonderful to be back in Missouri where our push for historic tax cuts all began. Six months ago I promised that we would cut taxes to bring Main Street roaring back – and that is exactly what is happening!"

What do we have here? Local voters being thanked for showing up at a rally. Community icons elevated for a moment or two. Praise bestowed on local folks who work hard. Ritualistic celebration of historical moments. Businesses applauded for doing business, heroes for being heroic, mothers for being maternal. These are things that all politicians say. One finds self-aggrandizement here but that is hardly uncommon in Washington, DC.

Twitter and Trump, a natural pairing. Trump doesn't "spend any time self-editing," say Harvard's Galen Stolee and Steve Caton, "which means he also [doesn't] take time to self-censor."[58] Like any good salesperson, Trump senses when to be brash and when to change direction. He knows that if he stumbles over a recalcitrant fact or two, his Twitter supporters will soon move on "to his next tweet or the next issue of the moment."[59] So Trump consigns himself to the moment, refusing to be intimidated by his often sordid past. A dozen tweets, a hundred tweets, will make such things go away, he reasons. For many Americans, they do.

Trump does not use Twitter to interact with voters even though Twitter is a quintessentially interactive medium. Instead, he hits and runs – to the next issue, to his next opponent, to another feeling state. "Trump tweets like a teenaged girl," says Fred Turner, "not just in frequency but in genre and diction."[60] His impoliteness, his political incorrectness, his grammatical mistakes make him authentic, a man with nothing to hide.[61] Trump's "incessant Twitter feed," says *Politico*'s Darren Samuelsohn, is "a place where secrets go to die."[62]

Donald Trump uses Twitter to make people feel less tired. He thumbs his nose at the establishment, making his supporters feel like renegades, part of something radical. While many of his backers wish he would curtail his use of Twitter, they also feel, as my surveys show, that his tweets speak directly to the average American, that they are refreshingly straightforward, and that they counteract the media's influence. To have Donald Trump in your Twitter feed is to feel energized.[63]

Typically, those who criticize politics attack its falseness and remoteness. How, then, could they complain about Trump's tweets? He is there from morning 'til night, telling you what he thinks even as he thinks it. "I'm your portable president," Trump seems to say, "my tweets follow you around – at work, at home, and in-between." Some columnists say all of this portrays "an undisciplined, capricious mind prone to laziness and emotional outbursts" and that the President should adhere to "a basic standard of properness and decorum."[64] Pish tosh, says Mr. Trump. Pish tosh, say his supporters.

Conclusion

Twitter is a world in which filtering shows weakness and where words are meant to be bold. Twitter respects the sanctity of the moment and assumes that truth lies within our loins. Twitter offers easy connections to practically anyone, new relationships at your fingertips. Brilliant thoughts are not needed on Twitter but cleverness is, unbridled repartee as well. Twitter is a communication medium but it is also a showplace. You can say anything you want on Twitter or you can just lurk. You can try out new ideas without real repercussions ensuing and you can watch your fellow humans being attacked by Twitter dogs.

Twitter is Donald Trump's world. He meets all its requirements. He is depthless and instinctual, saying whatever comes to mind. His policy preferences change in a nanosecond, so Twitter becomes a record of his whims and half-thoughts, all updated in real time. Trump has no interest in the past, so he is unthreatened by self-contradictions. In his former, corporate life, Trump shared everything he felt as soon as he felt it, and he was rewarded for doing so. Trump has all the money in the world and all the words in the world. If his tweets intimidate you, you have not yet evolved.

The Trump–Twitter world is not the press's world. They hate what Trump says, constantly stressing his negative tweets even though doing so misrepresents the Trump corpus. Naturally, reporters are incensed by his attacks on the Fourth Estate but that only inspires Trump to return fire. Still, Trump is good for the newspaper business, so commentators attack his morally besotted self day in and day out. CNN's Don Lemon and Anderson Cooper will live a thousand years because of the exercise they get when chasing after Trump.

"Enough!" declare most Americans. Trump's tweets – the ones they notice, that is – make a mockery of governance and waste their time. Most Americans want the President to get on with life instead of using Twitter to settle scores. Republican voters are slightly more tolerant of his Twitter indulgences but not by much. They have real jobs, after all, and, while they know that Trump has his adversaries, they are dismayed by the fisticuffs. "Be a president!" they demand. "Do some deals!" "Get over yourself!" Still Trump tweets.

One study by political scientist John Lovett and his colleagues notes that Donald Trump has three motivations for tweeting: (1) generating (or reacting to) media coverage, (2) pushing specific policy positions, and (3) protecting his self-image. My studies reveal a fourth reason: rallying the people. Voters need to be heartened when things go poorly, to be reminded of their common ties when things go well. Thus, even when President Trump celebrates his own success – for having passed a new law, for having attracted a grand audience – it is at least in part a people's victory. In these ways, at least, Trump's tweets can be considered a boon, even if a modest one.

Notes

1 As quoted in Susan Chiara, "Who Likes Trump's Tweets and Why," *New York Times*, June 29, 2017. Accessed at www.nytimes.com/2017/06/29/opinion/who-likes-trumps-tweets-and-why.html.

2 The preceding senatorial quotations can be found in Jessica Estepa, "Toxic Tweets Turn DC Stomachs: Trump's Own Party Urges Him to Stop Poisoning Political Discourse," *PressReader,* June 30, 2017. Accessed at www.pressreader.com/usa/the-signal/20170630/281767039240828.

3 Kathleen Parker, "Parker: Even Staunch Supporters Want Trump to Stop Tweeting," *Columbian*, June 8, 2017. Accessed at www.columbian.com/news/2017/jun/08/parker-even-staunch-supporters-want-trump-to-stop-tweeting/.

4 Dan Balz, "Loyalty, Unease in Trump's Midwest," *Washington Post*, May 10, 2018. Accessed at www.washingtonpost.com/graphics/2018/national/trump-voters/.

5 Christine Beswick, "Trump Approval Rating Drops as Some of His Own Voters Find Him 'Suspect' and a 'Liar,'" *The Inquisitr*, November 3, 2017. Accessed at www.inquisitr.com/4596553/trump-approval-rating-drops-as-some-of-his-own-voters-find-him-suspect-and-a-liar/.

6 Nate Silver, "Never Tweet, Mr. President: It Could Help Your Approval Rating," *FiveThirtyEight*, September 28, 2017. Accessed at https://fivethirtyeight.com/features/never-tweet-mr-president/. See also Marisa Fernandez, "Trump's Tweets Are Less Read and Influential Than People May Think," *Axios*, October 4, 2018. Accessed at www.axios.com/by-the-numbers-trumps-tweets-less-influential-fca7df91-4050-437e-9b4e-79748501e226.html.

7 As reported in Tom Jacobs, "Are Trump's Tweets Self-Defeating? New Research Finds Incivility Decreases Politicians' Public Approval, even in a Hyper-Partisan Environment," *Pacific Standard*, September 13, 2018. Accessed at https://psmag.com/news/are-trumps-tweets-self-defeating.

8 As quoted in Rachel Stoltzfoos, "Trump Fans Beg Him to Ditch 'Stupid Tweeting' and Focus on Hillary," *Daily Caller*, October 1, 2016. Accessed at https://dailycaller.com/2016/10/01/trump-fans-beg-him-to-ditch-stupid-tweeting-and-focus-on-hillary/.

9 As quoted in Pilar Melendez, "'MAGA Mom' Compiles All of Trump's Tweets in Bible-Like Book, Sells It for $35 a Pop," *Daily Beast*, October 23, 2018. Accessed at www.thedailybeast.com/maga-mom-compiles-all-of-trumps-tweets-in-bible-like-book-sells-it-for-dollar35-a-pop.

10 As quoted in Suzanne Presto, Brynn Gingras, and Chris Welch, "Trump Voters to President: Stop Twitter Rants," *CNN Politics*, March 29, 2017. Accessed at www.cnn.com/2017/03/28/politics/trump-tweets-supporters-ccntv/index.html.

11 Lawrence Douglas, "Donald Trump's Disregard for Words – and Truth – Is Finally Catching Up with Him," *Guardian*, March 18. 2017. Accessed at www.theguardian

.com/commentisfree/2017/mar/18/donald-trump-disregard-words-truth-finally-catching-up-with-him.

12 George Saunders, "Who Are All These Trump Supporters? At the Candidate's Rallies, a New Understanding of America Emerges," *New Yorker: American Chronicles*, July 11–18, 2016. Accessed at www.newyorker.com/magazine/2016/07/11/george-saunders-goes-to-trump-rallies.

13 Ibid.

14 As reported ibid.

15 Francisco S. Pérez, Irene A. Román, and Javier L. Rodriguez, "Seizing the Populist Rhetorical Toolkit: a Comparative Analysis of Trump and Clinton's Discourse on Twitter during the 2016 U.S. Presidential Campaign," in Michele Lockhart (ed.), *President Donald Trump and His Political Discourse: Ramifications of Rhetoric via Twitter* (New York: Routledge, 2019), pp. 13–32.

16 Frank Newport, "Deconstructing Trump's Use of Twitter," *Gallup.com*, May 16, 2018. Accessed at https://news.gallup.com/poll/234509/deconstructing-trump-twitter.aspx.

17 Scott Wallsten, "Do Likes of Trump's Tweets Predict His Popularity?" *Technology Policy Institute*, April 17, 2018. Accessed at https://techpolicyinstitute.org/2018/04/17/do-likes-of-trumps-tweets-predict-his-popularity/.

18 Scott Adams, "The Power of the Presidential Tweet: Trump's Online Missives Make His Supporters Laugh and Even His Opponents Think Past the Sale," *Wall Street Journal*, October 22, 2017. Accessed at www.wsj.com/articles/the-power-of-the-presidential-tweet-1508702456.

19 For more on this sense of interactivity, see Christian R. Hoffman, "Crooked Hillary and Dumb Trump: The Strategic Use and Effect of Negative Evaluations in U.S. Election Campaign Tweets," *Internet Pragmatics*, 1:1 (2018), 55–87.

20 Mathew Ingram, "The 140-Character President," *Columbia Journalism Review*, Fall 2017. Accessed at www.cjr.org/special_report/trump-twitter-tweets-president.php/.

21 As quoted ibid.

22 Adam Gopnik, "Trump's Tweets Are Ridiculous, but Perilous to Ignore," *New Yorker*, April 17, 2018. Accessed at www.newyorker.com/news/daily-comment/trumps-tweets-are-ridiculous-but-perilous-to-ignore.

23 Ibid.

24 Steven P. Nawara and Mandi Bates Bailey, "Analyzing Candidate Use of Social Media in the 2016 Presidential Campaign," in Jody C. Baumgartner and Terri L. Towner (eds.), *The Internet and the 2016 Presidential Campaign* (Lanham, MD: Lexington Books, 2017), pp. 79–108.

25 Colleen Elizabeth Kelley, *A Rhetoric of Divisive Partisanship: The 2016 American Presidential Campaign Discourse of Bernie Sanders and Donald Trump* (Lanham, MD: Lexington Books, 2018); Ann Crigler, Marion Just, and Whitney Hua, "Twitter News and Trails: A Hybrid Media Analysis of 2016 Presidential Campaign Communication," Paper presented at the annual convention of the International Communication Association, San Diego, CA, May 2017; Orin Tsur, Katherine Ognyanova, and David Lazer, "The Data Behind Trump's Twitter Takeover," *Politico*, April 29, 2016. Accessed at www.politico.com/magazine/story/2016/04/donald-trump-2016-twitter-takeover-213861.

26 Nawara and Bailey, "Analyzing Candidate Use of Social Media in the 2016 Presidential Campaign," p. 89.

27 As quoted in Jenna Johnson, "'I Wish He'd Quit Tweeting': Many Trump Backers Say It's Time for Him to Put Down His Phone," *Washington Post*, May 12, 2017. Accessed at www.washingtonpost.com/politics/i-wish-hed-quit-tweetingmany-

trump-backers-say-its-time-for-him-to-put-down-hisphone/2017/05/10/9e806526-319a-11e7-9534-00e4656c22aa_story.html?utm_term=.f9e35d273c5f.

28 Peter L. Francia, "Free Media and Twitter in the 2016 Presidential Election: the Unconventional Campaign of Donald Trump," *Social Science Computer Review*, 36:4 (2017), 440–55.

29 Christopher Wells, Dhavan Shah, Ayellet Pelled, Jon Pevehouse, and Zhonghai Sun, "Trump, Twitter, and Media Responsiveness: a Systems Approach," Paper presented at the annual convention of the International Communication Association, Prague, Czech Republic, June 2018.

30 For more on this matter of amplification, see Brian T. Edwards, "Trump from Reality TV to Twitter, or the Selfie-Determination of Nations," *Arizona Quarterly*, 74:3 (2018), 25–45.

31 Yini Zhang, Chris Wells, Song Wang, and Karl Rohe, "Attention and Amplification in the Hybrid Media System: The Composition and Activity of Donald Trump's Twitter Following during the 2016 Presidential Election," *New Media and Society*, 20:9 (2018), 3161–82.

32 Newport, "Deconstructing Trump's Use of Twitter," *Gallup.com*.

33 Patrick Fletchall, "This Halloween, the Scariest Monsters Are the Trump and Hillary Inside Us All," *The Federalist*, October 11, 2016. Accessed at http://thefederalist.com/2016/10/11/halloween-scariest-monsters-trump-hillary-inside-us/.

34 See Jasmine C. Lee and Kevin Quealy, "The 547 People, Places and Things Donald Trump Has Insulted on Twitter: a Complete List," *New York Times*, November 21, 2018. Accessed at www.nytimes.com/interactive/2016/01/28/upshot/donald-trump-twitter-insults.html.

35 Joseph Lowndes, "Trump, Twitter and the Authoritarian Presidency," *Huffington Post*, December 12, 2016. Accessed at www.huffingtonpost.com/joseph-lowndes/the-authoritarian-potenti_b_13558344.html.

36 These are the remarks of Silicon Valley founding father Jaron Lanier, as quoted in Maureen Dowd, "For Whom the Trump Tolls," *New York Times*, July 7, 2018. Accessed at www.nytimes.com/2018/07/07/opinion/sunday/trump-twitter-social-media.html.

37 Brian L. Ott, "The Age of Twitter: Donald J. Trump and the Politics of Debasement," *Critical Studies in Media Communication*, 34:1 (2017), 66. See also Sarah Smith-Frigerio and J. Brian Houston, "Crazy, Insane, Nut Job, Wacko, Basket Case, and Psycho: Donald Trump's Tweets Surrounding Mental Health Issues and Attacks on Media Personalities," in Lockhart (ed.), *President Donald Trump and His Political Discourse*, 114–130; Bethany A. Conway-Silva, Christine R. Filer, Kate Kenski, and Eric Tsetsi, "Reassessing Twitter's Agenda-Building Power: an Analysis of Intermedia Agenda-Setting Effects During the 2016 Presidential Primary Season," *Social Science Computer Review*, 36:4 (2018), 469–83; Ramona Kreis, "The 'Tweet Politics' of President Trump," *Journal of Language and Politics*, 16:4 (2017), 607–18.

38 Chris Cillizza, "Donald Trump Doesn't Really Care What You Think of His Twitter Obsession," *Washington Post*, March 16, 2017. Accessed at www.washingtonpost.com/news/the-fix/wp/2017/03/16/people-really-dont-like-donald-trumps-tweets-that-wont-stop-him/?utm_term=.9c07e20ab2de.

39 Steven Shepard, "Poll: Trump's Tweets Damage the Nation," *Politico*, May 31, 2018. Accessed at www.politico.com/story/2018/05/31/poll-trumps-tweets-damage-the-nation-614311.

40 Joshua Scacco and Lauren Copeland, "When the President Tweets: Exploring the Normative Foundations of Contemporary Presidential Communication," Paper

delivered at the annual meeting of the Midwest Political Science Association, Chicago, April 2018.

41 David Byler, "We Got Polling Data on 3,000 Trump Tweets: Here's What We Found," *Weekly Standard*, July 9, 2018. Accessed at www.weeklystandard.com/david-byler/yougov-releases-polling-data-on-3-000-tweets-from-trumps-twitter-account.

42 Cillizza, "Donald Trump Doesn't Really Care," *Washington Post*.

43 For additional details about the TMASS survey, see https://moody.utexas.edu/sites/default/files/2018%20Topline%20Results.pdf.

44 Statistical patterns for "tweet less often." Age: 18–$29 = 10.5\%$, 30–$44 = 18.9\%$, 45–$59 = 27.8\%$, $60+ = 42.8\%$; $\chi^2(1,5, n = 2066) = 22.149$, $p = 0.008$; Education: less than high school $= 6.3\%$, high school $= 25.1\%$, some college $= 29.7\%$, BA+ $= 39.0\%$; $\chi^2(1,5, n = 2066) = 22.789$, $p = 0.003$; Evangelical: yes $= 38.7\%$, no $= 61.3\%$; $\chi^2(1,3, n = 2066) = 20.939$, $p = 0.0008$; Facebook: yes $= 63.2\%$, no $= 36.8\%$; $\chi^2(1,3, n = 2066) = 21.401$, $p = 0.000$; Gender: male $= 48.666\%$, female $= 51.4\%$; $\chi^2(1,3, n = 2066) = 22.149$, $p = 0.008$.

45 All of these questions (and twelve others of the same sort) were pretested during the winter of 2018 with a smaller national sample (n = 620) that was slightly younger and slightly more Democratic than those in the final survey. Responses to both the pretest and the final survey were virtually identical.

46 Chris Cillizza, "Voters to Trump: Never Tweet," *CNN.com*, August 8, 2017. Accessed at www.cnn.com/2017/08/08/politics/trump-twitter-cnn-poll/index.html.

47 Nico Lang, "Dear Donald Trump: It's Time to Stop Tweeting," *Salon*, November 21, 2016. Accessed at www.salon.com/2016/11/21/dear-donald-trump-it-is-time-to-stop-tweeting/.

48 Philip Bump, "Most Americans Still Want Trump to Stop Tweeting – and Think He's Unfit for Office," *Washington Post*, September 27, 2017. Accessed at www.washingtonpost.com/news/politics/wp/2017/09/27/most-americans-still-want-trump-to-stop-tweeting-and-think-hes-unfit-for-office/.

49 As quoted in James Hohmann, "The Daily 202: Trump Voters Have Buyer's Remorse in North Carolina Focus Group," *Washington Post*, November 16, 2017. Accessed at www.washingtonpost.com/news/powerpost/paloma/daily-202/2017/11/16/daily-202-trump-voters-have-buyer-s-remorse-in-north-carolina-focus-group/5a0d0c8a30fb045a2e003078/.

50 As quoted ibid.

51 As quoted in Katharine Q. Seelye and Bill Pennington, "Here's What NFL Fans Think of Trump's Comments and Anthem Protests," *New York Times*, September 24, 2017. Accessed at www.nytimes.com/2017/09/24/sports/football/nfl-trump-patriots.html.

52 For the foregoing quotations, see Presto, Gingras, and Welch, "Trump Voters to President"; Johnson, "I Wish He'd Quit Tweeting"; and Rush Limbaugh, "CNN Finds Happy Trump Voters in Youngstown, Ohio," *RushLimbaugh.com*, January 18, 2018. Accessed at www.rushlimbaugh.com/daily/2018/01/18/cnn-finds-happy-trump-voters-in-youngstown-ohio.

53 Eric Hoffer, *The True Believer: Thoughts on the Nature of Mass Movements* (New York: Harper, 1951).

54 See the Trump Twitter Archive at www.trumptwitterarchive.com/.

55 Richard M. Weaver, *The Ethics of Rhetoric* (Chicago: Henry Regnery Co., 1953).

56 These tweets can be found in Peter Osborne, *How Trump Thinks: His Tweets and the Birth of a New Political Language* (New York: Head of Zeus, 2017), pp. 11, 61, 135, 137, 155, 157.

57 One study has shown that Trump's least popular tweets are those attacking other people, while his best received honor World War II veterans, first responders, and the U.S. Women's Hockey Team. Yet another study finds that his tweets on immigration became much more positive during the general election than they were during the primaries. See Ariel Edward-Levy, "Even Trump's Base Seems to Prefer His Less 'Trump' Tweets," *Huffington Post*, October 22, 2018. Accessed at www .huffingtonpost.com/entry/even-trumps-base-generally-prefers-his-less-trumpy-tweets_ us_5bca0217e4b0d38b5877b62f. For more along these lines, see Chris Haynes and Justin Sattler, "The Twitter Effect: How Trump Used Social Media to Stamp His Brand and Shape the Media Narrative on Immigration," in Jeanine E. Kraybill (ed.), *Unconventional, Partisan, and Polarizing Rhetoric: How the 2016 Election Shaped the Way Candidates Strategize, Engage, and Communicate* (Lanham, MD: Lexington Books, 2018), pp. 135–72; and Katherine Haenschen, Michael Horning, and Jim A. Kuypers, "Donald Trump's Use of Twitter in the 2016 Campaign," in Jim A. Kuypers (ed.), *The 2016 American Presidential Campaign and the News: Implications for American Democracy and the Republic* (Lanham, MD: Lexington Books, 2018), pp. 55–76.

58 Galen Stolee and Steve Caton, "Twitter, Trump, and the Base: a Shift to a New Form of Presidential Talk?" *Signs and Society*, 6:1 (2018), 147–64.

59 Ibid.

60 Fred Turner, "Trump on Twitter: How a Medium Designed for Democracy Became an Authoritarian's Mouthpiece," in Pablo J. Boczowski and Zizi Papacharissi (eds.), *Trump and the Media* (Cambridge, MA: MIT Press, 2018), p. 149.

61 For more on Trump's use of "authenticity markers," see Gunn Enli, "Twitter as Arena for the Authentic Outsider: Exploring the Social Media Campaigns of Trump and Clinton in the 2016 US Presidential Election," *European Journal of Communication*, 32:1 (2017), 50–61.

62 Darren Samuelsohn, "'The Guy's a F___ing Yenta': Trump Loose Lips Draw Fire," *Politico*, June 1, 2018. Accessed at www.politico.com/story/2018/06/01/trump-secrets-white-house-security-leaks-617961.

63 There may well be a limit to such effects, however. One study shows, for example, that even though Trump increased his tweeting over the course of his presidency, it generated less "uptake" (i.e., fewer retweets, fewer followers, etc.) as time went on. See Neal Rothschild, "Trump's Tweets Are Losing Their Potency," *Axios*, May 26, 2019. Accessed at www.axios.com/president-trump-tweets-engagement-4c6067a8-734d-4184-984a-d5c9151aa339.html.

64 Christian Schneider, "Donald Trump's Twitter Assault on the English Language Weakens Him and America," *USA Today*, May 29, 2018. Accessed at www .usatoday.com/story/opinion/2018/05/29/donald-trump-tweets-assault-english-lan guage-undermine-america-column/638888002/.

Part VI
FEELING RESOLUTE

10   TRUMP'S LESSONS

As the Trump administration entered its third year, everyone, it seemed, reviled the President. MSNBC's Chris Matthews regularly described him as a liar and Old Europe dismissed him as a man drunk on ego. Women throughout the United States complained about his misogyny and a newly elected Representative from the Bronx labeled him a racist. Late-night comics called him malevolent and probably deranged. Donald Trump didn't brush regularly. Everyone agreed.

And then there was the other half of the country. When Republicans were asked what they thought of Donald J. Trump in January of 2019, 87 percent of them said he was doing just fine. In recent years, only George W. Bush surpassed Mr. Trump's popularity among the party's faithful at the 500-day mark of his presidency (and that, no doubt, was partially a 9/11 effect). How could so many reasonable people, so many church-going, paper-recycling people, continue to plight their troth to such a preposterous fellow? How could a man so taken with himself turn the heads of so many fine Americans?

Those are the questions I have asked in this book. Although much of the data I report were gathered during the 2016 presidential race, the Trump campaign has never really ended and people's attitudes have never really changed. Americans are resolved – to hate Donald Trump, to love Donald Trump. "We are on the precipice of fascism," says political scientist Bonnie Honig, "he's Reagan, he's Hitler." Speaking on the same conference panel, William Connolly of Johns Hopkins University said that Donald Trump's policies were "assassinating democracy," after which a conference-goer proposed that Trump staffers not be served in local DC restaurants.[1] Cooler heads like Harvard's Dani Rodrik declared that, while it was OK to invite Trump administration officials to speak on college campuses, they should not be given an honorific title, allowed to deliver a keynote address, or be invited to campus by a senior university official. The average sophomore could listen to such people, said Rodrik, but under no circumstances should the speaker feel flattered at having been asked to speak.[2]

As the 2020 presidential election came into view, then, the United States found itself in a state of dynamic inertia: People's feelings were turbulent but no minds were being changed. So, for example, Barack Obama's former photographer, Pete Souza, regularly trolled the new president by reissuing photos from a calmer, saner era because, said Souza, things were "not normal" under Trump.[3] That, of course, was why The Donald was elected, his supporters replied. With the Left and the Right now in their respective bunkers, everyone watched the news that pleased them. On January 2, 2019, for example, folks could read a story about John Kasich possibly entering the 2020 presidential race or Donald Trump declaring that the government shutdown would last "as long as it takes" or a former Bush advisor predicting that Mr. Trump would resign the presidency in exchange for legal immunity or Mitt Romney auditioning for the job of Senate power broker.[4] January 3rd would bring additional stories.

In the midst of all this, Massachusetts Institute of Technology's David Gelernter wondered if it was really possible to hate Donald Trump and not hate the average American.[5] While Gelernter's point is overstated, he points to a kind of revulsion common in higher education.[6] For reasons such as these, this was a hard book to write. How could any self-respecting scholar spend three years analyzing the rhetoric of a man so opposed to the fundaments of the academy – reverence for truth, transparency, even-handedness, civility? Thus, when someone would ask me how I could take on such an enterprise, I told them that my book was not just about Donald Trump but also about their brother-in-law. A knowing look suddenly crossed their face. "Oh, yeah," they would reply, "my brother-in-law voted for the jerk."

This book has tried to turn Donald Trump into a question. Is it possible, I have asked, for perfectly decent people to have voted for Donald Trump for perfectly decent reasons? Must all brothers-in-law be shipped off to some distant island or could we learn something fresh by listening carefully to Trump and his supporters? I also asked if the

Trump presidency might be just another episode in the Continuing American Challenge – accommodating people we do not like. The Trump presidency brought these problems of accommodation to the surface, showing how hard it is to resolve issues of race, region, religion, gender, age, and class. The United States of America is a mess, and Donald Trump has made it only messier.

Making a question out of Donald Trump is not easy because so many people know all they can possibly know. Instead of focusing on cognitions, then, I have focused on emotions because emotions, too, have their reasons. "Finally," Mr. Trump's supporters declared, "I can vote for an elite individual who has non-elite feelings – anger, envy, revenge, pride, jealousy, lust – unpretty feelings but feelings I have witnessed." "America has yet to make sense of Trump," said the *Wall Street Journal*'s Holman Jenkins, but Trump's main contribution may be that he has made new things sayable.[7] He often did so with desultory results – racism in Charlottesville, anti-Semitism in Pittsburgh. But other Trump moments had broader appeal, as when he attacked media imperialism, faced down China, made fun of Elizabeth Warren, or hung tough on the southern border. Donald Trump liked hard-hitting emotions and his supporters liked him for liking them.

Throughout this book, I have argued that despite his legion idiosyncrasies, Donald Trump is a brilliant emotional manager, a political revolutionary of the first order. True, he is thin-skinned and often incorrigible but he is nonetheless the President of the United States. Where will Trump and his emotions take us as a nation? Is it safe to travel with him? Will Thanksgiving ever be the same again, now that he has stolen our brother-in-law's heart? Will anyone be left to pass the turkey?

My Challenge

The great challenge in writing about Donald Trump is explaining the multidimensionality of a unidimensional man. Trump's ideas are so outlandish and his emotions so close to the surface that he begs to be caricatured. Trump has lived out his life on the public stage so he is always his own center of attention. In some ways, he is just another pol who is afraid to admit what he does not know. His bluster is the obvious result, as is his bully-boy penchant for putting people down. "I used to come over that bridge and I used to say, 'I want to be in

Manhattan someday,'" said the young Donald Trump when selling shoddy pieces of real estate.[8] He eventually got to Manhattan but his psyche remained in Queens.

I have tried to honor Donald Trump's complexity in this book. Featuring hard evidence has helped in that regard, keeping me from being thrown off by his peculiarities. I found, for example, that Trump uses simple language because emotions are sometimes blissfully simple – I love you, I hate you. Trump's volubility is also elemental, a way of showing his supporters he cannot get enough of them. Trump's I-hear-you style suits the emotions of the road, whereas the White House's teleprompters take the Trump out of Trump, leaving him with mere words to say.

It may seem strange to call Donald Trump an artist but he is just that when addressing people's grievances. He used Anger and Hurt terms four to five times more than the political norm, and he used them more often as the 2016 campaign progressed. Trump is easily angered, even more easily hurt, so he constantly explores himself in the presence of others. Out there with the people, he grabs onto this emotion and then that, his arguments trailing along behind. All good populists have such skills. Bill Clinton felt individual pain; Donald Trump feels collective pain.

Trump is also a fine, if unsubtle, storyteller. His stories have predictable characters harboring obvious motives. Mexicans are rapists who will nab your daughter in an instant. Members of the Fed are incompetent and Democrats are stuffing the ballot boxes in Florida. Trump knows why you lost your job and he could give you the name of the Chinese bloke who took it if he had the time. Few Americans actually believed such stories but many liked the richness of Trump's imagination and his willingness to name names. Trump saw where things were going.

Trump is also thoroughly transactional. He came to politics from the business world, so moral abstractions were foreign to him. An interview with CBS' Lesley Stahl shows that. No matter what sort of question Stahl asked, Trump took refuge in a spreadsheet. The ethical dimensions of climate change? "I don't want to lose millions and millions of jobs," said Trump. Sanctions on Russia? "They are ordering [our] military equipment," the President replied. Refugee children at the southern border? "There have to be consequences for coming into our country illegally," Trump countered. Have you made any mistakes? "I could have been earlier with terminating the NAFTA deal."[9]

Trump is transactional about emotions as well. When Brett Kavanaugh launched an unconvincing defense of himself on Fox News while auditioning for the Supreme Court, the President was beside himself, wondering if he had made the wrong choice. Then came the Senate hearings where "Kavanaugh came roaring in, delivering the majority of his 45-minute opening statement at a volume level just shy of full shout," turning "red-faced and teary-eyed" while declaring "you may defeat me in the final vote, but you'll never get me to quit. Never."[10] Mr. Trump is said to have been "riveted" by the Senate hearings, telling his inner circle, "this is why I nominated him!"[11] Kavanaugh had met the Trump standard – using emotion to do what needed to be done. If you cannot feel something, Trump reasons, it does not exist.

For these reasons the Paranoid Style was Trump's go-to strategy. He understood people's sense of isolation and betrayal as their communities changed before their eyes because of foreign actors. He also identified with their sense of indignation based on his own prior experience as a wannabe. Trump was a billionaire, yes, but the business he was in – Manhattan real estate – was mercurial, requiring constant deal-making with people he did not know well. As a result, Trump has spent much of his life looking over his shoulder, and he brought that instinct to the campaign trail.

Trump grew up on the tabloids. They taught him how fickle the press could be, that you could never really count on them, so he became his own advance man. It angered him that he could not control the press's agenda so he made Twitter his 24/7 counterargument. Media coverage became his preoccupation as president, often causing him to get lost in the world of hoopla. My surveys show that voters overwhelmingly wanted Trump to curtail his tweeting, but he would hear none of it.

To this day, most journalists cannot understand how Donald Trump became president. The values they cherish – pursuing the truth, disclosing the facts, balancing different points of view – are values that Donald Trump routinely dismisses. Journalists are idealists, people who respect the Grand Virtues – justice, equality, fairness, reliability. Trump, in contrast, is a working postmodernist who markets the truth layer by layer and who sees the Grand Virtues as a dodge for undermining him.

Trump likes the Plain Virtues instead, virtues that are interpersonal in nature – loyalty, dependability, mutuality, friendship – the things one expects from one's teenage buddies. So, for example, Trump supported Big Luther Strange in the 2017 Alabama senate race because "he was so loyal and helpful to me" when running for the presidency.[12] Too, he continued to praise his former campaign manager, Paul Manafort, despite the latter's serial indictments. Trump also kept attorney Michael Cohen on his payroll even though, according to Trump, Cohen was "a weak person and not a very smart person." Why, then, keep him employed? "Because a long time ago, he did me a favor," Trump replied.[13]

There is also a dark side to the Plain Virtues. Trump once opined that he hates "flippers," those who reduce their legal liability by turning state's evidence on higher-ups. Similarly, the President became upset with General Motors' CEO, Mary Barra, when she shut down a plant in Lordstown, Ohio, thereby spoiling Trump's image as a savior of the working class. In another instance, Trump lashed out at CNN's Jim Acosta for mistreating Sarah Huckabee Sanders. "You're a very rude person," Trump remarked during a press conference. "You shouldn't treat people that way."[14] Not surprisingly, Mr. Trump's Plain Virtues were quickly set upon by journalists, with one declaring that his "thinly veiled threats" showed "an affinity for mobsters and their rhetoric." *Omertà* at 1600 Pennsylvania Avenue.

One of the problems in writing a book with *Trump* in the title is, well, that *Trump* is in the title, ready to dominate every discussion. I have tried to show that Donald Trump was not alone in 2016 or thereafter; 62.9 million Americans accompanied him on his trek. They, too, liked the Plain Virtues, especially those related to reciprocity and square-dealing. They too hated flippers as well as staffers who talked behind Trump's back. They did not like Christine Blasey Ford showing up with outrageous charges about Brett Kavanaugh but with insufficient corroborating evidence. They also understood rudeness, why Mr. Trump would get upset when a twenty-foot-tall blimp was sent aloft in London depicting him as an angry, diapered baby. They got it when Mr. Trump said, "I guess when they put blimps to make me feel unwelcome, no reason for me to [return] to London."[15]

It may seem strange that voters embracing the Plain Virtues would be drawn to Donald Trump, a notorious libertine who engineered more than his share of shady business deals. The simplest explanation is that the American people had only two choices in 2016 and saw Mr. Trump as the lesser of two evils. But that explanation overlooks his considerable strengths – his passions, his simplicity, his stories, his spontaneity. They also overlook how he made people feel acknowledged, better protected, less weary.

Because Donald Trump is the way he is, his presidency challenges the United States in unprecedented ways. The data I have presented here suggest three sets of challenges in particular – for Trump himself, for the nation's press, and for the American people. I discuss them in order of difficulty.

Trump's Challenge

Donald Trump knows nothing of the humanities. One despairs when hearing him mangle the English language or when displaying his ignorance of foreign lands, foreign people. Trump appears to have had no philosophical training either. If he has first assumptions, he quickly loses sight of them, speaking aimlessly and repetitively as a result. But these are an academic's complaints. The United States has had more than enough presidents unable to distinguish physics from metaphysics but who served the country well. Unlike Jack Kennedy, Ronald Reagan had no Harvard in him and yet he changed the world.

But lacking a sense of history is another matter entirely. An ahistorical president invents each day anew, a massively inefficient project. To be unable to draw on the past like Dwight Eisenhower or Barack Obama increases the chance of making your predecessors' mistakes your own. Trump seems not to know even the history of his own lifetime – the painful war into which he was born, the sacrifices of Korea, the great uprisings of class, race, and gender, and the dissolution of the Cold War. Without history, Trump has no ballast for his decisions, no ability to make comparative assessments.

A *de novo* president is also rhetorically shortsighted. Mr. Trump likes the term *nationalism*, for example, because it calls to mind patriotic bunting and a favorable balance of trade. Words have their histories, however, and Trump resents that. A man as rich as me, he reasons, should be able to make words do what you want them to do. Given that attitude, Trump often becomes spiteful about language: "You know, they have a word – it's sort of become old-fashioned – it's called a 'nationalist.' And I say, really, we're not supposed to use that word. You know what I am? I'm a nationalist, okay? I'm a nationalist. Nationalist. Nothing wrong. Use that word. Use that word."[16]

The fact that words pick up baggage over time also irritates the President. How can African-Americans and Jews hate *nationalism*, he queries? Would they rather live in Afghanistan? So Trump uses whatever words he likes regardless of their provenance. According to Vanderbilt's Sophie Bjork-James, this often creates a feedback loop between Trump's "Twitter feed and right-wing extremist movements."[17] Trump finds such criticisms absurd. If a given word gives you a bump in the polls, he reasons, why not use it?

Because Mr. Trump is such an emotional thinker, he consistently finds himself on the border of Fact and Possibility, a place where things feel true even when they are not true. His predecessor hates him, so Obama must have wiretapped the phones in Trump Tower ("This is McCarthyism!"). Muslim immigrants are coming to the United States from Syria ("Could be a Trojan horse!"). Antonin Scalia may have been smothered in his home ("A pretty unusual place to find a pillow!"). Vaccines are probably causing autism ("People that work for me, just the other day, two years old, a beautiful child, went to have the vaccine and came back and a week later got a tremendous fever, got very, very sick, now is autistic").[18] "Sometimes," says Trump, people "go to their car, put on a different hat, put on a different shirt, come in and vote again."[19] Hey, it could happen.

Trump is symbol-obsessed and that both helps and hurts him. "I want a parade like the one in France" on Bastille Day, Trump told his Defense Secretary in 2018.[20] Trump saw how powerful such an event could be, drawing people together and showing off some really great military equipment at the same time – American exceptionalism plus showmanship. But even a ceremony of this sort would have required grace, wisdom, nuance, and less Trump from Trump. Ay, there's the rub.

Donald Trump's biggest problem is that he is an immigrant in the world of politics. He thinks like an immigrant and he is clannish like an immigrant. He uses social media like an immigrant and has the enthusiasms of an immigrant. He is angry at not being accorded Old World deference, and he resents people who think they are better than him – reporters, academics, comedians, feminists. It is enough to make an immigrant seethe.

Trump also talks like an immigrant. His fractured patois is perfect for Twitter, a medium where even punctuation seems effete. Trump is a classic first-genner: If Ted Cruz lands a blow, put a hit on his dad. If Mitt Romney looks at you sideways, disembowel him in the kitchen. The things your average politician depends upon – astute waffling, a taste for irony – look like weaknesses to an immigrant. For a fellow new to politics, every slight demands a response, every shadow becomes a threat. Strange accents, unfamiliar neighborhoods. A doubled-up fist in each pants pocket. This is Donald Trump on the streets of Washington, DC.

Trump's fight-or-flight instincts may initially protect him but they are unlikely to advance his cause in the long run. Like any immigrant, he needs to make some friends, ask for advice, and combine his Old World skills with those demanded in the New World. He also needs to expand his emotional repertoire. He has mastered anger and resentfulness. For the good of the nation he needs to add comity and humility. Above all, he must become more comfortable with questions, the deeper the better. People come together when they are commonly perplexed but it takes a president to help them do so.

The Press's Challenge

The Trump era is the best of times and the worst of times for journalism. On the plus side, Mr. Trump's animadversions have given the press a new reason for being or, more accurately, they have reawakened its old reason for being. Never before have so many reporters in so many news outlets spent more time dissecting the outrageous things a president has said. When talking to reporters, one senses a mixture of anger and zeal among them, a thoroughgoing disgust with Trump's evasions and a renewed commitment to their profession.

But it is also a challenging time for journalism. The press's treatment of Trump supporters is a case in point. Says Adam Serwer: "Trump's fiercest backers enjoy his cruelty towards people they have decided deserve it. For them, the cruelty is the point."[21] Mr. Serwer enters people's hearts and minds here with nary a piece of evidence. Other reporters describe Trumpers as either addicts (Trump's "hokum" is said to be "heroin for his supporters") or as feckless (Trump's people want "their lodestar to give them absolute direction").[22] Occasionally, reporters find slivers of redemption ("civility is alive and well [among Trumpers] if you know where to look for it."). At best, such people are treated paternalistically: "The Trump supporters I spoke with were friendly, generous with their time, flattered to be asked their opinion."[23]

Journalists clearly foment too many "word eruptions" as well. What do we really learn, for example, when a reporter says that Trump called his tax cut the *biggest* in American history 100 times, surpassing the 60 times he chastised Democrats for their *open borders*?[24] What does such accountancy gain us? Why devote an entire column to Trump's use of the phrase *smocking gun* only to prove that presidents, too, produce typos?[25] Is Eric Trump really being anti-Semitic when using the word *shekels*?[26] Does the President deserve universal censure for calling a hurricane *tremendously big and tremendously wet*?[27] Is the First Soul really at risk when Mr. Trump sits quietly in church rather than recite the Apostles' Creed aloud?[28] "Wimp reporting" of this sort is causing many Americans to lose faith in journalism. Policy issues, the real stuff of governance, beckon.

Journalists should, of course, hold the President's feet to the fire when he makes misleading statements or fosters intolerance. But because Mr. Trump is so naturally injudicious, reporters themselves must be even more judicious when evaluating him. The *New York Times'* David Brooks says that the anti-Trump forces' "low-browism" often magnifies the political alienation already present in the country:

> The anti-Trump movement, of which I'm a proud member, seems to be getting dumber. It seems to be settling into a smug, fairytale version of reality that filters out discordant informa-tion. More anti-Trumpers seem to be telling themselves a "Madness of King George" narrative: Trump is a semiliterate madman surrounded by sycophants who are morally, intellec-tually and psychologically inferior to people like us. I'd like to think it's possible to be fervently anti-Trump while also not reducing everything to a fairytale.[29]

In many ways, the Trump presidency is a gift to journalism, inviting reporters to reflect on their own presuppositions and biases. The best of them are up to the task. Dan Balz of the *Washington Post*, Sarah Smarsh of the *Guardian*, James Fallows of the *Atlantic*, and Josh Saul of *Newsweek* have turned in brilliant field reports, getting close enough to Trump supporters to understand them but standing far enough back to gain perspective. Reporters of this ilk are especially needed on the cable news channels which have become far too predict-able. Fox's Chris Wallace and MSNBC's Ari Melber remind us, though, that real journalism is still possible in ideologically overdetermined news organizations. Journalism's greatest challenge is rediscovering its best self in the Age of Trump.

The People's Challenge

Ample research shows that political polarization in the United States is at an all-time high. According to one study, 72 percent of the American people said they found it "harder than ever" to talk about politics with people of opposing viewpoints, while 27 percent said they have lost friends because of their disagreements.[30] Barbara Weber is one such polarized voter, reveling in the fact that "Trump threw open the doors to the closed, clandestine workings of power." Kimberly Carpenter is polarized as well, admitting that she now assigns "character or intellect weaknesses to people based upon whether they endorse Trump."[31]

But some voters are caught in between, contributing to what Stephen Hawkins and his colleagues call the "hidden tribes" of U.S. politics.[32] These voters are roundly dispirited, people like Theodore D'Afflidio, who says "my family has decided no politics, period, at any event or meeting."[33] School counselor Marsha Newman of West Virginia agrees but mournfully so: "It's so heartbreaking that all we can do is bring each other down and cut into each other. I feel like I'm going to cry."[34] "It's like World War I," says Christopher Kershaw of New Jersey, "where you're pushing each other back and forth over the same quarter-mile of ground and nothing happens."[35] Political scientist Yascha Mounk predicts that "you can win in 2020 by promising that if you become president, people can go back to talking about football."[36]

During tumultuous times like these, a sense of history comes in handy. The United States has labored through many trials in the past and no doubt will again. That perspective reflects the "resiliency school of politics" which holds that democracies ultimately "snap back" because of their inherent strengths.[37] Who is a true American? Which religion should guide us? When will the revolution come? How much inequality can the nation allow? These questions have waxed and waned since the Founding. Remembering that can help voters get through this time of discord.

Donald Trump's greatest contribution has been to remind the American people that they do not know the American people. "Maybe we need more junior-year 'abroad' programs," says the *New York Times* Nicholas Kristof, "that sends liberals to Kansas and conservatives to Massachusetts."[38] Failing that, we can listen more carefully to people and, importantly, ask the next question. Says voter Andy Kobela of Pennsylvania: "I'd like to see [us] be friends with Vladimir Putin. I'd like to see the United States and Russia get together. We're the same people."[39] What does Mr. Kobela mean here? What sort of geopolitics does he have in mind? How much rapprochement would he accept? When would Vladimir Putin begin to worry him?

Another citizen, Michigan's Mark Sherhart, says "If you want free shit paid for by someone else, then do it where you live in California and leave the rest of us alone."[40] How far would Mr. Sherhart push that proposition? Would he support universal healthcare if the United States spent less of its money on naval destroyers? Would he be upset if California suddenly cut back on its highway tolls while the state of Michigan increased theirs threefold? What are the limits to his parsimony? How many chips would he throw into the pot? What is his hole card when it comes to government finance?

Donald Trump's supporters are often caricatured and that wastes everyone's time. Real people say complex things, so one must listen to them in complex ways. "Clinton tries to ally herself with the 'common folk,'" says one online commenter, "but she comes off as pandering and fake. Trump does it too, but at least he seems real, especially when he is eating KFC."[41] This voter lives in two worlds, in the world of appearances and in the world of desire. He wishes that Donald Trump were the genuine article but he is willing to settle for a helpful facsimile. Why is this an acceptable bargain to him? Another Trump supporter says, "I also think Trump doesn't give a shit about me (or almost anyone else) but at least he made the effort to be among the people."[42] What are the limits to such a trade-off between authenticity and action? When would it become dangerous for the nation?

But even if the American people learn to listen better, they will still be confronted with their differences. Said retired hairdresser Connie Tessler: "I just don't care for [Muslims] ... They want to take over America. Why can't they just come here and live like us? I want you to be an American. Do what we do. We were here first, OK. You're second."[43] Ms. Tessler epitomizes the "familiarity crisis" currently unsettling many senior citizens in the United States. Some Americans now feel like strangers in their own land, says sociologist Arlie

Rothschild, feelings that Donald Trump rode to the White House.[44] We need to become more sensitive to these tensions of generational replacement. Avoiding the internet's comment strings would help in that regard.

Those at the other end of the age continuum, the children of the digital age, also need to work harder at keeping their cynicism in check. Numerous studies show how reviled Donald Trump is among young adults, 80 percent of whom disapprove of him and his policies.[45] Popular entertainment explains at least part of that effect. As Andrew Breitbart once declared, politics is downstream from culture.[46] Young people, for example, are drawn to the pessimism of late-night talk shows.[47] Each evening, Donald Trump is raked over the coals, leaving viewers with an acid taste in their mouths. Institutional cynicism results, with Trump being cast as today's problem, the presidency itself as tomorrow's problem. What will happen when the laughter dies down? What beliefs will remain? Who will care?

The Trump presidency has created work for everyone. One can only pray that Mr. Trump will eventually become president of all the people and abandon his divisive rhetoric. Incumbent presidents have a natural advantage when running for reelection, after all, but only if they maximize the fruits of incumbency, the most important of which is gravitas. Can Donald Trump meet that standard? If he does, will the press notice it? Indeed, will the press permit it? And what of the people? Will they show up as they did during the 2018 midterms, all fiery and full of themselves, or will they turn back into taxpayers instead of voters? The Trump presidency, it seems clear, has challenges enough for all.

Conclusion

Everyone listens to Donald Trump. How could they not? Many listen with unbridled anger. Trump's self-centeredness, his willingness to mock others, and his disdain for the "losers" of the world make even normally placid individuals gnash their teeth. Trump's disdain for logical consistency and his unwillingness to take in new information – and, by God, to read a book – alienate still others. But they listen to Donald Trump anyway, tuning in each evening to watch Erin Burnett and Rachel Maddow take him down another peg. Trump-hating has become great sport.

President Trump's supporters also listen. Some do so for ideological reasons, rejoicing that someone remembers how things used to be, a time when values were values and you could say whatever came into your head. These people too are angry – about immigrants, to be sure, but also about secularism and egalitarianism and globalism and technology and people who kneel during the national anthem. Donald Trump loves his base and he feels more like himself when he is with them.

One would expect the arch-haters and the arch-lovers to listen to Trump but others did as well. Some 30 million Americans voted for Donald Trump in 2016 who were not part of his base – then or now. This group included country-club Republicans, the Chamber of Commerce folks, stay-at-home moms, a good many veterans, fans of *The Apprentice*, socially tolerant evangelicals, nouveau Reagan Democrats, and everyone who despised Hillary Clinton. Donald Trump brought this coalition together by tapping into their feelings of being pestered and ignored, of being trapped in a world of relentless change and constant worry. Trump licensed them to hate the know-it-all media and to feel clever when doing so. Such people reprised his tweets and yelled "lock her up" whenever they felt like it. Trump's great skill was to marry reason with emotion and to make that union compelling.

Trump has another great skill – connecting with voters at a deeply personal level. Identification, what critic Kenneth Burke calls the ability to "share an identity" with another human being, drove people into his camp who were not normally attracted to licentious billionaires.[48] Donald Trump's flaws, in some ways, were his greatest strength. Trump hates being laughed at and is typically ungracious. He knows no poetry or art, no science or mathematics, and so is easily intimidated by the Old Money folks and the Cambridge set. Trump knows he has bodily flaws and, perhaps, that he is losing a step mentally.

These feelings of not fitting in are the feelings of us all. Rather than hiding from them, Donald Trump modeled them – brazenly – showing that you can still get ahead in the United States despite your afflictions. Trump exchanged identities with voters, becoming their empath-in-chief. Trump's approach was unique. It is hard to imagine the emergence of a second Donald Trump. That thought will comfort many Americans, some of whom actually voted for him. A nation can only take so much turmoil after all, so the taste for Trump will eventually fade away. Before it does, we need to reflect on how he became president and what that experience says about us. This book has been a step in that direction.

Notes

1 The foregoing remarks were presented at a roundtable on "What Political Theorists Can Tell Us About the Trump Presidency," Annual convention of the American Political Science Association, Boston, MA, September 1, 2018.

2 Dani Rodrik, "No to Academic Normalization of Trump," *Project Syndicate*, Monday, August 7, 2018. Accessed at www.project-syndicate.org/commentary/no-academic-normalization-of-trump-by-dani-rodrik-2018-08?barrier=accesspaylog.

3 Lee Moran, "Obama Photographer Rips Donald Trump: Does 'Too Many Things' That Are 'Not Normal,'" *Huffington Post*, November 25, 2018. Accessed at www.huffingtonpost.com/entry/pete-souza-obama-photographer-donald-trump-lies_us_5bf9048ce4b0eb6d930e8f60.

4 Kevin Freking, "New GOP Rivalry? Romney Bolts into Washington, Blasts Trump," *The State*, January 2, 2019. Accessed at www.thestate.com/news/politics-government/national-politics/article223810720.html; Steve Peoples, Zeke Miller, and Jonathan Lemire, "GOP Confronts Anxiety about Primary Challenge," *Sacramento Bee*, January 2, 2019. Accessed at www.sacbee.com/news/politics-government/article223848605.html; Tim Marcin, "Donald Trump Will Resign the Presidency in 2019 in Exchange for Immunity for Him and His Family, Former Bush Adviser Says," *Newsweek*, January 2, 2019. Accessed at www.newsweek.com/donald-trump-resign-2019-family-immunity-1276990; Zeke Miller and Lisa Mascaro, "President Trump Says Shutdown Will Last 'as Long as It Takes,' as He Continues Push for Wall," *Time*, January 2, 2019. Accessed at http://time.com/5492255/trump-pushes-for-wall-amid-shutdown/.

5 David Gelernter, "The Real Reason They Hate Trump," *Wall Street Journal*, October 21, 2018. Accessed at www.wsj.com/articles/the-real-reason-they-hate-trump-1540148467.

6 For more on these matters, see Terry W. Hartle, "Why Most Republicans Don't Like Higher Education," *Chronicle of Higher Education*, July 19, 2017. Accessed at www.chronicle.com/article/Why-Most-Republicans-Don-t/240691.

7 Holman W. Jenkins, Jr., "America Has Yet to Make Sense of Trump," *Wall Street Journal*, October 19, 2018. Accessed at www.wsj.com/articles/america-has-yet-to-make-sense-of-trump-1539989072.

8 Michael D'Antonio, *Never Enough: Donald Trump and the Pursuit of Success* (New York: Thomas Dunne Books, 2013), p. 23.

9 Lesley Stahl, "Interview with President Donald Trump," *CBS*, May 22, 2018. Accessed at www.cbs.com/watch/.

10 Ashley Parker, Josh Dawsey, and Philip Rucker, "For Trump and White House, Kavanaugh Hearing Was a Suspenseful Drama in Two Acts," *Washington Post*, September 27, 2018. Accessed at www.washingtonpost.com/politics/for-trump-and-white-house-kavanaugh-hearing-was-a-drama-in-two-acts/2018/09/27/6b82f8c8-c276-11e8-a1f0-a4051b6ad114_story.html?utm_term=.36a8da98549e.

11 As quoted ibid.

12 As quoted in Michael Kruse, "I Need Loyalty," *Politico*, March/April 2018. Accessed at www.politico.com/magazine/story/2018/03/06/donald-trump-loyalty-staff-217227.

13 As quoted in Marc Fisher, "Trump Borrows His Rhetoric – and His View of Power – from the Mob," *Washington Post*, November 29, 2018. Accessed at www.washingtonpost.com/outlook/trump-borrows-his-rhetoric–and-his-view-of-power–from-the-mob/2018/11/29/d8d66e16-abb8-11e8-8a0c-70b618c98d3c_story.html?utm_term=.2f4c93399d27.

14 As quoted in Nikki Schwab and Bob Fredericks, "Trump Rails Against 'Rude' Media in Heated Press Conference," *New York Post*, November 7, 2018. Accessed at https://nypost.com/2018/11/07/trump-rails-against-rude-media-in-heated-press-con ference/.

15 As quoted in Felicia Sonmez, "Trump Suggests That Protesting Should Be Illegal," *Washington Post*, September 5, 2018. Accessed at www.washingtonpost.com/polit ics/trump-suggests-protesting-should-be-illegal/2018/09/04/11cfd9be-b0a0-11e8-aed9-001309990777_story.html?utm_term=.5a3f1263c89d.

16 As quoted in Aaron Blake, "Trump's Embrace of a Fraught Term – 'Nationalist' – Could Cement a Dangerous Racial Divide," *Washington Post*, October 23, 2018. Accessed at www.washingtonpost.com/politics/2018/10/23/trumps-embrace-fraught-term-nationalist-could-cement-dangerous-racial-divide/?utm_term=.358ed9c1ddbd.

17 As quoted in Kevin Roose and Ali Winston, "Far-Right Internet Groups Listen for Trump's Approval, and Often Hear It," *New York Times*, November 4, 2018. Accessed at www.nytimes.com/2018/11/04/us/politics/far-right-internet-trump.html.

18 The foregoing Trumpian observations can be found in Maxwell Tani, Michal Kranz, and John Haltiwanger, "Nineteen Outlandish Conspiracy Theories Donald Trump Has Floated on the Campaign Trail and in the White House," *Business Insider*, September 13, 2018. Accessed at www.businessinsider.com/donald-trump-conspir acy-theories-2016-5.

19 As quoted in Gary Fineout and Kelli Kennedy, "Florida Recount Nears Deadline," *Philadelphia Inquirer*, November 15, 2018. Accessed at www.philly.com/wires/ap/ floridas-ongoing-partisan-battle-over-recount-continues-20181114.html-2.

20 As quoted in Greg Jaffe and Philip Rucker, "Trump's 'Marching Orders' to the Pentagon: Plan a Grand Military Parade," *Washington Post*, February 6, 2018. Accessed at www.washingtonpost.com/politics/trumps-marching-orders-to-the-pentagon-plan-a-grand-military-parade/2018/02/06/9e19ca88-0b55-11e8-8b0d-891 602206fb7_story.html?utm_term=.dfoed4a419f8.

21 Adam Serwer, "Trump and His Supporters Thrive on Cruelty," *Atlantic*, December 13, 2018. Accessed at www.theatlantic.com/video/index/577960/trump-cruel/.

22 The preceding comments are reproduced in Andrew McMurry, "Trumpolect: Donald Trump's Distinctive Discourse and Its Functions," in Jeremy Kowalski (ed.), *Reading Donald Trump: A Parallax View of the Campaign and Early Presidency* (Cham, Switzerland: Palgrave Macmillan, 2019), pp. 39, 40.

23 The preceding can be found in George Saunders, "Who Are All These Trump Supporters? At the Candidate's Rallies, a New Understanding of America Emerges," *New Yorker: American Chronicles*, July 11–18, 2016. Accessed at www.newyorker .com/magazine/2016/07/11/george-saunders-goes-to-trump-rallies.

24 Linda Qiu, "Deciphering the Pattern in Trump's Falsehoods," *New York Times*, December 29, 2018. Accessed at www.nytimes.com/2018/12/29/us/politics/trump-fact-check.html.

25 Eugene Robinson, "What Has the President Been 'Smocking'?" *Washington Post*, December 9, 2018. Accessed at www.washingtonpost.com/opinions/what-has-the-president-been-smocking/2018/12/10/02e10810-fcbd-11e8-862a-b6a6f3ce8199_ story.html?utm_term=.88a196e68118.

26 Eli Rosenberg, "Eric Trump Said Claims that He Used an Anti-Semitic Dog Whistle are 'Nonsense': Others Beg to Differ," *Washington Post*, September 13, 2018. Accessed at www.washingtonpost.com/politics/2018/09/13/eric-trump-said-flap-over-his-use-anti-semitic-dog-whistle-is-nonsense-others-beg-differ/?utm_term=.3f47 7e33f935.

27 Royce Dunmore, "Wet Storms: Donald Trump's Most Ignorant Moments during Hurricane Relief Efforts," *Michigan Chronicle,* September 21, 2018. Accessed at https://michronicleonline.com/2018/09/21/wet-storms-donald-trumps-most-ignorant-moments-during-hurricane-relief-efforts/4/.

28 Carol Kuruvilla, "Trump's Evangelical Supporters on Apostles' Creed Gaffe: 'I Can't Sing Either,'" *Huffington Post,* December 7, 2018. Accessed at www.huffingtonpost.com/entry/trumps-evangelical-supporters-on-apostles-creed-gaffe-i-cant-sing-either_us_5c09b1fce4b0b6cdaf5d7920.

29 David Brooks, "The Decline of Anti-Trumpism," *New York Times,* January 8, 2018. Accessed at www.nytimes.com/2018/01/08/opinion/anti-trump-opposition.html.

30 Lisa Lerer, "On Politics with Lisa Lerer: These Divided States," *New York Times,* November 19, 2018. Accessed at www.nytimes.com/2018/11/19/us/politics/on-politics-trump-division.html.

31 As quoted ibid.

32 See Stephen Hawkins, Daniel Yudkin, Míriam Juan-Torres, and Tim Dixon, "Hidden Tribes: a Study of America's Polarized Landscape," *More in Common,* 2018. Accessed at https://static1.squarespace.com/static/5a70a7c30100277736a22740f/t/5bbcea6b7817f7bf7342b718/1539107467397/hidden_tribes_report-2.pdf.

33 As quoted in Lerer, "On Politics with Lisa Lerer: These Divided States," *New York Times.*

34 As quoted in Sabrina Tavernise, "These Americans Are Done with Politics," *New York Times,* November 17, 2018. Accessed at www.nytimes.com/2018/11/17/sunday-review/elections-partisanship-exhausted-majority.html.

35 As quoted ibid.

36 As quoted ibid.

37 See Chris Edelson, "Trump and Constitutional Democracy: Are Constraints on Power Holding Up?" Paper presented at the annual convention of the American Political Science Association, Boston, MA, August 2018.

38 Nicholas Kristof, "My Most Unpopular Idea: Be Nice to Trump Voters," *New York Times,* April 6, 2017. Accessed at www.nytimes.com/2017/04/06/opinion/my-most-unpopular-idea-be-nice-to-trump-voters.html.

39 As quoted in Josh Saul, "Why Did Donald Trump Win? Just Visit Luzerne County, Pennsylvania," *Newsweek,* December 15, 2016. Accessed at www.newsweek.com/2016/12/16/donald-trump-pennsylvania-win-luzerne-county-527861.html.

40 As quoted in Michael Levy, "What Are the Main Reasons Why People Voted for Trump? How Do Those Reasons Continue to Satisfy Trump Supporters Today?" *Quora,* July 16, 2017. Accessed at www.quora.com/What-are-the-main-reasons-why-people-voted-for-Trump-How-do-those-reasons-continue-to-satisfy-Trump-supporters-today.

41 Anonymous commenter no. 1 included in Hamilton Nolan, "Trump Voters Explain Themselves," *The Concourse,* January 3, 2017. Accessed at https://theconcourse.deadspin.com/trump-voters-explain-themselves-1790711999.

42 Anonymous commenter no. 2 included ibid.

43 As quoted in Asma Khalid, "GOP Insists It Doesn't Engage in Identity Politics: Researchers Disagree," *NPR: Morning Edition,* December 20, 2018. Accessed at www.npr.org/2018/12/20/678578358/gop-insists-it-doesn-t-engage-in-identity-politics-researchers-disagree.

44 Arlie Rothschild, *Strangers in Their Own Land: Anger and Mourning on the American Right* (New York: New Press, 2018).

45 Ed Kilgore, "Trump Is Really, Really Unpopular with Young People," *New York Magazine,* August 29, 2017. Accessed at http://nymag.com/intelligencer/2017/08/trump-is-really-really-unpopular-with-young-people/html?.

46 Wil S. Hylton, "Down the Breitbart Hole," *New York Times*, August 16, 2017. Accessed at www.nytimes.com/2017/08/16/magazine/breitbart-alt-right-steve-bannon.html.

47 For more on this matter, see Dominic Stephens, "The Ides of Laughs: the Politicization of American Late-Night Talk Shows over Time and under Trump," *Journal of Promotional Communications*, 6:3 (2018), 301–23.

48 For more on this topic, see Kenneth Burke, *A Rhetoric of Motives* (Berkeley: University of California Press, 1969).

INDEX

Note to the Index

References such as "178–79" indicate (not necessarily continuous) discussion of a topic across a range of pages. Wherever possible in the case of topics with many references, these have either been divided into subtopics or only the most significant discussions of the topic are listed. Because the entire work is about "Donald Trump," the use of this name (and certain other terms which occur constantly throughout the book) as an entry point has been minimized. Information will be found under the corresponding detailed topics.

Other Books in the Series (*continued from page ii*)